Bedford County
Tennessee

Bible Records

- Volume #1

I0091201

Compiled By:
Helen C. Marsh & Timothy R. Marsh

Southern Historical Press, Inc.
Greenville, South Carolina

Please Direct All Correspondence and Book Orders to:

Southern Historical Press, Inc.
PO Box 1267
375 West Broad Street
Greenville, S.C. 29602

ISBN # 0-89308-470-0

Printed in the United States of America

INTRODUCTION

After many hours of collecting, copying and traveling many miles, we have just completed our first
Volumn of BEDFORD COUNTY TENNESSEE BIBLE RECORDS.

We have had the pleasure to meet so many lovely
people in this endeavor. We wish to thank them for
the many courteous ways that they treated us in
their homes.

BEDFORD COUNTY TENNESSEE has so many Treasures, many
are not recognized until they are spotted by someone.

We shall continue to search for and copy any and all
Bible Records so that they will benefit the people
of Bedford County, Tennessee, and also to those who
live outside our County and State. As long as the
Bedford County Bible Records can be found, we will
continue this project.

Helen Crawford Marsh
Timothy Richard Marsh

ELIJAH FLOYD BIBLE

In possession of Mrs. Jean M. Pittman, Tullahoma, Tennessee
Publisher: A. J. Holman & Co., No. 930 Arch Street, Philadelphia
1873

BIRTHS:
Elijah Floyd was born Feb 15th 1798
Sallie Floyd was born Sept 1, 1799
Jane Floyd was born May 6, 1818
William Floyd was born Feb 13, 1820
Watson Floyd was born July 4, 1822
Elizabeth Floyd was born Nov 11, 1824
Sydney Floyd was born May 16, 1829
George W. Floyd was born Nov 20, 1831
Kindred N. Floyd was born Oct 9, 1834
James S. Floyd was born March 18 (or 13), 1837.
John D. Floyd was born Sept 1, 1839
Synthia Floyd was born Jan 10, 1827

Pauline I. Floyd was born March 10, 1848
Mary A. Floyd was born Nov 27, 1853
Fenitte J. Floyd was born Nov 1st, 1856
Nancy E. Floyd was born Nov 1st, 1860

Warren Thomas was born Oct 17, 1854

The above are Children of Walt Floyd who was killed in battle during
Civil War and buried in Richmond, Va.- Died May 17, 1864.

MARRIAGES:
Elijah Floyd and Sallie Watson was married April 10, 1817
William Floyd and Sallie Gowan were married April 17, 1840
John Bearden and Jane Floyd were married Nov 19, 1840
Howard Boone and Elizabeth Floyd were married Nov 14, 1844
Watson Floyd and Ann G. Price were married Jan 5, 1847
Wm. P. Floyd and Sydney Floyd were married Nov 27, 1853
John D. Floyd and Susan B. Motlow were married Dec 28, 1865
Wm. H. Howard and Pauline I. Floyd were married Feb 1, 1870

DEATHS:
Synthia Floyd departed this life Oct 25, 1835
Lacy Tilly departed this life July 18, 1848
James S. Floyd departed this life June 18, 1863
Kindred N. Floyd departed this life July 6, 1863
Watson Floyd departed this life May 17, 1864
Pauline I. Howard departed this life June 23, 1871
Elijah Floyd departed this life Sept 27, 1876
George W. Floyd departed this life Feb 14, 1870
Sarah Floyd died October 18, 1891
Elizabeth Boone died in Texas Sept 20, 1900

1

Sydney Gowen died July 10, 1896
Emma Floyd died Feb 20, 1919
Susan M. Floyd died June 28, 1919
J. D. Floyd died Nov 30, 1919
Warren Thomas died Nov 24, 1937
Fenitte Bashaw died Jan 26, 1925

BIRTHS, MARRIAGES & DEATH of 4 GIRLS of LT. COL. WALT. FLOYD:
Pauline I. Floyd was born March 10, 1848
Pauline I. Floyd married Wm. H. Howard Feb 1, 1870, Died June 23, 1871
    Buried in Wiseman Cemetery
Mary A. Floyd born Nov 27, 1853, married Jim L. Hutson, Buried in the
    Old Flat Creek Cemetery, Marker states: Mary A. Floyd, wife of
    J. L. Hutson and dau of Watson and Ann I.(Price) Floyd,
    Nov 27, 1853, Mar 10, 1876
    Also marker:
    Inf Son of J. L. & Mary A. Hutson (no dates)
Fenitte Floyd was born Nov 1, 1856, married Peter Bashaw, died Jan 26,
    1925, Buried in Manchester City Cemetery on Walder Lot. Peter
    Bashaw also buried on this Lot.
Nancy Elizabeth (Bettie) Floyd, born Nov 1, 1860, married Warren Thomas
    of Manchester, Tenn., who was born Oct 17, 1854, on Dec 1881
    Warren Thomas died Nov 24, 1937,
    Bettie Thomas died April 25, 1954, Buried in Manchester City
    Cemetery. Graves marked.

WILLIAM GRAY KNIGHT BIBLE

In possession of Mr. Gerald Pearson, Gainesville, Texas.
Published by: American Bible Society, Nashville, Tennessee   1859

BIRTHS:
William Gray Knight, son of Allen & Mary Knight, was born in Bedford
    County, Tennessee, December 26, 1829.
Quincy Adams Knight, wife of Wm. G. Knight & daughter of Hugh & Susan H.
    (McLean) Davidson, was born in Coffee Co., Tenn., November 28,
    1828.
Their Children:
John Allen Knight was born in Bedford Co., Tenn., August 12, 1855.
Charles Edward Knight was born in Bedford Co., Tenn., December 9, 1857.
Susan Mary Knight was born in Bedford Co., Tenn., February 7, 1859.
Martha Clementine was born in Bedford Co., Tenn., February 13, 1861.
Margaret Priscilla was born in Bedford Co., Tenn., August 2, 1863.
Lucy Ann Knight was born in Bedford Co., Tenn., February 22, 1866.
Louis William Knight was born in Independence Co., Arkansas July 31,
    1868.

Children of John A. Knight and Elizabeth Ann (Sarles) Knight (b. Feb 22,
    1857).

Eva May Knight was born in Cooke Co., Texas October 21, 1882.
Lewis Knight was born in Cooke Co., Texas July 15, 1885.
Grace Knight was born in Cooke Co., Texas July 15, 1885.
Quincy Knight born in Cooke Co., Texas September 6, 1889.

Children of John A. Knight and his 2nd wife, Jennie P. Hand, b. Oct 31,
    1865, Illinois.
Gertrude Knight was born in Cooke Co., Texas November 29, 1893.
"Baby" Knight was born in Cooke Co., Texas (no dates in Bible or on
    monument).

MARRIAGES:
William Gray Knight, son of Allen & Mary Knight of Bedford Co., Tenn.,
    was married to Quincy Adams Davidson, daughter of Hugh and
    Susan H. (McLean) Davidson of Coffee Co., Tenn., by H. S.
    Emerson, Esq., July 22, 1851.
John Allen Knight, son of Wm. G. & Quincy A. Knight, was married to
    (1st) Elizabeth Ann (Bettie) Sarles, daughter of John C. &
    Sarah (Emans) Sarles, December 15, 1881, by Rev. P. Garrett.
Lucy Ann Knight, daughter of Wm. G. & Quincy A. Knight, was married to
    Ben F. Witt, January 15, 1888 in Cooke Co., Texas by A. J.
    Harris, Pastor.
John A. Knight married (2nd) Jennie P. Hand, daughter of William C. &
    --------- (Emmons) Hand, January 1, 1891 in Cooke Co., Texas.
Eva May Knight, daughter of John A. & Elizabeth A. Knight, was married
    to James Turner Ball December 11, 1904 in Cooke Co., Texas by
    Rev. A. B. Ingram.
Grace Knight, daughter of John A. & Eliz. A. Knight, was married to
    William Nicholas Pearson, son of William E. & Arminda (Sanders)
    Pearson, March 20, 1910 in Cooke Co., Texas by C. B. Hines.
Lewis Knight, son of John A. & Eliz. A. Knight, was married to Edith
    Pearl Robb in Cooke Co., Texas May 5, 1915.
Gertrude Knight, daughter of John A. & Jennie P. Knight, was married
    to Walter W. Dawson, son of John C. & Mary Elizabeth (Wilson)
    Dawson on December 24, 1914 in Cooke Co., Texas.

DEATHS:
Susan Mary Knight died in Bedford Co., Tenn., March 22, 1860.
Charles Edward Knight died in Bedford Co., Tenn., August 15, 1865.
    (Edwin)
Martha Clementine Knight died in Bedford Co., Tenn. August 23, 1865.
Margaret Priscilla Knight died in Independence Co., Arkansas July 8,
    1868.
Lucy Ann Knight Witt died in Cooke Co., Texas December 1, 1888.
Elizabeth Ann Knight died in Cooke Co., Texas February 23, 1890.
William G. Knight died in Cooke Co., Texas April 15, 1890.
Quincy Knight died in Cooke Co., Texas August (?), 1890.
Quincy Ann Knight died in Cooke Co., Texas May 20, 1894.
John A. Knight died in Cooke Co., Texas December 21, 1910.
Jennie P. Knight died in Whittier, California September 28, 1933.

Louis William Knight (no death date in Bible, but he evidently died as a child-- in Independence Co., Ark.)

This Bible Record was submitted by Mrs. K. K. Stanfield, Forney, Texas.

W. T. KEELING BIBLE

In possession of John F. Morrison, Jr., Lawrenceburg, Tennessee
Published by: American Bible Society, New York, 1857
Submitted by Miss Mary Bass, Wartrace, Tennessee

BIRTHS:
W. T. Keeling was born August the 30th, 1836
Letticia V. Keeling was born April the 12th, 1841
William James Keeling was born January 28th, 1861
Eulalie Agnes Keeling was born January 16th, 1864
Mary Louise Keeling was born January 10th, 1866
Reginald Lycurgus Keeling was born December the 21st, 1867
Gustavus Clarence Keeling was born January 16th, 1870
Lillian Lee Keeling was born January the 11th, 1872
Bess Keeling was born Nov. 2, 18__
Victor Lowery Keeling was born November 19th, 1878
Verbena Octavia Keeling was born June 18, 1884
James Lowery Keeling was born Sept. 7th, 1807
Charlotte Keeling was born 15th of Dec. 1804
Mary Emely Keeling was born Nov. 15th, 1839
James H. H. Keeling was born Nov. 24th, 1844
Eliz. F. C. Keeling was born Nov. 15th, 1847
Nancy C. A. Keeling was born Sept. 16th, 1842
G. A. Hopkins was born Oct. 13th, 1819
Elizabeth Demarius Hopkins was born Feb. 27th, 1822
William McGrew was born August, 1776 in Pennsylvania
Nancy McGrew was born May 10th, 1779, in Virginia

MARRIAGES:
W. T. Keeling and Letticia V. Hopkins was married Sept. 15th, 1858
Samuel W. Butler and Mary E. Keeling was married 29th Sept. 1865
Fletcher Tarpley and Eliza F. Keeling was married Sept. 20th 1869
James H. Keeling & Jennie Dickerson was married Oct. 16th, 1879
John F. Morrison and Eula Agnes Keeling was married 30th May 1896
W. E. Jordan and Lillian Lee Keeling was married Sept. 7th, 1892
James L. Keeling and Charlotte McGrew was married April 15th, 1834
William McGrew and Nancy Goodwin was married Jan. 1st, 1800
Vincent Smith & Mrs. Mary Keeling was married Dec. 25th, 1850
        (One of the above was 74 years old & the other 71.)
G. A. Hopkins and Elizabeth Demarius Brown was married 19th Dec. 1838.

4

DEATHS:

William McGrew departed this life July 10th, 1851
Nancie McGrew Departed this life Jan. 4, 1861
Mary Smith departed this life June 13th, 1853
James Lowery Keeling Departed this life Dec. 14th, 1854
Thomas A. Keeling died July 24th, 1844
Edmond Keeling died Jan.   1845
Thomas Keeling (sen) died March -- 1840, in Arkansas
Nancy C. A. Keeling Died Oct. 16th, 1842
Dr. J. H. H. Keeling Died in Knoxville, Tenn., Dec 29th, 1891,
        of congestion of the brain, aged 47 years 1 month and five days.
G. A. Hopkins Died Jan. 6th, 1892, age 72 yrs., 1 mo., 23 days.
Wilson L. Hopkins Departed this life January --, 1862
Mira Louisa Hopkins Departed this Life   1862.
Charlotte Keeling Died in Pulaski, Tenn., September 27th, 1873,
        at 7-10 A.M., age 68 yrs. 9 mos. 12 days
James L. Keeling died in Fairfield, Tenn., December 14th, 1854,
        at 8 A.M., age 47 yrs. 2 mo. 7 days.
Mary E. Butler Died on Riley's Hill near Pulaski, June 17th, 1879,
        at 11 P.M., age 39 yrs., 7 mo., 2 days
Willie J. Keeling, died at Columbia, Tenn., April 18th, 1882, at
        8-40 A.M., age 21 years 2 months and 19 days
Mary Louise Keeling Died in Houston, Texas, May 2nd, at 7-50 P.M.,
        age 35 years, 3 mo. 22 days.
Elisabeth D. Hopkins Died Dec. 19th, 1903.

NOTES:

The Gustavus Clarence Keeling listed above signed his name C. G. Keeling,
        and a Will executed by him about 1924, and later revoked by an-
        other Will, is signed Clarence G. Hopkins.
The Bess Keeling listed above signed her name Elizabeth Keeling, and a
        Will executed by her about 1924, and later revoked by another
        Will, which was never probated, is signed Charlotte Elizabeth
        Keeling; and the date of her birth is November 2nd, and the
        year, according to the best information abtainable is 1875.
According to the marriage records of Giles County, Tenn., the date
        of the marriage of John F. Morrison and Eula Agnes Keeling is
        shown as May 24, 1896, and not May 30, 1896.

MORGAN SMITH BIBLE

In possession of Mrs. Harry Hoopes, Shelbyville, Tennessee
Publisher: American Bible Society, New York, 1851

FRONT PAGE: Tabitha Williams Smith Book
             This Book was the year 1858

This book was   To Morgan C. Webb
by his Grandmother Tabitha W. Smith in the year 1879
This book was to Floy F. Webb by his Father Morgan C. Webb in the year
1935
This book to Laura Amrette Webb Hoopes by her father Floy F. Webb, in
the year 1967

MARRIAGES:

Morgan Smith and Tabitha Williams Moore was married December the 23rd,
      1823.
Isaac B. Webb and Frances E. Smith was married Nov. the 24th, 1842.
W. G. P. Sharp and Ann Eliza Webb was married Jan the 20th, 1863.
John H. Ward and Tabitha Williams Moore Webb married Dec 18, 1866.
John Henry Harrison Thweatt and Martha Jane Webb married Feb 11, 1868.
Floy F. Webb was married to Emily R. Eagan, Apr 20, 1957.
Morgan C. Webb and Laura E. Shofner married Dec 13, 1876
Effie B. Webb, daughter of M.C. Webb married Ross Shearin, Mar 22, 1899.
Ross Shearin died 1904
Tina S. Webb, daughter of M. C. Webb was married to H. K. Morgan,
      Dec 10, 1898.
Floy F. Webb, son of M. C. Webb was married to Lillian Bell Ashley,
      Aug 6, 1905.
Nell Katherine Webb, daughter of M. C. Webb was married to Lee Clarence
      Pannell, May 12, 1909.
Amrette Webb, daughter of F. F. Webb married John W. Ailes, Mar 19, 1937.
John W. Ailes born June 20, 1894.
James H. Webb, son of F. F. Webb married Bernice Perry, May 6, 1936
Amrette Webb Ailes married Harry Hershel Leiter, born June 28, 1891
      on Nov 28, 1949.
Amrette Leiter married Harry Hoopes June 11, 1951, born May 12, 1898.
Charlotte Webb, daughter of F. F. Webb married Wallace E. Ott, June 20,
      1936, of Quincy, Ill.
Amrette Ott, born Feb 5, 1938
Charles Webb Ott, born Mar 26, 1941, birthplace St. Louis, Mo.
Mary Elizabeth Ott, born Jan 21, 1944
Paul Douglas Ott was born Nov 17, 1951, birthplace Palo Alto, Calif.
Amrette Ott married Mar   1957 to John Winston Cordell at Burlingame,
      California.
Dawn Cordell born Oct 7, 1957, Burlingame, Calif.
Catharine Cordell born Dec 12, 1960
Elizabeth Cordell born May 10, 1963, Redwood, Calif.

BIRTHS:

Morgan C. Webb was born Apr 16, 1853
Laura E. Shofner was born Jan 27th, 1856
Effie B. Webb was born Oct 16th, 1877
Tina Shofner Webb was born Nov 28, 1879
Floy F. Webb was born July 4th, 1885
Nellie K. Webb was born Jan 1, 1890
M. C. Webb, Jr. was born Dec 19, 1892
Loraine Webb was born May 10, 1896

Laura Amrette Webb was born May 3, 1907
James Howard Webb was born Oct 20, 1910
Charlotte Webb was born Mar 31, 1914
Frances Helene Pannell was born Feb 26, 1912, daughter of L. C.
        Pannell & Nell Pannell, his wife.

James Lester Morgan, son of H. K. Morgan & Tina S. Morgan, was born
        Feb 17, 1900
Alta Ernestine Morgan, daughter of H. K. Morgan and Tina S. Morgan,
        his wife, was born Sept 9, 1901
Henry Malcolm Morgan, son of H. K. Morgan & Tina S. Morgan, his wife,
        was born Oct 26, 1908
Raymon Morgan, son of H. K. Morgan & Tina S. Morgan, his wife, was born
        Jan 14, 1911
Lucile born July 28, 1915
Rebecca Morgan, born Oct 31, 1917
        Children of Morgan C. Webb, II and Lillian Card Webb:
Lillian Marion Webb born Oct 18, 1917
Jean Marie Webb, born Nov 21, 1918
Morgan Cofield Webb born Mar 4, 1920
Shirley Ann Webb born July 23, 1921
John Card Webb born Mar 4, 1923
Phyllis Lincoln Webb born Feb 12, 1925
Gordon William Webb born Sept 7, 1926
James Howard Webb, II, born Nov 26, 1938
Sarah Lillian Webb born Jan 22, 1942
Perry Ashley Webb born Sept 2, 1945
Sarah Lillian Webb married

DEATHS:
John Moore departed this life Jan the 6th 1842
Mary Ann Eliza Sharp departed this life April 14th, 1866
J. Emmie Florence Sharp departed this life on the July 15th, 1866
Morgan Anderson Sharp departed this life Oct 16, 1868
Morgan Smith departed this life Nov the 20th, 1875
Tabbitha W. Smith born 1800, departed this life Oct 14, 1882
Laura Shofner Webb departed this life Sept 12, 1935
Morgan C. Webb, Sr., departed this life July 8th, 1942
John Walter Ailes died April 7, 1947
Harry Herschel Leiter died May 9, 1950
Lillian Ashley Webb died Apr 5, 1952, age 63 yrs.
Tina Webb Morgan died Dec 14, 1962
Wallace Edwin Ott died Sept 15, 1966, Palo Alto, Calif., Age: 55 yrs.
Floy F. Webb died Mar 8, 1967
Rev. J. W. Gernert, Lutheran Minister at Jenkins Chapel Church died
        July 27, 1964, aged: 75 yrs. Lytle grave yard, Rutherford
        County, Tenn.
James E. Webb, Esq., died July 9, 1873
Martha An Webb, wife of James E. Webb, died Oct 3, 1872.

SHOFNER BIBLE

In possession of Mrs. Prentice Cooper, Shelbyville, Tennessee
Publisher: The Holy Bible, by Zeigler, McCurdy & Co.,
Philadelphia, Penn.   1868

MARRIAGES:
J. M. Shofner & M. E. Landis were married July 27, A.D., 1862
R. D. King & Miss Alice Shofner were married Mch 13 A.D., 1884
E. B. Maupin & Emma Shofner were married Oct 7, 1884. A.D.
W. P. Cooper & Argentine Shofner were married Oct 25th, 1894

BIRTHS:
J. M. Shofner was born August 2nd. Anno Domini 1841
Melissa E. Shofner was born September 4th A.D., 1844
Alice Shofner was born May 30th A.D., 1863
Emma Shofner was born October 31st, A.D., 1864
Edna Shofner was born March 26th, A.D., 1867

DEATHS:
Jacob Morton Shofner died July 8, 1916
Melissa Shofner died August 28th, 1912
Edna died Oct 17th, 1868

BIRTHS:
Argie Shofner was born, April 3rd, A.D., 1873
Hoyt D. King was born March 11, A.D., 1885
Dale King was born May 23, A.D., 1861
E. B. Maupin was born Oct 15, A.D., 1860
Edward Bowlin Maupin was born July 15, 1886 A.D.
Morton Brandon King was born September 8th A.D., 1887

DEATHS:
Hoyt D. King died March 18, 1902
Redden Dale King died July 4th, 1895
E. B. Maupin died Aug 17, 1900

BIRTHS:
Redden Douglass King was born March 27 h, 1892
Wm. Prentice Cooper was born September 27th, 1870
Wm. Prentice Cooper, Jr., was born September 28th, 1895
Mildred Cooper was born Sept 29th, 1898
Major A. L. Landis was born Aug 31, 18?3 and died June 6, 1896

DEATHS:
Douglas died October 6, 1896
Mildred died October 11, 1895
Nancy Carter Landis was born March 20, 1826 & died Feb 6, 1901

COLEMAN BIBLE

In possession of Mrs. Prentice Cooper, Shelbyville, Tennessee
Publisher: The Holy Bible, by H. Cowperthwait & Co.   1856

PARENTS:
Father: W. E. Coleman was born February the 17th, 1820
Mother: Elizabeth F. Coleman was born March the 7th, 1821

BIRTHS:
Alexander E. Coleman was born Jan the 7th, 1853
Martha Willeford Coleman was born October the 27th, 1872

MARRIAGES:
W. E. Coleman & Elizabeth F. Alden was married January the 4th, 1849
W. E. Coleman and E. J. Wardlaw was married Nov the 29th, 1871
Alex. E. Coleman and Anna Belle Shofner was married Sept 22, 1874

DEATHS:
Wilford E. Coleman departed this life April 11th, 1879 at 12:15
    o'clock at night
Emily Jane Hester died Oct 30, 1911 abt 1 o'clock A.M.
Elizabeth F. Coleman departed this life Sept the 11th, 1870,
    abt Sun Rise.

NORMAN BIBLE

In possession of Mrs. Prentice Cooper, Shelbyville, Tennessee
Publisher: C. Alexander & Co., Philadelphia, Pa.   1834

BIRTHS:
Wesley Norman, son of Benjamin Norman and Judy his wife was born June
    28th, day in the year of our Lord, 1794.
Elizabeth Norman, daughter of Joseph B. Arnett & Agnes, his wife, was
    born Oct. 31st, in the year of our Lord, 1798.
Eliza H. Norman, daughter of Wesley Norman & Elizabeth his wife was
    born May 20th in the year of our Lord, 1817.
Joseph C. Norman, son of Wesley Norman & Elizabeth his wife was born
    Jan 7th in the year of our Lord, 1819.
Agnes A. Norman, daughter of Wesley Norman & Elizabeth his wife was
    born 6th Aug. in the year of our Lord, 1820.
Nancy H. Norman, daughter of Wesley Norman & Elizabeth his wife was
    born Nov 20th, in the year of our Lord, 1822.
George T. Norman, son of Wesley Norman & Elizabeth his wife was born
    Sept. 12th in the year of our Lord, 1824.
Betsey Ann T. Norman, daughter of Wesley Norman & Elizabeth his wife
    was born Jan 15th in the year of our Lord, 1826.

Wesley G. Norman, son of Wesley Norman & Elizabeth his wife was born
     June 10th in the year of our Lord, 1827.
Martha R. Norman, daughter of Wesley Norman & Elizabeth his wife was
     born Feb 28th in the year of our Lord, 1829.
Mary Jane F. Norman, daughter of Wesley Norman & Elizabeth his wife
     was born Jan 22nd in the year of our Lord, 1839
Cornelius A. Norman, son of Wesley Norman & Elizabeth his wife was
     born July 31st in the year of our Lord, 1841

MARRIAGES:
William Royster & Eliza H. Norman were married Jan 18th, 1833
Joseph C. Norman & Virginia R. Brooks were married Feb 17th, 1841

DEATHS:
Nancy H. Norman, daughter of Wesley Norman and Elizabeth his wife
     died July 15th in the year of our Lord, 1826
Wesley Norman, son of Benjamin Norman and Judy his wife died August
     26th in the year of our Lord, 1843
Elizabeth Norman, wife of Wesley Norman died Sept 2nd, 1852
Mary F. Norman, daughter of Wesley & Elizabeth Norman died Sept. 3rd,
     1852
George T. Norman, son of Wesley & Elizabeth Norman died Feb 25th, 1845
Mrs. Martha R. Earle, daughter of Wesley Norman & Elizabeth, his wife
     died Dec 18th, 1851

Laura Denman was born March 29th, 186_.

WILLIAM ROYSTER BIBLE

In possession of Mrs. Prentice Cooper, Shelbyville, Tennessee

William Royster and Eliza his wife, late Eliza H. Norman, was married
     on the 17th day of January, 1833.

(piece of paper):
Bro. Alexander Royster was born in Mecklenberg Co., Va. June 1799,
     removed to Henderson Co., Ky., Oct 1818. Professed Religion
     about the year 1820, Licensed to preach in the year 1837.
     Died August 7th, 1871. Aged: 72.

BIRTHS:
William Royster was born September 30th, 1809
Eliza H. Royster was born May the 20th day, 1817
Wesley Wilkins Royster was born June 24th day, 1834
Joseph Cliff Royster was born November 16th day, 1836
William Thomas Royster was born in the year of our Lord January 8th
     day, 1839

DEATHS:
William Royster died January 23rd, 1896 at 6 p.m.
Eliza H. Royster deceased July 22, 1889 at 5:20 p.m.
Wesley Wilkins Royster died August 14th, 1912 at 2:30 p.m.
J. C. Royster died September __, 1863.
William Thomas Royster deceased October 11th, 1840.
Joseph Royster died July 19th, 1863

BIRTHS:
William E. Royster was born in the year of our Lord, April 23rd, 1841
George M. Royster was born Oct 21st, 1843.
Ireneaus F. Royster was born Dec 16th, 1845.
Eliza Ann Frances Royster was born Oct 22nd, 1848.
Leander A. Royster, son of Wm. Royster and Eliza, his wife, was born
        February 2nd, 1851.

DEATHS:
Wm. E. Royster died September 19th, 1921 at 10:30 A.M. of _____
George M. Royster died January 13th, 1863
J. H. Royster died November 25th, 1864.
Leander A. Royster, M.D., died July 8th, 1898 between 4 & 5 o'clock p.m.

BIRTHS:
John N. Royster, son of Wm. Royster and Eliza his wife, was born
        January 31st, 1853.
James Henry Royster born January 17th, 1856.
A Bebe was born September 10th, 1858 and deceased Sept 12, 1858.
Levin C. Royster was born July 19th, 1860.

DEATHS:
John N. Royster died November 2nd, at 11 o'clock, 1893.
Levin C. Royster died Aug 14th, 1909 between 12 & 1 o'clock p.m.

NEGRO'S AGES:
Clay born October 9, 1834
Phillis born in year 1835
Nelson born January 8th/10th, 1841
Benjamin born February 28, 1849
Louis born August 4, 1856
Amanda born March 27, 1868
Theodore born May 2, 1856
Florence born July 7th, 1858
Babe born August 6, 1860 & deceased Aug 6, 1866
Victoria Addalane was born October 18, 1861
Marcia Augusta was born February 1863
Hayward G. was born October 1863.

11

COOPER BIBLE

In possession of Mrs. Prentice Cooper, Shelbyville, Tennessee
Publisher: American Bible Society, 1871   New York

MARRIAGES:
James W. Cooper and Eliza A. Royster were married November 3rd, 1869
Wm. Prentice Cooper and Argentine Shofner of Shelbyville, Tenn., were
    married October 25, 1894.
Henry Lee Cooper and Lucie Higgins were married November 27th, 1895.
Eliza C. Cooper and W. W. Agnew were married August 22nd, 1900

BIRTHS:
James Wm. Cooper was born April 27th, 1841
Eliza A. Royster was born October 22nd, 1848
Wm. Prentice, son of James W. and Eliza A. Cooper was born September
    27th, 1870.
Henry Lee Cooper was born February 27, 1873.
Eliza Corine Cooper was born on September 22nd, 1877.
Miller Marvin Cooper was born January 14th, 1880.

DEATHS:
Wm. Prentice, son of James W. and Eliza A. Cooper was baptised by
    Rev. E. Thurman August 1871
Henry Lee Cooper was baptised by Rev. E. Thurman December 3, 1874.
Eliza Corine Cooper was baptised by J. C. Petrie on September 22nd, 1878.
Miller Marvin Cooper was baptised by Rev. Wm. T. Moore on September
    25, 1881.

BIRTHS:
Wm. Prentice Cooper, Jr. was born September 28, 1895
Mildred Cooper was born September 29, 1898 & died October 9th, 1898.
Carolzor Cooper was born on December 10, 1898.
Henry Lee Cooper, Jr., was born September 4th, 1906
Thomas A. Cooper was born October 24, 1913.
William N. Agnew was born October 4, 1901
Wm. Walter Agnew was born November 24th, 1903
James W. C. Agnew was born February 14th, 1908

DEATHS:
Miller Marvin Cooper died September 21, 1883 at about 6 o'clock a.m.
James W. C. Agnew died June 29, 1916 at 11:15 a.m.
Henry Lee Cooper died in Denver, Colorado, September 29th, 1925 at
    7:48 a.m.
James Wm. Cooper, M.D., died in Henderson, Ky., August 13th, 1928
    at 9 p.m.
Eliza A. Royster Cooper died December 31, 1928 at 9 p.m.

LANDIS BIBLE

In possession of Mrs. Prentice Cooper, Shelbyville, Tennessee
Publisher: H & E Phinney, Cooperstown, N.Y.,   1840

Jas. R. P. Landis, son of Abel J. Landis born February 20, 1867
Abel H. Landis, 2nd son of Abel J. Landis born September 22nd, 1868
Letitia Bennett, 1st child of J. M. and M. E. Bennet born June 27,
    1860
James S. J. Albert Bennet   2nd of J. M. and M. E. Bennet born Nov-
    ember 25, 1863
Virginia Bennet, 3rd of J. M. and M. E. Bennet born December 10, 1866

MARRIAGES:
John Landis and Mary Lowe was married November 18th, A.D. 1820
A. L. Landis and Nancy Carter was married June 27th A.D. 1843
J. M. Bennett and Margaret E. Landis was married _____
Jacob M. Shofner and Melissa E. Landis married July 1862

BIRTHS:
John Landis was borned April 19th A.D. 1795
Mary Lowe was borned October 14th A.D. 1796
Sarah Landis was borned March 19th, 1822
Absalom L. Landis was borned August 31st A.D., 1823
Eran Landis was borned October 15th, A.D., 1826
Phebe A. Landis was borned June 27th A.D., 1830
Robert W. Landis was borned December 13th, A.D., 1832
James H. P. Landis was borned October 3rd, A.D., 1835
Abel J. Landis was borned October 18th A.D., 1837
Margaret E. Landis was borned December 18th A.D., 1839
Nancy Carter now Nancy Landis was borned March 20th A.D., 1826
John Coble Holt Benton Dallas William Landis was borned July 18th A.D.,
    1845
Joseph Thomas Shofner, 3rd son of A. J. and Eran Shofner born February
    3rd, 1863.
Robert Newton Shofner, 4th son of A. J. and Eran Shofner was born
    March 28th, 1865
Doctor Jenkins Shofner, 5th son of A. J. and Eran Shofner born
    March 15th, 1864.
Albert Lowe was borned September 24th A.D., 1827
James K. P. Landis returned from Louisiana November 16th 1855, was
    absent 13 months for ____ in lease of friends in October 1856.
James K. P. Landis was borned February 20th 1857 (or 1867)
John P. Koonce, 1 son of Jno. and Eran Koonce born May 6th, 1854
Jas. A. Koonce, 2nd son of Jno. and Eran Koonce born September 18th 1855
Frederick Landis Shofner, 1st son of A. J. and Eran Shofner born July
    15, 1858, 1st
William Coble Shofner, 2nd son of A. J. and Eran Shofner born April 20th
    1861- 2nd.

13

Absalom's children:
Melissa Emma Landis borned September 4th A.D., 1844
Absalom Melville Landis borned April 3rd A.D., 1846
Helen Narcissa Landis borned Jany 1st, 1848
Melville Alonzo Landis borned Dec 12th, 1849
Solon Lee Landis was borned Feby 26th, 1852
Lavoy P. Landis borned March 9th, 1854
Abb S. Landis borned August 9th, 1856
Sallie N. Landis borned May 10th, 1860
Lenora Landis borned November 10th, 1863
John T. Landis borned August 4th, 1866
Leelan Landis borned October 27th, 1868

DEATHS:
Phebe A. Landis departed this life October 11, A.D., 1839, aged: 9 years
        3 months   14 days
Robert W. Landis departed this life October 25, A.D., 1839 aged: 6 years
        9 months   25 days
Absalom Melville, son of A. L. and Nancy Landis departed this life
        September 20, 1847 aged: 1 year 5 months 17 days
Lavoy P. Landis, 4th son of A. L. and Nancy Landis departed this life
        August 9th 6:20 p.m., 1868 aged: 14 yrs 5 mos __days
Edora Shofner, 3 dau of J. M. and Melissa Shofner and grand daughter of
        A. L. and Nancy Landis departed this life October 17, 1868

DEATHS:
A. J. Shofner born March 21, 1828 and died July 27th, 1868.

Major A. L. Landis died June 6, 1896
Nancy Carter Landis died February 6, 1901
John Landis departed this life July 4, 1854 aged: 59 yrs, 2 mos, 15 days
Mary Landis departed this life December 14th 8:30 p.m., 1868
        aged: 72 years, 2 months, died suddenly after long sleep.
Martha Troxler departed this life 11th October 1868 aged: 74 years.
Jas. K. P. Landis departed this life Jany 17th 1866 at 7:30 a.m.
        aged: 30 years 3 months 14 days
Eran Shofner departed this life at 5 o'clock a.m. June 21st, 1869
        aged: 42 years 8 months & 6 da. born October 21, 1826.

Margaret E. Bennett died February 20th 1877 a.m. at
Abel J. Landis died at his brother's, A. L. at 12 midnight Wednesday
        16th day of February, 1876.
Helen Nascissa Green died October 25, 1887

Phebe Lee Landis	1774-1841
John Landis	1794-1854
Mary Lowe Landis	1795-1868
Phebe Landis	1830-1839
Robert Landis	1832-1839
Abel J. Landis	1837-1876

Margaret Landis Bennett	1839-1877
Eran Landis Shofner	1826-1869
Wm. Shofner	1861-
John P. Koonce	1854-
Absalom Landis	1846-1847
Melville A. Landis	1849-1914
Lavoy P. Landis	1854-1868
Martha Lowe Troxler	1794-1868
Albert Lowe	1827-1899

BRADEN BIBLE

In possession of Mrs. Helen C. Marsh, Shelbyville, Tennessee
Publisher: Date and Publisher missing

John W. Braden was born Dec 5th, 1804 in South Carolina and
Sintha Porter was born Feb 14th, 1806, was married in 1824.
Children:
Mary Malinda Braden was born Jan 22, 1825
Sintha Porter was born Oct 16, 1827
Narcissa Ellen was born Nov 27, 1825

DEATHS:
Sintha P. Braden died Dec 10, 1827, aged: 21 years
Mary Malinda died Feb 1, 1825, aged: 11 days
Sintha Porter Braden died Nov 4, 1839 aged: 12 years & 19 days

John W. Braden and Rachel married in 1829
Rachel was born May 15, 1812
Irene Angeline Braden was born Oct 12, 1830
Eliza Jane Braden was born April 3, 1832
James Wiley Braden was born July 27, 1836
Lucinda Clementine Braden was born Dec 31, 1837
Casander Abbetine Braden was born Feb 3, 1840
Perry Columbus Braden was born April 9th, 1842
Nancy Parthenia Braden was born Feb 18th, 1844
John Wesley Braden was born Dec 29, 1846
Francis Orlena Braden was born Feb 28, 1848
Thomas Green Braden was born July 21, 1850
Leroy Calvin Braden was born Aug 16, 1852

Rachel Braden died Aug 27, 1854
Patrick Harvy died Aug 14, 1854

MARRIAGES:
Narcissa Ellen Braden married William Huffman August 12, 1843
Irena Angeline Braden married Thomas F. Mitchell
Eliza Jane Braden married W. D. Gill, July 8th, 1852

15

James Wiley Braden married Sarah B. Gill, September 12, 1857
Lucinda Clementine Braden married M. M. Story, August 29, 1857
John Wesley Braden and E. L. Williams, September 11, 1872
Leroy Calvin Braden married N. A. Cole, December 18, 1873

John W. Braden and Sarah A. Taylor was married May 20, 1855
Sarah A. Taylor Braden was born Oct 28, 1821
Giles Whitfield Braden was born Dec 10, 1856
William Henderson Braden was born May 26, 1858
Susan Jane Braden was born July 8th, 1859
Sintha Alis Braden was born Jan 1, 1861
Temple Albine Braden was born Mar 21, 1862
Harvey Lafayette Braden was born July 7th, 1863

MARRIAGES:

Giles Whitfield Braden and Mattie _____ was married in Anson, Texas
William Henderson Braden and Minnie S. McCrory was married at Spring-
      place, Marshall County, Tenn.
Susan Jane Braden and James Buchanan Edwards married at Cornersville,
      Tenn., Marshall County.
Temple Albine Braden and Cora Turner married in Marshall County, Tenn.
Harvey Lafayette Braden and Jennie Evert Ray was married July 4th, 1900
      at Fayetteville, Tenn.

DEATHS:

John W. Braden died August 29, 1871 at Ostella, Marshall County, Tenn.
Sarah A. Taylor died November 17, 1898 at Ostella, Tenn.
Giles Whitfield Braden died 1926 in Anson , Texas.
William Henderson Braden died 1937, Springplace, Tenn.
Susan Jane Braden Edwards died 1938 at Cornersville, Tenn.
Sintha Alis Braden died January 5, 1865
Temple Albine Braden died in Nashville, Tenn., 1922
Harvey Lafayette Braden died at Flintville, Tenn., April 27, 1914
Eliza Jane Braden died September 23, 1909
Patrick Harvy Braden died August 14, 1854
James Wiley Braden died in Chattanooga, September 25, 1864, Battle of
      Chickamauga, C.S.A., Corpl. Co. I, 32 Inf.
Perry Columbus Braden died February 14, 1862, C.S.A., Pvt Co. I., 32 Inf.
Thomas Green Braden died November 9, 1898, Clardyville, Lincoln Co.,
      Tenn.
Jennie Evert Ray Braden died December 23, 1956, Flintville, Tenn.,
      aged: 77 years.
Vera Braden died July 2, 1902, Ostella, Tenn., aged: 3 mos & 3 days
(Twin to Vertna Mae Braden Crawford, born Mar 31, 1902)
Henry Clark Crawford died November 29, 1953, Flintville, Tennessee,
      aged: 54 years. Vertna M. Crawford died Mar. 29, 1990, Shelbyville, TN.
Rachel Crawford died October 30, 1920, aged: 6 weeks, Concord Church
      Cemetery, nr. Hazel Green, Ala.
Lizzie C. Wells Ray died July 7, 1903. Marshall County, Tennessee
      Wells Cemetery.
Charles Harvy Ray died Nov 19th, 1934, aged: 84 yrs. Wells Cemetery.

Robert Lee Ray died May 18, 1969, Flintville, Tennessee. Vet of W.W.I

MARRIAGES:
Vertna Mae Braden and Henry Clark Crawford married November 29, 1919
Helen Joe Crawford and Timothy Richard Marsh married July 24, 1941, in
    Huntsville, Ala.
Lee Earl Crawford and Jean F. Burba married May 12, 1955 in Waukegan,
    Illinois.
Marsha Joan Marsh and Arthur Ray Edwards married Feb 12, 1960, at
    Shelbyville, Tennessee. Divorced July 1, 1976
Leslie Devons Marsh and Betty Jane Foster married Oct 4, 1968, at
    Huntsville, Ala. Divorced abt 1972
Leslie Devons Marsh married Shirley Frances Farris, Sept 12, 1972
    Rover, Tennessee. Divorced 1973
Marsha M. Edwards and Raymond Markiewicz married March 11, 1977

BIRTHS:
Jennie Evert Braden born October 14, 1878
Vertna Mae and Vera Braden born March 31, 1902, Marshall Co., Tenn.
Henry Clark Crawford born December 25, 1897, Howell, Lincoln Co., Tenn.
Rachel Crawford born September 17, 1920, Plevna, Alabama
Helen Joe Crawford born November 21, 1921, Flintville, Tenn.
Lee Earl Crawford born April 29, 1925, Flintville, Tennessee
Charles Harvey Ray born July 14, 1850
Robert Lee Ray born Dec 9, 1894
Marsha Joan Marsh born in Chicago, Illinois, October 6th, 1942, Cook Co.
Leslie Devons Marsh born in Jackson, Tenn., October 13, 1945, Madison Co
Timothy Richard Marsh born at Lincoln, Tenn., June 12, 1921, Lincoln Co.
Melissa Michele Edwards born at Lewisburg, Tenn., January 10, 1963, in
    Marshall Co.
Timothy James Edwards born at Lewisburg, Tenn., October 19, 1968, in
    Marshall Co.
Sally Rachel Edwards born & died August 11, 1971, Lewisburg, Marshall
    Co. & buried in Willow Mount Cemetery, Shelbyville, Tenn.

WILLIAM CRAWFORD BIBLE

By Helen C. Marsh, Shelbyville, Tennessee

William Robert Crawford was born November 3, 1867
Minnie Grantland Crawford was born October 28, 1868
Mary Emma, eldest daughter of Wm. and Minnie Crawford was born June
    22, 1894
Joseph Warren, eldest son, was born November 5, 1895
Henry Clark, second son, was born December 25, 1897
William R. Crawford was born September 12, 1899
Exie Lee Crawford was born June 3, 1902
Blanche Fuller Crawford was born September 13, 1904

Alice Ellen Crawford was born December 11, 1907
Richard Grantland Crawford was born July 23, 1909
William Crawford and Minnie Grantland was married December 27, 1892
Mary Emma Crawford died September 2, 1895 aged: 1 year, 2 mos, 10 da.
Joseph Warren Crawford died June 11, 1897 aged: 1 yr, 7 mos, 7 da.
Infant Boy died 1905 (Born & Died)
Infant Girl died 1910 (Born and Died)
William Robert Crawford died September 3, 1936
Minnie Grantland Crawford died January 7, 1948
Henry Clark Crawford and Vertna Mae Braden was married November 29,
     1919.
Exie Lee Crawford and Andy Jackson married 1919
Blanche Fuller Crawford and Desso Cowley was married Nov 24, 1921.
Alice Ellen Crawford and Charlie Jackson married..
Richard Grantland Crawford was married December 25, 1929 to
     Margie Ella Foster.

CRAWFORD BIBLE

By- Mrs. Helen C. Marsh, Shelbyville, Tennessee
Publisher: George Grierson, Dublin   MDCCXXXIX (1739) Ireland

Rachel M. B. Titus, deceased Oct the __ the year of our Lord, 1795, at
     4 o'clock in the morn. aged sixty three years, after bearing
     seven children, she lived til after the death of three, to wit,
     John, Arthur and Moses Bowen.

Titus Crawford was born in Sept. the 13, 1803
Rebecahah Crawford was born Dec the 23, 1804
Evaline Crawford was born March 12, 1806
Rachel Sawyers Crawford born Aug 30, 1807
Nancy T. P. Crawford was born Sept 11, 1810
John James Crawford was born Nov 12, 1812
William Alexander Crawford was born June 17, 1816
Phebe Titus Crawford was born Sept 20, 1819
Elizabeth Ann Crawford was born Jan 30, 1822
Sally Sellers Crawford born May 2, 1825
"Children of William and Rachel Titus Crawford"

Titus Crawford died Oct 8, 1817
Rachel Sawyers Crawford Bell died Sept 4, 1820, aged: about 70
Ebenizer Titus died Sept 14, 1807. Aged: 80 yrs.
Pheby T. Rednick died Sept 2, 1815. Aged: 35 yrs.
Elizabeth A. Crawford Banet died June 15, 1824. Aged: 57 yrs.
Nancy B. Frazor died May 7, 1835 Aged: 71 yrs.
William Crawford died Oct 19, 1792 Aged: 48 yrs.

Offsprings of William and Nancy Crawford:
Margaret Ann Crawford born Aug 17, 1844
George Gibson born Jan 10, 1846, died Sept 6, 1896, aged: 50 yrs,
       7 mos, 26 days.
Joe Warren Crawford born Sept 17, 1847, died Jan 31, 1871, aged: 23 yrs
       4 mos 14 days.
Mary Etta Crawford born Aug 6, 1853, died Mar 12, 1870, aged: 16 yrs,
       7 mos 6 days.

William Crawford born Feb 13, 1780 married Rachel Titus, born Aug 19,
       1782, married April 1802, Nashville, Tennessee.

James Titus born Dec 10, 1775
George Titus born Feb 10, 1777
Phebe Titus born Aug 2, 1779
Rachel Titus born Aug 19, 1782

John Titus born
Arthur Titus born
Moses Bowers born

Rachel Crawford, daughter of Ebenezer Titus, died June 25, 1841, aged:
       58 yrs, 10 mos, 24 days.
Nancy T. P. Arendale, daughter of Ebenezer Titus.
Rachel Crawford died Sept 9, 1843, lacking one day being 33 years.
Rachel T. Hamton died June 30, 1843, aged: 41 yrs & 10 Mos.
Sally S. Eastland died May 12, 1850. Aged: 25 years & 10 days.
William Crawford died Mar 7, 1859, aged: 80 years.

George G. Crawford and Fannie E. Kimes were married Jan 9, 1872

WILLIAM CRAWFORD BIBLE

By Helen C. Marsh, Shelbyville, Tennessee
Publisher: missing   Date: 1841

Nancy R. Gibson, daughter of John and Margaret Gibson born in Lincoln
       County Tennessee May 23, 1814 and was united in marriage to
       William Crawford Oct 16, 1843.
Children:
Margaret Ann Eliza Crawford born Aug 17, 1844
George Gibson Crawford born Jan 10, 1846
Joseph Warren Crawford born Sept 17, 1847
Mary Etta Frances Crawford born Aug 6, 1853
Ellen B. Strother born May 29, 1847

William Crawford and Nancy R. Gibson married Oct 16, 1843
John B. Tigert and Margaret Ann Crawford married Oct 19, 1858
Joseph Warren Crawford and Emma N. Harris married Dec 24, 1864

George G. Crawford and Frances Ellen Kimes married Jan 9, 1872
Virgil Green Crawford and Emma Laura Dickey married Nov 27, 1906
George Nelson Harris and Georgie Crawford married Dec 22, 1903
Charles S. Crawford and Lola Clyde Buchanan married May 20, 1902
George G. Crawford and Ellen B. Strother married Oct 21, 1874
Carrie Emma Crawford and James Calvin Ellis married Dec 22, 1899

DEATHS:
William Crawford died Mar 7, 1859
Nancy R. Crawford died Aug 6, 1868
Mary Etta F. Crawford died Mar 12, 1870
Joseph Warren Crawford died Jan 31, 1871
Frances Ellen Crawford died Aug 9, 1873
George G. Crawford died Sept 6, 1896
Maggie Ellen Crawford died abt 1884
William Duvergne Crawford died abt 1904/05
George Nelson Harris died May 10, 1936
Charles Strother Crawford died Sept 14, 1942
Carrie Crawford Ellis died May 17, 1951
Virgil Green Crawford died Feb 12, 1943

George Gibson Crawford's Children:
Fannie Etta Crawford, daughter of G. G. & Frances Ellen Crawford
        born Dec 15, 1872
Charles Strother Crawford, son of George G. & Ellen Bowers Strothers
        Crawford born Sept 13, 1875
Carrie Emma Crawford, daughter of George G. & Ellen B. Crawford born
        Nov 20, 1877
Georgia Anna Crawford, daughter of George G. & Ellen B. Crawford born
        Nov 21, 1879
Maggie Ellen Crawford, daughter of George G. & Ellen B. Crawford born
        Jan 30, 1881
Virgil Green Crawford born Apr 30, 1884
William Duvergne Crawford born May 22, 1886

Charles Strother & Lola Clyde Crawford descendants:
Helen Crawford born June 9, 1903
Meredith Crawford born Aug 15, 1905

James Calvin & Carrie Emma Ellis' descendants:
George Benton Ellis born Feb 4, 1901
Fredna Mae Ellis born July 29, 1903
James Orin Ellis born July 9, 1907
Charles Crawford Ellis born Oct 4, 1913

George Nelson & Georgia Anna Harris descendants:
Julian Nelson Harris born Mar 13, 1905
Harold Crawford Harris born Nov 2, 1905

Virgil Green & Emma Laura Crawford's descendants:
Joe Kyle Crawford born May 31, 1908

Merrill Davis Crawford born Dec 3, 1911

Joseph Warren and Nancy Emma Harris Crawford descendants:
William Robert Crawford born Nov 3, 1869
Josie Crawford born Feb 28, 1872

Helen Crawford and Harry Wickstrom, married June 18, 1926, their
        descendants:
Charles C. Wickstrom born June 19, 1927
Joanne Helene Wickstrom born Aug 23, 1928

Meredith Crawford married Nestor Duguay, Mar 4, 1932, their descendants:
Richard Crawford Duguay born Aug 15, 1936
Stephen Buchanan Duguay born Nov 23, 1940

DEATHS:
Charles Crawford Ellis died Mar 13, 1930
Fredna Mae Kuney Crawford died Apr 6, 1931

John Bowen Deceased August 11th, at 9 o'clock in the morning in the
        year of our Lord, 1760. Aged: thirty one years.
Nancy B. Mathews died July __, 1807, aged: 47 yrs.
William Bowen died __ October 1828, aged: 62 yrs.
Rebecca B. Frazor died May 7th, 1835, aged: 71 years.

John Bowen was born May the 21, Saturday, in the year of Our Lord, 1746.

John Bowen was marryed March 5, 1756
John Bowen was born Aprile 10th 1757
Arthor Bowen was born August 23rd, 1758
Ann Bowen was born Aprile 26th, 1760
Mosses Bowen was born June 10th, 1762
Rebacha Bowen was born January 28th, 1764
William Bowen was born March 6th, 1766
Elizabeth Bowen was born November 30th, 1767

James Titus was born December 20th 1775
George Titus was born February 10th, 1777
Pheby Titus was born August 2nd, 1779
Rachel Titus was born August 19th, 1782

RICHARD CASWELL BIBLE

Copied by Miss Mary Bass, from a Bible in the possession of Mrs.
        Thomas F. Bates, Oct 6, 1968.
NOTE: This Bible and other items has been sent to North Carolina
        Library and Archives, Raleigh, N.C.
Publisher: John Baskett, Printer of the University, Oxford MDCCXL

21

Richard Caswell, son of Rich'd Caswell & Christian his wife was married
to Mary Mackilwean on Tuesday the 21st day of April 1752
The said Rich'd & Mary had a daughter Still born the 15th day of Sept-
ember 1753.
William, son of said Richard & Mary was born on Tuesday the 24th day of
September 1754.
Mary, wife of Richard Caswell was delivered of a Daughter on Friday
night the 4th Day of February 1757 and on Monday the 7th of said
Month she (said Mary) Departed this life in the 25th year of her
age and was Interr'd on Wednesday following.
Richard Caswell was maried to Sarah Herritage on Tuesday the 20th day
of June 1758.
Richard, son of the above Rich'd & Sarah Caswell was Born on Saturday
the 15th of September 1759.
Sarah, Daughter of Rich'd & Sarah Caswell was Born on Tuesday the 26th
Day of February 1762.
Winstone, son of said Rich'd & Sarah Caswell was Born on Monday 7th of
May 1764.
Anne, Daughter of Rich'd & Sarah Caswell was Born on Thursday the 4th
Day of December 1766.
Dallam, Son of Rich'd & Sarah Caswell was Born on Thursday the 15th
Day of June 1769.
John, Son of Rich'd & Sarah Caswell was Born on Friday the 24th of
January 1772.
Susannah, Daughter of Richard & Sarah Caswell was Born Thursday the 16th
of February 1775.
Christian intended, Son of Richard & Sarah Caswell was Born at Newington
the 7th of January (Wednesday) and died the 9th following, 1779
and was buried there.

Joseph Winstone Caswell (Mentioned later) Departed this life on Wednesday about 12 o'clock at night the 21st of January 1761 in the
22d year of his age & was Interr'd the Saturday following, by
his Father.

Anne Caswell (Mentioned later) Departed this life on Sunday (about noon)
the eleventh day of January 1784 & was interr'd the Tuesday
following by her Father.
                    "The End of The Prophets"

Christian Caswell who had been the wido. of Richard Caswell upwards in
the 83d year of her age of 31 years Departed this life at Newington on Sunday night or the morning of the 18th of February
1787 and was Interred by her said husband at the ----(4 letters,
illegible) on Tuesday following.

Richard Caswell arrived in Maryland on the 2d Day of February in the year
of our Lord 1712
Richard Caswell and Christian Dallam were married the 12th day of
January 1723.
Elizabeth, Daughter of Richard & Christian Caswell was born the 27th Day

of October 1724, and she Departed this life the 25th Day of
   November 1725.
William, the first son of Richard & Christian Caswell was Born the __
   of ___ember 1726 (page frayed, day & month cannot be read).
Richard, the 2nd Son of Richard Caswell & Christian (page frayed) was
   Born the 3rd Day of August 1729.
Mary, the 2nd Daughter of Richard Caswell & Christian (page frayed),
   wife was born the 1st Day of August 1731.
Martin, third Son of Richard Caswell & Christian his wife was born the
   15th Day of February 1733.
Joseph (Intended), the 4th Son of Rich'd Caswell & Christian his wife
   was Still Born 3d of May 1736.
Christian & Benjamin, Daughter & Son of Rich'd & Christian Caswell
   were Born 20th of April 1737.
Joseph Winstone, the Sixth Son of Rich'd Caswell & Christian his wife
   was Born 1st of December 1739. (In Margin): See his Death Prior
   to this page.
Samuel & Anne, Son & Daughter of Rich'd Caswell & Christian his wife
   were Born the 28th May 1742. (In Margin): See the next side
   before this.
Richard Caswell Departed this life on Thursday the 24th Day of April
   1755 (2 o'clock afternoon) and was Interr'd Saturday following.
William Caswell, (Son of Rich'd & Christian) Departed this life the
   10th Day of August 1755 A Quarter past Seven in the morning,
   on Board Capt. Jacob Walters on his passage from Barbadoes to
   Maryland.
Christian Caswell (Daughter of Rich'd & Christian) was married to
   William Williams the 16th Day of August 1757 by whom she had a
   Daughter named Elizabeth Born the 23rd Day of June 1758 and she
   the said Christian Departed this life on Tuesday the first Day
   of August 1758 and was Interr'd on Thursday following by her
   Father.
Samuel Caswell & Mary Irons were married on Friday the 26th Day of
   October 1764.
John Caswell, Son of Samuel & Mary his wife was born on Friday 23rd
   November 1765.
Mary, Wife of Samuel Caswell Departed this life on Friday the 26th
   Day of June 1767 and was Interr'd on the Sunday next following.
Samuel Caswell & Eleanor Shine were married on Thursday 22d of June
   1775.
Charlotte Caswell, Daughter of Samuel & Eleanor his wife was Born on
   Sunday the 3d Day of March 1776.
Sally Caswell, 2d Daughter of Samuel & Eleanor his wife was Born on
   Friday the 23rd July 1778.
Elizabeth Caswell, third Daughter (this line was crossed out)
Shine Caswell, first Son of Sam'l and Eleanor Caswell was Born the
   23rd of March 1782.
Elizabeth Caswell, third Daughter of Sam and Eleanor his wife was Born
   July 22d Day of July 1783.
Samuel Caswell departed this life at Doziers Old field Wednesday the
   5th Day of January 1785.

EDWARD EVERETT DEAN BIBLE

Copied by Mrs. Sara Dean Carothers, Wartrace, Tennessee &
          Mrs. Dollie Dean Wolford, Wartrace, Tennessee
Publisher: Central Publishing House, Nashville, Tennessee 1881

This Certifies that EDWARD EVERETT DEAN and SALLIE VIOLA ESLICK
were solemnly united by me in the Holy Bonds of Matrimony at
SALEM CHURCH on the twenty eight day of December in the year of
          our Lord, One thousand Eight Hundred and Eighty Four.
          Conformably to the Ordinance of God and the Laws of the State
          in the presence of Large Assembly At Church Old Salem.
          Signed by ELDER JOHN FLOYD.

MARRIAGES:
Margaret Lee Dean was married to J. G. Gillespie Dec 23 at home by
          Eld. Shelborn 1913
Adlaid Anderson was married to Dewey Hix Kimbro Sept. 1920 by
          Eld. Shelborn.
Edward Elam Dean was married to Minnie E. Locke May 18, 1921 by
          Eld. Gowan.
Frederick Murphy Eslick was married to Anna Francis Martin.
Nancy G. Dean was married to Harrison Stewart April 1st, 1937 by
          Eld. Largen.

BIRTHS:
Edward Everett Dean was born A.D. 1855 Oct 30.
Sallie Viola Anderson was born A.D. 1862 May 2.
Fred Murphy Eslick was born A.D. 1879 July 3.
John Thomas Dean was born A.D. 1888 Jan 18.
Margaret Lee Dean was born A.D. 1890 Nov 26.
Edward Elam Dean was born A.D. 1892 March 23.
Nancy G. Dean was born May 16, 1894
Adlaid Anderson Dean was born Jan 8, 1897

DEATHS:
Edward Everett Dean died May 14 in the year 1913.
          age: 55 years.   A Christian.
John Thomas Dean died April 24, 1928.
A loving and obedient son. A pure Christian.
Minnie Locke Dean, wife of Edward died March 14, 1941
          51 years of age.
Edward Elam Dean died Nov 15th, 1963
Margaret Dean Gillespie died Nov 6th, 1966

MEMORANDA:
Amanda H. Anderson was born in S.C. in the year of our Lord April 25,
1842, died July 29, 1919. Confessed her faith in Christ in her fifteenth year.
John Moutlrie Anderson born Oct 19, 1837 died Dec 13, 1925.

CLEMENT CANNON BIBLE

In possession of Mrs. Morton King, Shelbyville, Tennessee
Publisher: Stereotyped by B & J Collins   New York   1816

BIRTHS:
Clement Cannon, Sen, was born April 15, 1783.
Susannah Locke was born 29th June 1793.

Henry Cannon was born May the 29th 1811
Charles Locke Cannon was born February the 14th 1813
Thomas Batte Cannon was born May the 28th 1815
Letticia Thompson Cannon January the 30th 1817
Mary M. Cannon was born April the 18th 1819
Clement Cannon was born April the 1st 1823

DEATHS:
Mary Cannon departed this life March the 12th 1823
John Cannon departed
Clement Cannon Sen departed this life June 19th 1860
Susannah Cannon Slept in the Arms of Jesus on Sunday March 15th 1874,
        about 4 o'clock p.m.
Emily Janette Little, wife of Thos. B. Cannon, departed in peace on
        February 25, 1895.

MARRIAGES:
Clemment Cannon and Susannah Locke was maried 9th August 1810
Charles L. Cannon & Mary An Hooser were married on the 15th December
        1842.
Thos. B. Cannon & Emily Janette Little were married March 12th 1844
Henry Cannon and Sallie C. Tillman were married Jan. 10, 1833.
Samuel S. Moody and Lettitia T. Cannon were married Oct. 29, 1840.

Family Record:
BIRTHS:
George Whorton Moody Born November 5th 1847 at Huntsville Ala.
Georgie Etta Strong Moody Born July 24th 1860 at Shelbyville, Tenn.,
        married March 16th 1881 at Shelbyville, Tenn.
Children of the above:
Winston Gill Moody Born January 2nd 1882 at Shelbyville, Tenn.
Samuel Shaw Moody August 29th, 1884 at Shelbyville, Tenn.
Margaret Moody, August 6th 1889, at Shelbyville, Tenn.
Winston Gill Moody & Margaret Love Wilson Moody married October 21, 1902
Samuel Shaw Moody & Martha Elizabeth Weatherly married November 6th 1915

MOODY BIBLE

In possession of Mrs. Morton King, Shelbyville, Tennessee
This is a Bible Record which has been removed from the Bible.

Rev. Samuel Shaw Moody May 1, 1810 ╳
Lettitia T. Moody   Jany 30, 1817 ╳

Dr. George Mastin Strong   1832   ╳
Margaret B. Strong   1835   ╳

Dr. George Whorton Moody Nov 5, 1847 ╳
Georgie E. Moody   July 24, 1860 ╳

Winston Gill Moody   Jany 2, 1882 ╳
Margaret Wilson Moody   ╳

Samuel Shaw Moody Jr Aug 29, 1884

Margaret Moody Aug 6, 1889
Morton B. King Sept 8, 1887
Morton B. King, Jr. March 24, 1913
Mary Dale King Feby 4, 1920
George Moody King Aug 12, 1922

Clement Cannon Sr April 11, 1783
Susan L. Cannon June 29, 1793
Gen Wm. Moore
Elizabeth R. Moore
Rev. T. L. (Thomas Lipscomb) Moody Nov. 30, 1842

Clement J. Cannon July 2, 1845
Sallie C. Moody Aug 18, 1859
Samuel S. Moody 2nd Feby 20, 1850
Mary E. Moody March 13, 1855
Hugh Lawson Strong Jany 1856
Charles R. Strong Nov 30, 1858

MARRIAGES:
Rev. Samuel S. Moody & Lettia T. Cannon, were married Oct. 29, 1840
Dr. George M. Strong & Margaret B. Moore were married April 18, 1855
Dr. George W. Moody & Georgie E. Strong were married March 16, 1880
Winston G. Moody & Margaret L. Wilson were married Oct 21, 1902
Margaret Moody & Morton B. King were married Nov 22, 1911
Samuel S. Moody & Martha E. Weatherly were married Nov 6, 1915

DEATHS:
Rev. Samuel S. Moody, May 7, 1863
Lettitia T. Moody, July 26, 1880
Dr. Geo. M. Strong, April 1860

Margaret B. Strong, Oct 15, 1861
Georgie E. Moody, April 2, 1922

Clement Cannon Sr, June 19, 1860
Susan L. Cannon, March 15, 1874
Genl. Wm. Moore
Elizabeth R. Moore
Mary Erwin Moody, July 24, 1876
Samuel S. Moody, 2nd., May 16, 1902
Hugh L. Strong, June 1858
Charles R. Strong
Rev. T. L. Moody, Sept 23, 1916 (Thomas Lipscomb)

MICHAEL FISHER BIBLE

In possession of Mrs. W. Nowlin Taylor, Shelbyville, Tennessee
PUBLISHER: Page missing.

Thomas T. Parson was marred to Mary F. Clardy September the 14 1852

MARRIAGES:
Michael Fisher was married to Christiana Earnhart November 23rd, 1786

Jacob, son of Michael and Christiana Fisher was married to Sarah Smith
    July 9th, 1813.

Philip Fisher was married to Phoebe Dice April 1813.
Elizabeth Fisher was married to Edward Wade. Feby 26th 1807.
Christiana Fisher was married to Thompson Thompson June 13th 1811
Margaret Fisher was married to George Parsons July 18th 1811
Thomas T. Parsons was married to Mary F. Clardy, Sept 14, 1852.
Mary Fisher was married to Michael Fisher January 2d 1812
Martin Fisher was married to Margaret Earnhart June 24th 1813
Anna Fisher was married to Jacob Morton August 31st. 1815
George Fisher was married to Permelia Parsons November 14th 1817
Sarah Fisher was married to Samuel Sloan Aug 29th 1816
Amy Fisher was married to Newcomb Thompson July 6th 1820
Mary Ann Fisher was married to Silas Tilgman Sept 28th 1820
Michael Fisher was married to Elizabeth Turrentine July 5th 1822
John Fisher was married ..... illegible....... 182_

Michael Fisher was born May 20, 1766
Christiana Fisher was born February 19th 1764
Children of the above:
Jacob Fisher was born July 10th 1787
Philip Fisher was born July 15th 1788
Elizabeth Fisher was born September 29th 1789
Christiana Fisher was born November 6th 1790

Martin Fisher was born January 6th 1792
Margaret Fisher was born July 23rd, 1793
Mary Fisher was born February 19th 1795
George Fisher was born May 9 1796
Anna Fisher was born April 27th 1798
Michael Fisher was born October 13th, 1799
Sarah Fisher was born August 5th, 1801
Mary Ann Fisher born March 22nd 1803
Amy Fisher was born May 22nd 1805
John Fisher was born July 23rd 1808

                                        Finis

Rebecca Shearon was born January 18th 1823
John F. Thompson was born November 24th 1813

George W. Tilmon was Born January the 25 1821
Cristena A. Tilmon was born 14 day of April 1824
Nicholas Harris was born december the 23, 1815 and was married to
        Mary Ann Parsons July the 12, 1838
Silas M. Tilmon was born May the 15, 1829

M. F. Parsons was marred to Y(Z). W. Thomas in April the 22, 1836.
A. C. Parsons was marred to Eliza More August the 3, 1834.
J. M. Parson was mard to Lusinda Crowell August 16, 1841

DEATHS:
Martin Fisher exit December 10th 1828
Charley Fisher exit November 13th 1828
Christiana Fisher exit the 9th day of April 1830
Michael Fisher exit December 18th 1833
Mary An Clardy exit April the 30, 1839 3 o'clock in the morning.
George Parsons departed this life 16th November 1842, at 9 o'clock
        night.
Michael F. Parsons Departed this life April 2nd 1849 3 'clock in
        New Orleans.
Amey Thompson Departed this life March 20, 1886

George Parsons was born December 27, 1787

Michael F. Parsons was born June the 30, ____.
A. B. Parsons was born the 10 of September 1815

Mary An Parsons was born March the 1, 1816
Amie Parsons was born November 1st, 1817
Martha T. Tilmon was born April 13th, 1825, daughter of Silas Tilmon.

DEATHS:
Jacob M. Parsons was Born August 29th, 1819.
George W. Parson was born April 19th 1821

John W. Parsons was born January 3rd, 1824

Elizabeth J. Parsons was born April 14th, 1825

Newton B. Parsons Born October 23rd, 1826
Thomas J. Parsons was Born February 16th, 1827

Benjamin S. Parsons was Born February 3rd, 1831
Margaret C. Parsons was Born December 17th, 1832
Philip A. Parsons was born April 12th, 1835

NELSON BIBLE

In possession of Mr. Lawson Boone Nelson, Copied by Mrs. S. D. McGrew,
    Shelbyville, Tennessee
Publisher: Butler's Edition   1847

Matthew Nelson born in Virginia, April 7, 1781
M. Nelson departed this life July 13, 1856, age: 75 years, 3 months,
    6 days.
Nancy C. Nelson born Virginia, April 1792
James L. Nelson born Newcastle, Kent.
Wm. D. Nelson born Murfreesboro
H. L. Nelson born Shelbyville, Kent.
Thomas R. Nelson   Louisville, Kent.
C. L. Nelson   New Orleans
S. B. Nelson   Clairmont
J. F. Nelson   Murfreesboro
M. L. Nelson   Murfreesboro
E. C. Nelson (Elizabeth) Carth Indolener
N. B. Nelson   H. & P.
Mary H. Wilson   Memphis
M. F. (F. M.) Nelson Hurricane Creek

    Nov. 6, 1855 (fin)
Napoleon B. Nelson born March 31, 1829
Eliza M. Cannon born Nov 1, 1829
Ida Ann Nelson January 22, 185_
Elizabeth Scales Nelson born Dec 28, 1853, died March 14, 1905.

NELSON BIBLE

In possession of Lawson Boone Nelson, copied by Mrs. S. D. McGrew,
    Shelbyville, Tennessee
Publisher: The Holy Bible by Carey   1818

Samuel B. Nelson and Sarah H. Moore were married June 5, 1845
Samuel B. Moore was born Oct.   , 1821, died March 21, 1898
Sarah H. Nelson was May 5, 1823, died Feb 5, 1908

Matthew F. Nelson was born August 5, 1846, died Jan 5, 1868 (unmarried)
Frederick Nelson was born Sept. 6, 1848
Lewis M. Nelson was born Nov. 24, 1850, died Aug 3, 1930 (unmarried)
Lucy Nelson was born May 30, 1853, Died May 27, 1932 (unmarried)
S. B. Nelson, Jr. was born Sept 9, 1855
Charlie Nelson was born Jan 19, 1858 (female), died July 12, 1941,
        (unmarried)
Sally Nelson was born Aug 3, 1860
Jeffey Nelson was born May 4, 1864 (Jefferson Davis)

Jeff Nelson and Ida Boone were married Aug 6, 1897, in Shelbyville,
        Tenn.

page: 678
Sarah H. Moore was born May 5, 1823
Thomas D. Moore was born Sept 15, 1825
Nancy M. Moore was born August 28, 1827
Augustus·F. Moore was born June 24, 1829
        Grandchildren:
Lewis Melone Nelson was born Oct 14, 1898
Lawson Boone Nelson was born Dec 9, 1901
Gladys Lorraine Nelson was born Mar 15, 1904
Newton Tillman Nelson was born Aug 8, 1908

page: 679
Lucinda Moore died March 10, 1847
Frederick A. Moore died Sept 1, 1846
Nancy M. Moore died Jan 1, 1842

FRANKLE BIBLE

In Possession of Mrs. Bryant Woosley, Sr., Shelbyville, Tennessee
Publisher: American Bible Society, New York   1898

Front: From Uncle Ed, and Aunt Jessie
        To George Y. Frankle- Sept 12th 1899

Family Records:
MARRIAGES:
A. Frankle and Lizzie Yancey were married Jan 4, 1886

BIRTHS:
Clarence Wilhoite Frankle was born Oct 1, 1888
George Yancey Frankle was born Sep 12, 1890

Clarence Wilhoite Frankle was born Oct 1, 1888 Baptised when an
    infant, joined the Methodist Church, May 21, 1905.
George Yancey Frankle was born Sep 12, 1890, Baptised when an infant,
    joined the Methodist Church March 9, 1909.
Clarence and George both baptised by Rev. J. B. Stewart.

A. Frankle was born in Poland, June 24, 1847
Lizzie Yancey Frankle was born in Shelbyville, Tenn., April 6, 1858.
A. Frankle died Mar 28, 1928
Elizabeth Yancey Frankle died October 17, 1945

MARRIAGES:
Lizzie Yancey & A. Frankle were married Jan 4, 1886

BAIRD BIBLE

In possession of Mrs. S. D. McGrew, Shelbyville, Tennessee
Publisher: J. B. Lippincott & Co. Philadelphia   1859

MARRIAGES:
William E. Baird and Martha E. Gordon was married 8th day of January
    1856.

James H. McGrew and Ella May Baird was married 23rd day of April 1884.

Zenas Baird and Jane E. Black was married 8th day December 1829.

BIRTHS:
William E. Baird was born 15th October 1830
Martha E. Gordon was born 6th January 1838
Robert Gordon was born
Mary Hinton Lane was born on Thursday the 5th of June 1817.
Horace Ney Baird was born 24th March 1857
Willie Eugene Baird was born 24th February 1859
Robert Gordon Baird was born 7th May 1861
Ella May Baird was born 16th September 1863
Ann Pointer Baird was born 5th November 1865
Sarah Jane Baird was born 22nd April 1871
William Edward Baird was born 7th October 1876

DEATHS:
Horace Ney Baird Died 28th day of July 1863
Robert Gordon Baird Died 2nd day of August 1863
Willie Eugene Baird Died 6th day of August 1863
Zenas Baird Died 1st day of March 1874
Jane E. Baird Died 4th day of August 1874
Robert Gordon Died Sunday Dec. 23rd 1855

31

JOHN W. THOMPSON BIBLE

In possession of Mrs. S. D. McGrew, Shelbyville, Tennessee
Publisher: & sold by Kimber and Sharpless, No. 8 South 4th Street,
       Stereotyped by E. White, New York

Front Page: William Thompson
        Initials: E, J, F, B.
           John W and
           John W. Thompson

John W. Thompson
born January the 8th 1831
this January the 8th 1848

Inside Front Cover: J. T. Brittain   May 8th 1878
Jason T. Brittain.. illegible name..., Maria Brittain and Jesse Newton.

MARRIAGES:
Newcom Thompson, Cener and Amey was mared on the 6 day of July in the
      year of our Lord 1820.
George W. Thompson and Marthey (Cannon) was marred on the 18th day of
      May 1843
Jason T. Brittain & Mary Ann Thompson was married on the 4th July A.D.
      1844.
Newcom Thompson, Junr.; and Catherine Davis was maried on the 13 day of
      September 1844.
Michel F. Thompson and Marthey Hollen was mared on the 13th day of
      February 1848.
Samuel A. Thompson & Marthey Fisher was mared on 13 day of April 1848.
John Thompson 1848 was mared to Jane Pannel 31 day of December 1848.
Elizabeth Jane Thompson was married to William Griffis on the 5th day
      of february 1852
Newcom Thompson & Frances Dixon was married on the
(Frances J. Thompson was wife of Newcomb Thompson, 3rd & daughter of
      James Dixon)
Newcom Thompson, Cener, was born on the 27 day of December our Lord 1792
Amey Thompson was born on the 22nd day of May our Lord 1805
Mary Ann Thompson was born on the 28th day of december 1821
George Washington Thompson was born on the 1st day of February 1823
Newcom Thompson, Jun, was born on the 20th day of July 1825
Samuel A. Thompson was born on the 17th day March 1827
Michel Fisher Thompson was born on the 26th day November 1828
John Westley Thompson was born on the 8th day of January 1831
Jacob Fisher Thompson was born on the 12th day of June 1833
Elizabeth Jane Thompson was born on the 23rd day of January 1835
William M. Thompson was born on the 29th day of March 1837
Martha Washington Thompson was born on the 31th day of January in the
      year of our Lord 1839
Joseph Adrian Glastobury Thompson was born on the 3rd April 1861
Jennie Alvas Thompson Thompson was born on the 12th day of February 1843

BIRTHS:
Jason T. Brittain was born December 1st A.D. 1821
Mary Ann Thompson was born December 28th A.D. 1821
Martha Washington Thompson was born January 31, A.D. 1839
Jennie Alvis Thompson was born February 12th 1843

DEATHS:
Eliza J. Thompson died the 9th day of July 1854
Michel F. Thompson died the 25th day of October 1855
N. Thompson, Sr., died Sept 8th 1869
Newcomb Thompson died Sep 9th 1869, aged 77
Jacob F. Thompson died June 8, 1880
Amey Thompson died March 20, 1886
Jenie Woods died the 8 of March 1898
Nicholas Graham was born on the 9th day of March 1809
Mary Ann Brittain departed this life April 13th, 1900, age 79 years

----

KNOTT BIBLE

In possession of Mrs. S. D. McGrew, Shelbyville, Tennessee
Formerly in the possession of the late Mrs. Henry L. (Ada Landers)
        Hanson, who was a daughter of the Flavius S. Landers in the
        Bible Record.
NOTE:_ Mrs. Amie C. McGrew says: "I found these Bible Papers on the
        floor of a basement-room in the Hotel where Mrs. Hanson had
        once kept a trunk".

MARRIAGES:
Albert F. Knott and Malinda Ann Hoskins was married Oct 31, 1848
John H. Anderson and Susannah E. Knott was married 26 July 1866
F. S. Landers and Sallie J. Knott was married Sept 13th, 1870
J. R. Batte and Ella A. Knott was married Dec 17th, 1872
C. B. Neal
Charles B. Neal and Algie S. Knott was married Feb 20th 1879
J. W. Knott and Sarah J-------- Tarpley was married Dec the 23, 1879
W. L. Clary and Laura F. Knott was married September the 30, 1883
Thomas J. Jackson and Mary Ann Thomas Knott was married Oct 26, 1886

BIRTHS:
Susannah E., daughter of Albert F. Knott & Malinda Ann his wife, was
        born Feby 4, 1850
Sarah Jane Knott, daughter of Albert F. Knott & Malinda his wife, was
        born Feby 15, 1852
James W., son of Albert F. Knott & Malinda his wife, was born Oct 11,
        1854.
Lieullor Almancyy, daughter of Albert F. Knott and Malinda his wife,
        was born Oct 16, 1856.

33

Virginia Tennessee, daughter of Albert F. Knott & Malinda his wife, was
    born Oct 18, 1858.
Alga Matilda, daughter of A. F. Knott & Malinda his wife, was born
    20th Jan 1860.
Mary Ann Thomas, daughter of A. F. & Malinda his wife, was born
    8th Decbr. 1863.
Laura Frazer, daughter of A. F. Knott & Malinda his wife, was born
    22 May 1866.
Alfred Ransom Knott, son of Albert F. Knott & Malinda his wife, was
    born Oct 14, 1868.
Charles Rufus Knott, son of Albert Knott & Malinda Knott his wife,
    was born April 14th, 1871.
Albert F. Knott, son of William Knott & Elizabeth his wife, was born
    12 March, 1819.
Malinda Ann, daughter of Redman Haskins & Susan his wife, was born
    12 Nov. 1832.
John Henly, son of Charles M. Anderson and Margaret his wife, was born
    17 June, 1847.
Thomas Jefferson Jackson, son of James L. Jackson was born Dec 24, 1860
Flavius S. Landers, son of Anderson & Sarah Landers, was born Dec 12th,
    1842.

DEATHS:
William Knott departed this life Feby 27, 1828.
Elizabeth Knott, consort of Wm. Knott, departed this life Oct 21st,
    1854. aged 70 years and six months.
Virginia Tennessee, daughter of A. F. Knott & Malinda his wife, departed
    this life Sept 10th, 1862. aged 3 years, 10 months & 23 days.
Charles Rufus Knott, son of A. F. Knott and Malinda his wife, departed
    this life June 19th 1907. aged 36 years, 2 months and 2 days.
Albert F. Knott departed this life Aug 11th 1879. aged 60 years,
    4 months & 29 days.
Malinda Ann Knott departed this life July third, 1919, aged 86 years,
    8 months & 21 days.
Sarah Jane Landers, daughter of A. F. & Malinda Ann Knott, departed
    this life April 1913.

PICKLE BIBLE

Copied by Mrs. Amie C. McGrew, Shelbyville, Tennessee
NOTE: The information below was copied from a Bible owned by Mrs.
    David Cliff Daughtrey (Malissa Pickle). She made the entries
    from her own knowledge, or from records available to her.

Mother's Father: Bryant Anderson
Mother's Mother: · Pylant

Parents:
Betty and Thomas Pickle, born 1850 (Her) & 1840 (His), Bedford Co.,
    & died 1912 (Hers) & 1918 (His), Wheel.
Thomas and Alsie Daughtrey born 1848 Bedford Co., & died 1912, Wheel
Children: (all born in Bedford Co.)

Names:	born:	Married:	Died:
Mollie Pickle	July 12, 1873	1889, Monroe Burlin	May 10, 1895
Ella Pickle	Sept 15, 1875	1892, Dock Haskins	
Mag. Pickle	June 20, 1877	1902, John Lee Perryman	
Will Pickle	April 12, 1880	1906, Lora Lentz	
Malissa Pickle	Jan 13, 1883	1902, David Daughtrey	
Charlie Pickle	Aug 3, 1885	1909, Rose Cook	
John Pickle	Feb 15, 1888	1934, Hattie Louis Fallon	
Winnie Daughtrey	June 15, 1871	1893, Louis Cox	Sept 18, 1928
David Daughtrey	Feb 2, 1878	1902, Malissa Pickle	Mar 25,1952
Tommie Daughtrey	Nov 3, 1885	1912, Bonnie Gamble	Nov 1921
Ray Clifford Daughtrey	Oct 16, 1902	1928, Pearl Kingree	
Thomas Franklin Daughtrey	July 15, 1905	1930, Sarah Davidson	
John Calvin Daughtrey	Jan 11, 1909	1934, Lillian Hames	
Susie Beatrice Daughtrey	Feb 7, 1912	1930, Dryden Davidson	(Dec 26,1935)
Susie Beatrice Daughtrey		1938, Hugh Searcy	

Dryden Davidson died with T.B., Shelbyville, March 26, 1935.

CLIFFT BIBLE

Copy by Mrs. Amie C. McGrew, Shelbyville, Tennessee
NOTE: The Frontis page of the New Testament section shows that it was
    translated from the Original Greek: That it was published in
    New York, and has the date 1865. It also says American Bible
    Society, instituted in the year MDCCCXVI. The first part of the
    Bible, to Exodus, has been destroyed.

David L. Clifft and Diania Burlin was married the 7 day of March 1841
    (Mrs. Daughtrey says her name was Diana).
D. L. Clifft was Bornd September 20, 1818.
Diania Clifft was Bornd September 19, 1819.
Jane D. Clifft was Bornd May 15, 1842.
John W. Clifft was Borned February 16, 1844.
Mary E. Clifft was Bornd September 29, 1848.

David L. Clifft was bornd September the 20, 1818 and departed this life
    July the 12, 1885.

Asley Clifft and Thomas Daughtrey was married september the 5, 1870.
Thomas Daughtrey was bornd August the 8, 1849.
Tommie Daughtrey and Bonnie Gambill was married March 24, 1912.

Winey Daughtrey was bornd June the 15, 1871.
Willey Cox was bornd January the 1, 1894.
Grady Cox was bornd Aprile the 29, 1895.
Flora Cox was bornd february the 17, 1899.
Davy C. Daughtrey was bornd february the 2, 1878.
John thomas Daughtrey was bornd november the 3, 1885.
Bonnie Daughtrey was bornd November 27, 1890.
Dianah Clifft was bornd september the 19 and 1819, departed this life
    March the 20, 1900.
Tinny Daughtrey was born December the 6, 1913.
Harvie Daughtrey was born April 3, 1916.

HARRIS BIBLE

Copy by Mrs. Amie C. McGrew, Shelbyville, Tennessee
In 1964, Bible is owned by G. L. Harris, Nashville, Tennessee
Publisher: Kimber and Sharpless Steretype Edition, Stereotyped by
            E. White, New York   (no date)

MARRIAGES:
John T. Harris and Gillie P. Orr, daughter of David and Jane Orr was
    married on the 30th day of August A.D., 1827. Bedford County,
    Tennessee.
John T. Harris and Sarah W. Brown was married on the 1st day of
    November A.D., 1831. Williamson County, Tennessee.
John T. Harris and Catharine B. Wallis was married on the 4th day
    June A.D., 1857 in Shelbyville, Bedford County, Tennessee by
    the Rev. Saml. S. Moody.

FAMILY RECORDS
BIRTHS:
John Thomas Harris was born on the 6th Day of July A.D., 1804, North
    Carolina, Rowan County.
Gillie Perry Orr, wife of John T. Harris, was born on the 22nd day of
    December A.D., Summer County, Tennessee. (no year given)
Martha Gillie Ann Harris, daughter of John T. and Gillie P. Harris
    was born on the 2nd day of September A.D., 1828 b.c.t.(Bedford
    County, Tennessee)
Safrona Ann Harris, Daughter of John T. Harris and Sarah W. Harris was
    born on the 16th Day of November A.D., 1832, Bedford Cty, Tens.
Melissa Elizabeth Harris was born on the 9th Day of November A.D., 1834.
Mary Neil Harris was born on the 18th day of November A.D., 1836.
Sarah W. Harris was born on the 9th day of March A.D., 1806 Williamson
    Cty, Tens.
Luiza Marian Harris was born on the 17th Day of October A.D. 1838.
Nancy Thompson Harris was born on the 14th Day of September A.D., 1840,
    Baptised 7th Day April 1844 by Joseph Smith.

Margaret Almeida Harris was born on the 29th day of January A.D.,
	1843, M.C.T.(Marshall County, Tenn.), Baptised Apl 7th,
	1844 by Jas. Smith.
William James Harris was born on the 17th day of May A.D., 1846,
	Marshall Cty, Tens.
Sarah Francis Harris was born on the 15th day of May A.D. 1848,
	Marshall Cty, Tens.
John Brown Harris was born on the 28th Day of July A.D., 1850,
	Marshall County, Tennessee.
Watson Randolph Harris was born on the 15th July 1858.
Mary Isabella Harris was born on the 24th of March A.D., 1860
Alfred Wallis Harris was born on the 12th day of October A.D., 1861.
Cyntha Cathrine Harris was born on Sept 4th, 1863.

DEATHS:
Gillie Perry Harris, wife of John T. Harris, Departed this life on
	the 20th Day of September at 4 & 20 m 6°o'clock in the evening
	A.D. 1828 after 19 days illness, aged 22 years, 8 months and
	28 days with a hope of blessed immortality.
Mary Neil Harris, infant daughter of John T. & Sarah W. Harris,
	Departed this life on the 6th Day of December 1836, aged
	18 days.
Louiza Marian Harris, Daughter of John T. Harris and Sarah W. Harris,
	departed this life on the 11th Day of September A.D. 1839,
	aged ten months and twenty five Days.
Sarah W. Harris, Departed this life on the fifteenth day of February
	A.D., 1856, after 2 months and five days illness of Tyfoid
	fever with a confident certainty of blessed immortality at
	10 min. before 2 o'clock A.M.
John T. Harris, Departed this life on the thirtyeth of October after
	protracted illness A.D. 1864.
Catherine B. Harris departed this life on the fourth of July 1912,
	aged 87 years, 10 months, and 21 days.

MOTLOW FAMILY RECORD

From: "The Motley Family" by Motlow, 1949

John Motlow and Elizabeth his wife were married April the 19th, 1781,
	She was wounded by the Indians the 3rd day of June and the 7th
	she died of her wounds.
John Motlow and Agness his wife was married the 26th day of February
	in the year 1784.
November the 2nd, 1786, Mary Motlow deceased this life, was buried the
	3rd day of Nov.
Elizabeth Motlow daughter of John Motlow and Agness his wife was born
	in May 15th 1785.
Wm. Motlow son of John Motlow and Agness his wife was born March 12th,
	1787.

Zadock Motlow son of John Motlow and Agness his wife was born in September 6th, 1789.
Laraet Motlow daughter of John Motlow and Agness his wife was born the 9th of June in the year 1791.
James McElhaney Motlow son of John Motlow and Agness his wife was born the 1st day of May in the year 1784.
John Motlow son of John Motlow and Agness his wife was born in October 29th, 1797.
Felix Motlow son of John Motlow and Agness his wife was born the 13th day of June 1801 on Saturday.

DEATHS:
July 27th 1802, Jo Thompson departed this life laying seventeen days in fever.
John Motlow departed this life May 25th, 1812, aged 54 years, 9 months and 28 days.
Agness Motlow his wife departed this life August 14th, 1825.

NEGROES:
Cate, Dick and Rhine's daughter, was born the 12th of April in the year 1797.
Sew, Dick and Rhine's daughter, was born 17th of May in the year 1795.
Fred was born October the 12, 1798, Dick and Rhine's son.
Daisa, Dick and Rine's daughter was born 10th October 1787.
Roan, Dick and Rine's daughter was born 24th June, 1800.
Chaney, Dick and Rine's daughter was born the 24th of May 1803.
Easter, Dick and Rine's daughter was born November the 3, 1805.
Dick, the son of Dick and Rine, was born September 3, 1806.
_____ 1791 this little book was made _____
black and white.

signed: "J. Motlow"

_____

WM. & ELIZABETH REED RECORD

From: "A Reed Family in America" by Reed, 1962, page 43.

William Reed was born in Lancaster Co., S.C., Dec 23, 1818, son of John & Jincy Coffee Reed.
Elizabeth Moore Wilson, born September 13, 1825 in Florence, Alabama, daughter of Robert L. & Ann Hartgrove Wilson.
William Reed and Elizabeth Wilson were married October 9, 1843.

1: William Washington Reed. Born September 16, 1844 & died March 16, 1931
2: Andrew Marion Reed. Born January 23, 1846 & died in 1874.
3: James Henderson Reed. Born November 2, 1847 & died January 8, 1848.
4: John Larmer Reed. Born November 25, 1848 & died in 1887.
5: Robert Argyle Reed. Born October 26, 1850 & died September 14, 1851.
6: Madison Lafayette Reed. Born August 15, 1852 & died February 28, 1937.

38

7: Cordelia Victoria Reed. Born December 23, 1853 & died June 16, 1940.
8: Benjamin Franklin Reed. Born January 19, 1856 & died May 18, 1944.
9: Mary Isabella Reed. Born July 30, 1857 & died October 25, 1932.
10: Infant Daughter. Born December 10, 1858 & died January 10, 1859.
11: Elizabeth Loucinda Reed. Born June 9, 1860 & died January 27, 1937.
12: Alice Josephine Reed. Born July 17, 1863 & died March 18, 1946.
13: Samuel Edward Reed. Born July 2, 1865 & died January 28, 1933.
14: Charles Nathaniel Reed. Born October 5, 1867 & died January 10, 1942.
15: Prentiss Reed. Born about 1869 & died about 1872.

ANDREW ERWIN, JR., BIBLE

In possession of Mrs. Richard P. Knight, Jr., Helena, Alabama

FAMILY RECORD
MARRIAGES:
Andrew Erwin, Junr. was married to Elvira Julia Searcy, October 12th,
      1820- in Nashville by the Revd. William Hume, at the residence
      of John P. Erwin.
Andrew Erwin was married the second time on the 25th November 1847 at
      9 o'clock a.m. to Mrs. Mary J. Camp at her residence in Hunts-
      ville, Ala., by the Revd. S. S. Moody.
Anne C. Erwin & George W. Bridges were married in Shelbyville, Tenn.,
      Dec 24, 1889.
C. Coldwell Bridges & Lena Katherine Sch------, married Birmingham,
      Ala., Sept 12, 1925.
Shirley Anne Bridges & Richard Posey Knight were married at 4 P.M.
      Sunday Dec 18th 1955 at St. John Evangelical Church, Birming-
      ham, Ala., Rev. Herman Rithie (?) officiating.
Frances Anne Erwin was married on the 2nd of September 1841 to William
      H. Pope of Huntsville, Alabama, at the residence of Danl. B.
      Turner.
Elizabeth Jane Erwin was married to John R. Eakin of Bedford County
      Tennessee at the Presbyterian Church in Huntsville, Ala., by
      the Revd. W.   on the   1848.
Henry Hitchcock Erwin was married at the residence of George Davidson
      in Shelbyville, Tennessee by the Revd. Dr. Dashielle to Miss
      Sarah Coldwell on the 21st May 1850.
Mrs. Frances Anne Pope was married to the Revd. John T. Edgar of
      Nashville, to Genl. Lucius J. Polk of Maury County, Tennessee
      at the residence of her father at Beechwood, Bedford County
      Tennessee at 9 o'clock A.M., on the 15th Sept. 1853 and left
      same day for Maury County.

BIRTHS:
Andrew Erwin, Jr., was born May 27th 1800 in Wilkes County, N.C. on
      (omitted) fork.
Elvira Julia Erwin was born October 12th 1801 in Nashville.

Robert Searcy Erwin was born Sept. 9th, 1821 at the Old Brick House
in Bedford County, Tenn.

Frances Anne Erwin born February 23rd, 1823 at the Old Brick House
in Bedford County, Tenn.

Elizabeth Jane Erwin was born March 12th, 1825 at the Old Brick House
Bedford County, Tenn.

Henry Hitchcock Erwin was born May 13th, 1827 at the small Brick House
on Knob Creek, Bedford County, Tenn.

Thomas Yeatman Erwin was born December 21st, 1829 at the small Brick
House on Knob Creek, Bedford County, Tenn.

James Porter Erwin was born July 27th 1832-about ½ past 10 o'clock A.M.
at the Framed House of the Revd. Geo. Newton on Knob Creek, Bedford Cty, Tenn.

Andrew Patton Erwin was born in Nashville August 22nd 1836 at the House
of Jno. P. Erwin.

Elvira Julia Erwin, youngest child of Andrew & Elvira J. Erwin, was born
in Nashville on College St., near the corner of the Public
Square in a house owned by the Heirs of Thos. Yeatman, dec'd,
and then occupied by A. B. Robertson-on the 25th June 1838, about
10 o'clock P.M.

Anne Coldwell Erwin, daughter of H. H. Erwin & Sarah Coldwell Erwin,
was born March 5th 1860. Cumberland Iron Works, Maury County,
Tenn.

Sara Roony Bridges, born Nashville, Tenn., Oct 4th, 1890.

Ethel Madalin Bridges, born Nashville, Tenn., Oct. 7, 1894.

H. Erwin Bridges, born near Nashville, Tenn., Sept 24, 1896.

James Erwin Bridges, born in Nashville, Tenn., June 27, 1899.

C. Coldwell Bridges, born Antioch, Tenn., Oct. 30, 1902.

Shirley Anne Bridges, daughter of Coldwell & Katherine Bridges, born
Birmingham, Ala., August 15, 1931.

Richard Chadwell Knight, born 6 A.M. today- June 29, 1957- Son of
Richard P. Knight, Jr & Shirley Anne Bridges Knight.

Karl Coldwell Knight, born 7:59 p.m., Dec 30, 1958- Second Son of
Richard & Shirley Knight, Southside Hospital, B'ham, Ala.

DEATHS:

Andrew Patton Erwin- died at the Family residence in Bedford County,
on the 19th July 1837, aged 10 mos & 27 days.

Elvira Julia Erwin wife of Andrew Erwin, Jr.- died at Nashville in a
House on Cherry Street belonging to Jno. P. Erwin and then
occupied by the Revd. Thomas Stringfield- on the 6th July 1838
about 20 minutes before 6 o'clock A.M.

Elvira Julia Erwin, youngest child of Andrew & Elvira J. Erwin died at
the Family residence in Bedford County (of Scarlet Fever) on
the 7th day of June 1839- about 8 o'clock P.M.- aged 11 months
and 12 days.

Robert Searcy Erwin Eldest son of Andrew & Elvira J. Erwin died at
the residence of Wm. H. Pope in Huntsville, Ala., of Consump-
tion, on the 7th December 1842, between 2 & 3 o'clock P.M.

Thomas Yeatman Erwin died at the residence of the Honorable John Bell
in Nashville on the 26th Apr, 1847 at 3 o'clock A.M. He was

40

first attack'd with measles which soon disappeared and a week after
the attack of measles when he was thought to be almost entirely well he went out at night to a large Temperance meeting
at the Methodist Church and was attack'd the next evening with
brain fever which produced delirium and of which he died in 60
hours after he was attack'd.
Frances Anne Polk, Eldest daughter of Andrew & Elvira J. Erwin and wife
of Genl. Lucius J. Polk, died at the residence of her husband--
Hamilton Place, Maury County, Tennessee, on the 28th May 1858
at 2 o'clock P.M.- disease Pneumonia followed by inflamation of
the stomach or Bowels--
Andrew Erwin Jr. Died at the residence of Mr. Ware in Lafayette, Ala.,
"His former residence since the year 1863 until the fall of ,
1871, he sold it to Mr. Ware"- on the 30th day of May 1872.
Aged 72 years & 3 days. His disease was dropsy of the heart.
Henry Hitchcock Erwin died of disease of heart & liver at Commercial
Hotel, Nashville, Tenn., Aug 15, 1875.
James P. Erwin Died of Flux at Mineral Springs, Arkansas- Oct 26th 1883.
Elizabeth J. Erwin Died of Paralais in Washington, Ark., May 21, 1885.
Sarah C. Erwin Died at No. 98 Maurry St., Nashville, 10 Feb 1899 of
Paralais.
Mrs. Sarah C. Erwin, died Nashville, Tenn., Feb 10, 1899.
Sarah R. Bridges, died Nashville, Tenn., Dec 15, 1890.
James Erwin Bridges, died at Willow Beck(?), July 5, 1900.
Anne Erwin Bridges, died at 211 Jernigan Ave., Chattanooga, Tenn.,
April 28, 1929= 12:15 P.M.   Age: 69
George W. Bridges died Birmingham, Ala., Thursday April 11, 1940, at '
8:15 P.M.   Age 82
Ethel Madalen Bridges Seyforth died at 11:45 P.M. at the Baptist Hospi-
tal, Birmingham, Ala., 11-18-1954.

May 19, 1950, _____ I loved him so.

BLAKE-PRICE-ROBERTSON FAMILY BIBLE

From: The North Carolinian   Vol III, No. 4 Dec 1957, No. 12

Family Record of Thomas Price (1775-7 Dec 1830), of Oak Grove, Wake Co.,
N. C., owned 1956 by Mr. Prentiss Price, Rogersville, Tenn.

Rebekah Robertson, now the wife of Thomas Price, was born the 14 day
February 1779; Thomas Price & Rebekah Robertson was married the
18 day of February 1800; Rebekah Price died the 18 day of February 1826; Scheherazade Price the first was born 10 december
1800, died the 10 december 1802; Washington Price was born 17
of October 1803; Scheherazade Price the 2nd was born the 12th
december 1805; Needham Price was born 8 day April 1808; Fetney
Price was born 7 day July 1810; Caswell Epps Price was born the

30 day of August 1813 & died the 28 October 1828; Fetney Price and Bennett Blake was married 21st February 1828".

Notes by Prentiss Price.

Additional data on the six children of Thomas and Rebekah (Robertson) Price:

1: Scheherazade Price, born 10 December 1800 and died 10 December 1802.
2: Washington Price, died 21 Oct. 1855 Lafayette Co., Miss., married (I) 2 Oct 1823 (Bond) in Orange Co., N.C., to Susan Webb, no issue; (2) 8 Feb 1837, in Madison Co., Tenn., to Frances Bushrod Harris, born 4 Feb 1818, Randolph Co., N.C., & died 16 Mar 1856, Lafayette Co., Miss. 9 children.
3: Scheherazade Price, died 25 May 1853, Raleigh, N.C., married (1) 11 May 1821 in Wake Co., N.C., to Thomas Mial, died June 1830 in Wake Co., N.C. 1 son. (2) 17 Feb 1837, Wake Co., N.C., to Rev. Bennett Taylor Blake, born 3 Jan 1800 Southhampton Co., Va., died 28 May 1882, Wake Co., N.C. 1 son.
4: Needham Price, died 19 Feb 1870, White Oak Grove, Wake Co., N.C. & married 29 Dec 1830 in Johnston Co., N.C., to Nancy Peters Sanders born 19 June 1810, Johnston Co., N.C. & died 25 July 1874 Wake Co., N.C. 3 daughters.
5: Fetney Price, died 22 Jan 1836 Wake Co., N.C., married 21 Feb 1828 Wake Co., N.C., to Rev. Bennett Taylor Blake (see No. 3, above) 2 children.
6: Caswell Epps Price, died 28 Oct 1828 Wake Co., N.C.

JOSIAH MARTIN BIBLE
(A REVOLUTIONARY SOLDIER)

From: The National Archives, Washington, D.C. W.1.047

Parents of Josiah Martin lived in Cumberland Co., Pa., Indians became so troublesome, they moved to a County nearby. (County not known).

Josiah Martin was born February 1757
Josiah Martin has an Older Sister (not named).
When Josiah Martin was about 2 years old, they moved back to Cumberland County, Pa., until 2765, they moved to Lincoln County, North Carolina. Josiah Martins' parents not named.

Josiah Martin volunteered in Spring of 1780.
Josiah Martin lived in Lincoln County, North Carolina until 1803 when he moved to Rutherford County, Tennessee. Both Josiah and his wife are Presbyterians. They had 8 children in all.
1: Abigail, born March 28, 1784
2: William, born December 8, 1786
3: Robert, born November, 1793
4: Clarissa, born Aug. 1796

5: Hannah, born 20 October 1790
6: Marilla, born September 29, 1799
7: Polly McDowel, born November 16, 1806
8: Matilda, born Feb 15, 1808

Nephew, William Martin, aged 76 years, in Marshall County, Tennessee
    (this age was in March 26th, 1845)
Nephew, William Martin witnessed their marriage in Mecklenburg County,
    North Carolina, at the house of Robt. McClary and her mother,
    together with 7 or 8 others, to the wedding, which was about
    20 miles from the said Josiah Martin's father and believes
    that the marriage was solemnised by the Rev. Jas. McGee, D.D.,
    about sixty one or two years ago, in the month of May, an
    incident that makes him recollect it is, when he returned home
    from the Wedding, his Father's house was burned.
                                        William Martin.

                            ANTHONY BIBLE

In 1950, this Bible Record was sent to Mr. John T. Lane, now deceased,
    by W. D. Anthony, Manchester, Tennessee.

William H. Anthony, Father of Robert H. Anthony, was born Aug 8, 1819,
    died May 11, 1884.
Robert H. Anthony, son of William H. Anthony, was born July 2, 1838,
    Died January 29, 1910.
W. D. Anthony, son of Robert H. Anthony, was born March 14, 1866.
Cornelia L. Anthony, wife of R. H. Anthony, was born 1840, Died March
    28, 1866. Her maiden name was Rich.
NOTE:
Mr. W. D. Anthony told Mr. John Lane on May 26, 1950 by phone from his
    son's, Carl Anthony:

    "Will D. Anthony, born at Anthony's Mill (which was built 1848),
    born March 14, 1866. Anthony's Mill was built by his father's
    brothers, one mile below Cumberland Springs on same Creek. He
    said his father's name was Robert H. Anthony, married in North
    Carolina and he or his father was a Methodist Preacher, son of
    William H. Anthony, born Aug 8, 1819 & died May 11, 1884 (this
    was his Grandfather). Nick Anthony (great-grandfather), Great-
    great-grandfather was a Dutchman and both great-grand mother &
    father spoke German well and were short and heavy built. Robert
    H. Anthony married in North Carolina, born July 2, 1838 & died
    Jan 29, 1910, to Miss Cornelia Rich, daughter of Daniel and _____
    (Clapp) Rich, daughter of Mr & Mrs. _____ Clapp.
    To Robert & wife:
    girls names unknown.
    W. D. Anthony, born March 14, 1865 & his mother died 14 days

                                43

later on March 28, 1866.
Father married 2nd _____
and went to Victoria, Texas and died there.
Will D. Anthony of Manchester, married Susan Dance, daughter of
John & _____(Price) Dance. He believes the Dances came from
Virginia, with the Gowans, Prices and Dances whom they, each
family intermarried with the other families, that the Funeral
Home & Court House Gowans' were related to Dances.
Anthony's from Virginia and North Carolina, he thinks.
Father's cousin (old bachelor) used to write and once mentioned
writting family history, is dead now but if any records, may be
in possession of W. D.'s Cousin, Mrs. Glenn McPherson, Burlington,
N. C., Route 6."

ANTHONY RECORDS

The following supplied by Mrs. Glenn P. McPherson, Burlington, N. C.,
and sent to Mr. John T. Lane, September 12, 1950.

From: Northeast of Graham, is Alamance County, the Southern boundary of
Caswell County, N.C.

"Jacob Anthony is the first of the name that we know of is this
section of North Carolina. There is a tradition in the families
that he was of German parentage. He married the only daughter of
Michael Shoffner, the progenitor of the Shoffners in this State
and Tennessee.
Jacob Anthony married Magdalena Shoffner. Born to this union:
1: Henry Anthony married Mary Garrett.
2: Adam Anthony married Sara Moser, went west.
3: Nicholas Anthony, went to Tennessee.
4: Dorothy Anthony married John Ingold.
5: Margaret Anthony married Frederick Moser.
6: Sallie Anthony married Daniel Thomas.
7: Betsy Anthony married Henry Thomas.
8: Eve Anthony married Daniel Sharp.
9: Katie Anthony married Thomas Steele.
10: Mary Anthony married Henry Moser.
11: Barbara Anthony married David Holt.

RICH FAMILY RECORD

Mrs. G. P. McPherson, Burlington, North Carolina, sent this Record to
Mr. John T. Lane, Shelbyville, Tennessee, on September 12, 1950.

Daniel Rich, born Feb 25, 1801 and died Sept 3, 1867
Barbara Clapp, born Jan 12, 1804.
Daniel Rich married Barbara Clapp Sept 17, 1826.
To this union was born:
1: Mary A. Rich, born July 9, 1827, died Aug 15, 1867, age: 45.
2: Emily E. Rich, born March 5, 1829, married Hardie S. Rike on
   Nov 1, 1866, died.....
3: Eliza Jane Rich, born Oct 3, 1830, married William Anthony on
   Jan 1, 1850, died Mar 28, 1921
4: Henry M. Rich, born Feb 18, 1833, married (1) Mary Jane Muse
   on June 2, 1859, (2) Unie C. Rike, Feb 15, 1866
5: Elizabeth Caroline Rich, born Dec 28, 1834, married (1) Daniel
   E. Sharp, May 17, 1855, (2) Mabe Ingle (no dates)
6: Barbara Harriett Rich, born Oct 2, 1836, married (1) Peter
   Fogleman (no date), (2) Jerome Riggins, Nov 28, 1868.
7: James R. Rich, born May 29, 1838, Returned from Civil Was
   with fever and died June 11, 1862.
8: Cornelia L. Rich, born Aug 8, 1840, married Robert H. Anthony,
   Feb 5, 1865.
9: Sarah Malinda Rich, born Sept 3, 1842, married Ruphus Washington Ingle on June 7th 1866 & died Mar 28, 1921, born to this
   union: William Thomas Ingle, dead; James Washington Ingle;
   Alonza Seymore Ingle, dead; Ernest C. Ingle; Benny Ingle and
   Ernest C. Ingle married Belle Clendinin.
10: Margaret T. Rich, born Oct 26, 1844, married Thadeus Ingle on
    May 27, 1889.
11: Martha Francis Rich, born March 15, 1848, married Caleb Trikle

DEATHS:
James R. Rich died June 11, 1862
Cornelius L. Rich Anthony died Mar 28, 1866
Mary C. Rich, died August 15th, 1867
Daniel Rich died Sept 3, 1867
Barbara Harriett Riggins died March 29, 1892
Eliza Jane Anthony died March 28, 1921
Sara Malinda Rich Ingle died March 1921
(both died same night about 3 hours apart)
Martha Francis Trikle died Feb 5, 1934

MORTON BIBLE

In possession of Mr & Mrs. Glenn Curtis Morton, Wartrace, Tennessee
Publisher: American Bible Society, New York   1866

FAMILY RECORD
William H. Morton was borned Nov the 14, 1839
Lucy H.(Harriet) A.(Arnold) Morton was borned April the 1, 1843
James B. Morton was borned June 24, 1864

George M. Morton was born Aug the 25, 1866
William H. Morton was married to Lucy H. Arnold, Sept the 9, 1863
J. R. Morton and L. B. Koonce was married June the 27, 1887

FAMILY RECORD:
L. B. Morton was borned Oct 14, 1869
James H. Arnold was born Sept the 3, 1806
Louisa H. Arnold was borned Dec the 15, 1816
Willie Evans Morton was born April 29, 1888
Robert Fulton Morton was borned June the 10, 1890
J. H. (John Holt) Morton was born March the 14, 1892
Eldridge L. Morton (Lee) was borned Feb 9, 1894
Earl Hobert Morton was borned Sept the 25, 1896
George Moody Morton departed this life December the 20, 1867, aged 1 yr,
    3 mo, & 25 da
G. W. C. Morton departed this life August the 12, 1880, aged 52 y, 3m,
    29 days
Willie Evens Morton this life July 15, 1889
Julia B. Morton died Dec the 23, 1891, aged 68 y, 10m, 5 da.
James H. Arnold departed this life May 10, 1873, aged 66 y & 9 m.
Fanny Allice Morton died January the 30, 1884
Lucy H. Morton departed this life Jan the 23, 1899, aged 55y, 9m, 28da.
Louisa H. Dean departed this life April the 5, 1890. aged: 73 yrs, 3 mos,
    & 21 days.
William H. Morton died 17th day of July 1902.

Seperate page of paper within this Bible:
Geo. W. C. Morton was born A.D. 14th day of April, 1818.
Julia B. Morton was born the 18th day of Feb A.D., 1823.
Wm. H. Morton was born the 14th Nov A.D. 1839.
Saphronia A. Morton was born the 12th day of May A.D. 1842.
James C. Morton was born the 11th day of Jan A.D. 1845.
Martha Jane Morton was borne the 6th day of March A.D. 1850.
Julia E. Morton was born the 19th day of May A.D., 1852.
Mary Minerva Lee Morton was born the 29th day of March A.D., 1860.
Fannie Allice Morton was born the 29th Dec A.D., 1864.
Fanny Allice Morton died the 30 of Jan, 1884, aged 20 y & 1 day.

GLENN AND GRACIE MORTON BIBLE

In possession of Mr & Mrs Glenn Morton, Wartrace, Tennessee
Publisher: The World Publishing Co., Cleveland, Ohio- New York

Presented by "Pa" James Robert Morton, Dec 25, 1942

This Certifies that Glenn Curtis Morton and Gracie Francis Word were
united in Holy Matrimony on the 12 day of Jan in the year of our Lord
1930, at Methodist Parsonage, Shelbyville, Tennessee by Dr. Aiken.

Witness: Mrs. Mary Hurt
Witness: Louise Arnold

BIRTHS:
Robert Curtis Morton born Oct 27, 1930
Francis Louise Morton born Apr 2, 1932
Margaret Annie Morton born Dec 28, 1934
Patsy Marie Morton born Nov 5, 1938
Betty Lou Morton born Dec 7, 1940
Nancy Belle Morton born Feb 28, 1944
Wanda Lee Morton born July 1, 1946
Wayne Lucus Morton born Sept 14, 1947
James Robert Nowlin, Jan 21, 1955
Michael Steven Nowlin, June 27, 1956
Mark Lee Nowlin, Oct 13, 1958
John David Morton, Jan 28, 1959
Timothy Glenn Walker, May 10, 1961
Jeffrey Howard Lovvorn born Apr 23, 1964
Laura Lee Thorneberry, born May 24, 1965
Larry Dean Morton, born Jan 3, 1964
Christopher Wayne Walker, born Sep 24, 1970
Debra Lynn Csuy, Jan 24, 1972
Steve James Csuy, Dec 28, 1973

MARRIAGES:
Margaret Ann Morton to Jerry Edward Nowlin, Apr 24, 1954 in Rossville,
     Ga.
Patsy Marie Morton to Guy Elam Thorneberry on Feb 2, 1957 in Ringgold,
     Ga.
Robert Curtis Morton to Mary Ellen Gordon on Sept 14, 1957 in Ring-
     gold, Ga.
Francis Louise Morton to Orlin C. Walker on June 24, 1960, in
     Nashville.
Betty Lou Morton to William Thomas Porterfield on May 26, 1961 in
     Nashville.
Nancy Belle Morton to Thomas Howard Lovvorn Sept 19, 1963, in M'boro.
Wanda Lee Morton to James Csuy, Nov 30, 1968 in Phenix, Ariz.
Wayne Lucus Morton to Shirlene Taylor in Oct 1969.
Robert Curtis Morton to Betty Holt, July 9, 1974, in Rover, Tenn.

DEATHS:
Wayne L. Morton- 1-4-70(1970)

L. B. MORTON BIBLE

In possession of Mr & Mrs Glenn Curtis Morton, Wartrace, Tennessee.
Publisher: Southwestern Publishing Co., Nashville, Tenn.
Presented by J. R. Morton, Oct 23, 1890.

This Certifies that J. R. Morton of Bedford County, Tenn., and L. B. Koonce of Bedford County, Tenn., were united by me in the Bonds of Holy Matrimony at the Residence of S. Swing on the 23rd day of June in the year of our Lord 1887. In Presence of Salie Swing & Clay Arnold. Witnesses: Maggie Hines & Percy Brandon. Signed: W. B. Rippetoe

DEATHS:
Willie E. Morton died the 15th day of July, 1889 A.D.
Hobeart Morton died the 4th day of Feb, 1900, A.D.
Bessie Mai Morton died the 24th day of Feb, 1930, wife of John H. Morton
Jack B. Morton died the 5th day of Nov, 1934, son of Ralph B. Morton & Hazel.
Lady Belle Morton died the 23rd day of Apr, 1952
John Holt Morton died the 6th day of Aug. 1956
James Robert Morton died 27th day of Dec 1959
Eldridge Lee Morton died 25th day of Feb, 1963.
Robert F. Morton died 29th day of March, 1967,• son of Glenn C. Morton & Gracie.
Wayne L. Morton, died 4th day of Jan, 1970
Julia Anne Morton, died 18th day of Oct, 1973, wife of John Holt Morton.

MEMORANDA:
J. R. Morton was born the 24th day of June 1864 A.D.
L. B. Morton was born the 14th day of Oct, 1869 A.D.
Willie E. Morton was born the 29th day of April, 1888 A.D.
Robert F. Morton was born the 10th day of June, 1890 A.D.
John H. Morton was born on the 14 day of March 1892 A.D., Bedford Co., Tenn.
Eldridge L. Morton was born on the 9th day of Feb, 1894 A.D.
Hobeart Morton was born 25th day of Sept 1896 A.D., Bedford Co., Tenn.
Ralph B. Morton was born 11th day of June 1903 A.D.
Glenn C. Morton was born 28th day of Aug 1909

SEARCY BIBLE
This Bible is in the pulpit of Mt. Olivet Methodist Church, Wartrace Pike.
Publisher: Nelson & Phillips Superfine Edition, Pictorial Family Bible, No. 803 Broadway, New York

"This Bible is lovingly presented to the Congregation of Mount Olivet Methodist Church, Wartrace, Tenn., by Miss Lucile Searcy, Norman, Oklahoma, in rememberance of her grandfather, The Rev. Daniel P. Searcy, original owner of the Book and one time Pastor of this Church. It is given also in the name of Mrs. Hattie E. Searcy Slater of Nashville, her Aunt, and Mrs. Reba Thomas of Nashville, her cousin, daughter of Mrs. Roxie Searcy Conwell."

The donor wishes to thank the Reverand J. E. Jones, Pastor of Mount Olivet, 1953, for receiving the Book and dedicating it to use on the Alter.

May this Sacred Volume, printed eighty-one years ago, continue
to interest, guide, comfort and inspire any who may read its pages.
                    signed: Lucile Searcy, May 1953

MARRIAGES:
Daniel P. Searcy and Mary L. Robinson were joined together in Holy
     Matrimony. Sept 11, A.D., 1856.

BIRTHS:
Daniel P. Searcy was born May 7, 1828
Mary L. Searcy was born May 2, 1832
Laura B. Searcy was born Apr 25, 1858
Alice E. Searcy was born Nov 3, 1859
Vinson E. Searcy was born Oct 18, 1861
Ada R. Searcy was born Mar 7, 1863
Hattie E. Searcy was born Aug 5, 1864
Emmett _. Searcy was born Nov 27, 1865
Martha Lucille Searcy born June 24, 1898
Sarah Catherine Searcy born May 20, 1866

DEATHS:
Alice E. Searcy died July 1, 1860, aged 8 mo.
Vinson E. Searcy died May 19, 1863 aged 1 yr & 7 mo.
Daniel P. Searcy died Oct 9, 1883 Grandpa-54 y & 4m (day was 17)
Mary L. Searcy died May 9, 1899   Grandma- 67 y lacking a week.
Ada R. Searcy Conwell died Mar 11, 1910   Aunt Roxie - 47 y lacking 4 da.
Laura B. Searcy died Dec 30, 1924   Aunt Belle   66 y
Emmett C.(Coldwell) Searcy died Sept 13, 1945 dad - 79 y
Sarah Catherine Searcy died Feb 22, 1953   Mother - 86
Martha Lucile S. died
Hattie E. Searcy died June 20, 1955
Ada Reba Thompson died Oct 25, 1969, daughter of Ada Roxie Searcy Conwell

----

RUFUS GRAY ARNOLD, JR. BIBLE

In possession of Mrs. Marvin (Lois Arnold) Claxton, Shelbyville, Tenn.

Rufus Gray Arnold, Jr. was born Sept 16, 1892
Gracie Lee Arnold was born April 17, 1892
Lois Vilma Arnold was born Tuesday Aug 15, 1916

MARRIAGES:
Rufus Gray Arnold, Jr. and Gracie Lee Flippo were united in marriage
     Dec 28, 1910
Lois Arnold & Marvin Claxton were united in marriage the 14, Sept 1940

DEATHS:
Gracie Lee Flippo Arnold died Mar 12, 1925
Ruffus G. Arnold died July 5, 1937

ARNOLD-REAVES BIBLE

Copy in possession of Mrs. Marvin Claxton, Shelbyville, Tennessee

Marvin Creasy Arnold borned January the 14, 19__
Aubry Dee Arnold borned March the 10, 192_
Laura Beatrice Arnold borned Oct 24, 1923
Gladis Lee Arnold borned December 6, 1925
Rufus Dayton Arnold born April 13, 1936
William Reaves born June 4th, 1814
Elisebeth Reaves born Dec 24, 1819
Sarah A. Reaves born Sept 3rd, 1842
Isham D. Reaves born Dec 4th, 1845
John Reaves born March 26th 1848
Elisebeth Reaves born Feb 6th, 1850
Priscilla Reaves born July 4th, 1852
Mary B. Reaves born June 9th, 1856
Chaney G. Reaves born April 22nd, 1859
Wm. H. Reaves born June 2nd, 1861
William Marcus Arnold born August 24, 1917
Rufus Gray Arnold was borned September the 16, 1892
Willie Clay Arnold was borned September the 16, 1892
Argie Maggie Arnold was borned September the 3, 1896
Edward Tomas Miles was borned October 26, 1907 & died October 1910
Mary Margaret Elizabeth Word was borned March the 1, 1908
Margrett Luease Miles was borned August the 28, 1909
Gracy Frances Word was borned April 14, 1911
Lois Velma Arnold was borned August 15, 1916
Grady _____ was borned June 16, 1926 at   & died June 16,
       1926, lived 5 hours.
Dayton Ruffus Arnold borned April 13, 1936
Robert Curtis Morton was borned October 27, ___
Frances Louise Morton was borned April 2, 1932
A. Y. (Acton Young) Snell was borned December the 1, 1839
M. E. Snell was bornd January the 12, 1844
Clara Ursula Arnold was borned October 25, 1888
Bertha Leola Arnold was borned March the 14, 1888
Horal M. Arnold borned August 28, 1928
Odis Gray Arnold borned August 16, 1931
Mary E. Snell was bornd March the 27, 1865
Willie Ursula B. Snell was bornd Jan. _____
Rufus G. Arnold was borned June the 20, 1865
Rufus Claton Arnold borned Dec the 11, ____
Ruffus Dayton Arnold borned April 13, 1930

MARRIAGES:
A. Y. (Acton Young) Snell and M. J. Reeves was married March the 28, 1860
Mary E. Word and Earl H____ married Oct 28, 1924
Rufus G. Arnold and Mary E. Snell was married December the 16, 1884
Lois Velma Arnold & Buck Claxton (Marvin) married Sept 14, 1940
Clara Arnold and Henry Word was maried February the 28, 1904

Bertha Arnold and Floyd Miles was married December the 1, 1906
Rufus G. Arnold and Gracy Flippo was married December the 28, 1910
Argie M. Arnold & Estelle Arnold were married Dec 24, 1915
Louise Miles and Grady Arnold married August 8, 1925
Gracie F. Word and Glenn Morton married Jan 12, 1930

DEATHS:
Willie Ursula B. Snell died May 20th, 1882
Mr. A. Y. Snell died March 2nd, 1883
Margaret Jane Snell borned Jan 12th, 1844, died Dec 5, 1929
Mrs. R. G. Arnold died Feb 3, 1941 Monday at 6:15 morning in Miami,
     Fla., arrived here Tuesday afternoon, funeral at Thompson's
     Funeral Home.
Willie Clay Arnold died Monday November the 22, 1909. 1:20 P.M.
Bertha Arnold Miles died January 9, 1918
Gracie Lee Arnold died March the 12, 1925
R. G. Arnold died July the 8, 1925
Rufus G. Arnold, Jr., died July the 5, 1937 at six o'clock eve.

WILLIE BELL SNELL BIBLE

Copy by Mrs. Marvin Claxton, Shelbyville, Tennessee

Father: Willie B. Snell was born April the 30th, 1798.
Mother: Elisabeth Snell was born August the 12th, 1796

Acton Young Snell was born December 1st, 1839

MARRIAGES:
Willie B. Snell and Elisabeth Cross was married February 16th, 1816.
J. C.(James Cross) Snell and Sarah H.(Hinton) Brown was married Feb-
     ruary the 16th, 1843.
A. G.(Albert G.) Snell and Casander Caldwell was married October 30th,
     1845.
W. P. (Warren) Bridges and Mary Snell was married September 25th, 1844.
John Brown and Nancy Snell was married October 8, 1846.
Willis(e) C.(Calvin) Snell and Casander Williams was married October
     2nd, 1853.
A. Y.(Acton Young) Snell and Margaret Reeves was married March 28, 1861.
Willie T.(Thomson) Snell and Emlia Burrow was married February 7th, 1850
Benjamin F. Reed and S. J.(Sary Jane) Snell was married December the 7,
     186_.

BIRTHS:
James C.(Cross) Snell was born December 8th, 1816
Frances Snell was born November 13th, 1818
Albert G. Snell was born July 22nd, 1820
Mary Snell was born February 5th, 1822

51

Asahel C. Snell was born February 3rd, 1824
Nancy Snell was born April 20th, 1826
Willie T. (Thompson) Snell was born May 28th, 1828
Elisabeth Ann Snell was born July 21st, 1830
Willis C. (Calvin) Snell was born November 11th, 18__
William R. Snell was born December 3rd, 1836
Acton Y. (Young) Snell was born December 1st, 1839
Sary Jane Snell was born February 2nd, 1843

DEATHS:
Asahel C. Snell died Sept·16, 1852
Albert G. Snell died November 15th, 1855
Wm. R. Snell died August 27th, 1859
Elizabeth Snell, wife of H. B. Snell, died November the 7th, 1861
Frances Snell died January 4th, 1865
Nancy Brown died Sept 22, 1868
Warren P. Bridges died August 29th, 1871   •
Mary Bridges died April 11th, 1879
W. B. (Willie Bell) Snell died January the 18, 1881
A. Y. (Acton Young) Snell died March the 2, 1883

The following is written on a seperate piece of paper:
"Willie (pronounced Wiley) B.(Bell) Snell and Elizabeth Cross Snell
        and their Descendants."
Willie B. Snell was born April 30th, 1798, in Orange County, North
Carolina, the names of his parents are not known. He married Elizabeth
Cross on February 16th, 1816. The Bedford County Census for 1850 states
that she was born in Kentucky, the date of her birth was August 12, 1796.
It is believed that she was the daughter of Asel (also spelled Asahel)
Cross. An Asel Cross is listed in the Census of 1790 of North Carolina.
It is known that in the 1790's, there were members of the Cross family
living in Madison County, Kentucky, but not definitely known that Asel
Cross lived there. Willie B. and Elizabeth lived in the 23rd Civil
District of Bedford County in the vicinity of Pisgah Church. They were
the parents of the following children:
James Cross Snell, born December 8, 1816; married Sarah Hinton Brown
        on February 16th, 1843; died April 7th, 1887.
Frances Snell, born Nevember 10th, 1818, died January 4th, 1865.
Albert Snell, born July 22nd, 1820, married Casander Caldwell on Oct-
        ober 30th, 1845, died November 15th, 1855.
Mary Sue Snell, born February 5th, 1822, married Warren Bridges Sept
        25th, 1844, died April 11th, 1879; Mr Bridges died August 29th,
        1871.
Asahel C. Snell, born February 3rd, 1824, died September 16th, 1852.
Nancy Snell, born April 20th, 1826, married John Brown (son of Paschal
        and Kittie Pollard Brown) October 8th, 1846, died September
        22nd, 1868.
Willie Thomson Snell, born May 28th, 1846, married Emlia Burrow on
        February 7th, 1850, died December 30th, 1902.
Elizabeth Ann Snell, born July 21st, 1830, never married, died Sept-
        ember 30th, 1905. Aged: 75 years.

Willis Calvin Snell, born November 11th, 18--, married Casander Williams
    on October 2nd, 1853, died June 24th, 1898.
William R. Snell, born December 3rd, 1836, died August 27th, 1859.
Acton Young Snell, born December 1st, 1839, married Margaret Reeves on
    March 28th, 1861, died March 2nd, 1883.
Sary Jane Snell, born February 2nd, 1843, married Ben F. Reed on Dec-
    ember 7th, 186-, died September 27th, 1914.
NOTE: The above Records of the Snell Family were taken from Willie
    Bell Snell's Bible, which is now in the possession of Fred Reed,
    a Grandson of Willie Bell and Elizabeth Cross Snell. Mr Reed lives
    in Shelbyville, Tennessee = 1974.
    Beside their own Family, Willie Bell and Elizabeth Snell reared
    Wiley Johnson whose parents died when he was an infant. Wiley
    married Mary Elizabeth Brown, a sister of John Brown, who married
    Nancy Snell. Wiley was born in March, 1836 and died May 12th, 1902.

    Willie Bell Snell and Elizabeth Cross were married February 16th,
    1816, their son, James Cross Snell and Sarah Hinton Brown were
    married February 16th, 1843; their daughters, Gartha Ann and
    Mary Adaline were married under a double ceremony on February 16th,
    1870 to John W. Lewellyn and Amzi Jenkins Gordon. Margaret Ray
    Prince, great-granddaughter of Mary Adaline and Amzi Jenkins Gord-
    on was married to James Marion Smith on February 16th, 1946, at
    Huntsville, Alabama.

    "An Aged Father In Isreal Gone"
Rev. Willie Bell Snell, a venerable soldier of the Cross, died at his
home in the 23rd District, Tuesday January 18th, 1881. He was born in
Orange County, North Carolina, April 30, 1798. His Parents (names unknown) came to this County (Bedford) while he was yet a child. At an
early age, he made a profession of religion and joined the M. E. Church,
South. He took an active part in the upbuilding of the Church and the
fruits of his labor has been great. He was engaged in preaching and
exhorting for about 60 years of his life and many have been the souls
that were turned to Christ by his earnest entreaties and fervent pray-
ers. How many Redeemed souls will rise at the last Great Day and call
him blessed.
About 35 years ago he became afflicted with cancer of the nose, which
slowly, stealthily, but surely took his life away. For 18 months Prev-
ious to his death, he was unable to leave his home and during that time
his suffering were great; but he bore them with that resignation and
patience characteristic of the true Christian.
He raised to adult age 12 children, 7 sons and 5 daughters, but 6 of the
12 have preceeded their sire to the grave. The faithful wife who bore
his children and shared his joys and his sorrows for so long, was called
from his side 19 years ago, since which time he has looked anxiously for-
ward to the day when he would follow her to the bright beyond.
Uncle Willie, thou who labored long in Thy Masters Cause, who has so often pleaded with the wayward and called him into the Lord, who has lived
to see thy third generation serving Him whom thou dids't glory in serving; We drop a tear on the spot where thou sleepest, and say,"Aged father,

faithful friend, servant of the Lord, Farewell, O, Farewell."
                                    --- H. L. Boone.---

The above was copied from the original obituary which was published
in a Bedford County Newspaper at the time of his death. The Obituary
rests between the pages of his own Bible.
Copied by Macon Brown Prince (a great-great granddaughter) on April
15th, 1944.

                "Epitaph of Rev. Willie Bell Snell"
"He was a Sincere and devoted Christian, lived by all who knew Him."

He was buried at Old Pisgah Churchyard, 23rd Civil District, Bedford
County, Tennessee.

        Willie Bell Snell's youngest son was named Acton Young, we had
often wondered why-- when copying the 1850 census Record of Bedford
County, Tennessee, we found that Acton Young, who was then 39 years old,
and born in Tennessee, was operating a Hotel in Shelbyville at that time.
It is possible that Willie Bell's son was named for him.

                            SWING BIBLE

Family Record in the possession of Mrs. Marvin Claxton, Shelbyville, Tenn.

MEMORANDA:
E. C. and Rebecca King moved to Eugene, Oregan in April 1894.
J. E. Koonce went to Texas on Jan the 12, 1885.
John H. Koonce departed this life Jan 27, 1914.
Rebecca Koonce King was married to G. B. Collis in 1904. In Oregan.
Rebecca Koonce King Collis was married to Harry Kissell in 1923.
        In Canada.
Rebecca Collis Kissell departed this life June 1, 1948.
John H. Morton was married to Bessie Mai Thaxton, March 2nd, 1929.
Bessie Mai Morton departed this life Feb 27, 1930.
Glenn C. Morton and Gracie F. Word was married Jan 12th, 1930.
Rebecca Collis was borned Aug 11th, 1864.
Harry Kissell was borned March 18th, 1882.

MARRIAGES:
Martha A. Koonce (Swing) & William W. Koonce was married A.D., March 16,
        1854 (error) (as written-Eds.)
William W. Koonce and Martha A. Swing was married A.D., March 16, 1854.
Joel E. Koonce and N. C. Scales were married A.D., Apr 3rd, 1877.
E. C. King and R. T. Koonce were married A.D., Dec 2nd, 1886.
Geo. Collis, Jr. was borned April 28th, 1908.
J. R. Morton and L. B. Koonce were married A.D., June 23, 1887.
J. E. Koonce and Emma Pittman were married Oct 23, 1888.

J. E. Koonce and were married 1894.
John H. Koonce departed this life Jan 27th, 1914.
Ralph Morton and Hazel Appleby were married Jan 11th, 1924.
Jack was borned July 2nd, 1925.
Dorothy was borned June 16th, 1927.

BIRTHS:
W. W. Koonce was borned A.D., May 1st 1828.
Martha A. Swing was borned A.D., Feb 8th, 1839.
Joel E. Koonce was borned A.D., Dec 27th, 1854.
John H. Koonce was borned A.D., April 3rd, 1857
George W. Koonce was borned A.D., June 22, 1859.
Sarah J. Koonce was borned A.D., April 18th, 1861.
Rebecca L. Koonce was borned A.D., August 11th, 1864.
Mollie F. Koonce was borned A.D., April 21st, 1867.
Ladie B. Koonce was borned A.D., Oct 14th, 1869.
Joel Coggins was borned A.D., Dec 7th, 1819
Sallie Swing was borned A.D., Jan 15th, 1815 (Martha Swing's mother)
Lottie Koonce was born A.D., Nov 30, 1857, wife of J. E. Koonce.

DEATHS:
George W. Koonce departed this life A.D., Dec 23rd, 1859.
Sarah J. Koonce departed this life May 1st 1870
Mollie F. Koonce departed this life May 10th, 1870.
Joel Coggins departed this life A.D., Sept 15th, 1865.
Martha A. Koonce departed this life Mar 14th, 1881 (mother of Lady Bell
      Koonce).
W. W. Koonce departed this life June 23rd, 1902.
Nancy C. Koonce departed this life Jan 5th, 1875.
Sallie Swing departed this life Nov 4th, 1894.
Earl C. King departed this life Aug 7th, 1894.
Willie E. Morton departed this life July the 15, 1889.
Hobeart Morton departed this life Feb 4, 1900.
J. E. Koonce departed this life July 9th, 1909.

YOUNG BIBLE

In possession of Mrs. S. M. Martin, Shelbyville, Tennessee.
Publisher: A. J. Holman & Co., No. 1222 Arch Street, Philadelphia,
      Pa.   1885

BIRTHS:
Mark M. Young was borned April 30, 1830
Malinda E. Young was borned Oct 13th, 1838
Margarett Josephine Young was borned Mar 29, 1853
Mary Frances Young was borned Sept 23, 1857
James M. Young was born Dec 18, 1859
Sarah E. Young was born June 16, 1862

Emily K. Young born March 31st, 1865
Gotha A. Young born Dec 31, 1868
Virgie C. Young born May 11, 1871
Martha E. Young borned Sept 5, 1874.
Eddie C. Young born Sep 18, 1877
Nettie Young born May 13, 1880
Willie A. Young born Sept 8, 1883
Ethel Young born Feb 2, 1887

MARRIAGES:
James Young and Bernice Richmond was married Jan 17th, 1894.
Noah Darnell and Lizzie Young was married August 23rd, 1883.
W. T. Sorrells & Fannie Young was married Sept the 11, 1884.
L. O. Nichols and Gothie Young was married July 6th, 1893.
J. R. Nichols and Ella Young was married August 24, 1893.
Charlie Pyrdom & Nellie Young was married May 28, 1899.
Edward Young & Addie Pearson was married Sept 19, 1900.
Will Young & Nona Brown was married July 13th, 1902.

DEATHS:
Emily K. Young died Aug 23, 1873.
Bernice Young died Dec 9, 1900.
M. M. Young died Feb 25, 1904.
Gothie Young Nichols died May 19, 1907.
Ethel Young died April 16, 1909.
Francis Jones died Feb 23, 1909.
Eddie C. Young died Jan 8th, 1913.
W. A. Young died Oct 23, 1918.
Sarah Elizabeth Darnell died Sept 12, 1921.
Melinda E. Young died Aug 25, 1923.
Katherine Woosley Young died Aug 1, 1923.
James Minous Young died April 10, 1929.

OBIT: "Burned to Death, Mrs. Bernice Young falls into the fire at her
        home near Singleton."
Singleton, Tenn., Dec 15, 1900.
        Mrs. Bernice Young met her death in a horrible manner at her home
near this place. No one was present but her little son, 6 years old, so
precisely how the accident occured cannot be definately stated.
        After dinner, her husband, James Young, went out for a walk, and
could not have been gone very long. His wife had cracked some walnuts and
was sitting before the fire in a low rocking chair eating them. It is
supposed she fell from the chair into the fire, as she was found near the
fireplace and the rocker turned over in such a way as to indicate she had
fallen from it. Her little son, with a bucket of water, did all he could
to extinguish the burning clothing of his mother, but was unsuccessful.
        The little fellow then ran to the house of a neighbor some quarter
of a mile distant, and told what had occured. They went immediately to
the scene, but arrived only to find her dead, with every particle of
clothing burned from her body and it burned to a crisp. It is supposed
she inhaled the flames when her clothing first caught fire, and at once

became unconscious.

Mrs. Young was born in Lynchburg, being the eldest daughter of Mr. & Mrs. H. B. Richmond. She was 27 years old and leaves a husband and one child."

HUGHSON BIBLE

In possession of Mrs. Beatrice Dickens, Atlanta, Georgia.
Publisher: American Bible Society, 1890

MARRIAGE:
J. S. (James Samuel) and E. M. (Myrtle Effie) Hughson on Feb 14th, 1884

BIRTHS:
James S.(Samuel) Hughson born Jan 22, 1857
Effie M.(Myrtle) Hughson born Sept 2, 1866 and died June 23, 1946.

Children:
      G. C.(Gifford Cleveland) Hughson, born Feb 11, 1885
      H. E.(Hummie Estelle) Hughson, born Oct 22, 1887
      T. M.(Thomas Marks) Hughson, born Aug 19, 1890 and died Feb 11, 1952.
      M. S.(Mary Sue) Hughson, born April 4, 1892
      W. F.(William Fred) Hughson, born Aug 26, 1894
      J. C.(Jimmie Cleo) Hughson, born Feb 5, 1897

DEATHS:
James S. Hughson died Sept 1, 1896
Jimmie Cleo Hughson died May 10, 1913.
Effie Myrtle Hughson, died June 23, 1946
T. M. Hughson died Feb 11, 1952
G. C. Hughson died   1962
W. F. Hughson died Dec 27, 1972
M. S. Hughson Shearin died Oct 1, 1972
J. C. Hughson died   1913
H. E. Hughson Wilson died   1955

DICKENS BIBLE

In possession of Mrs. Beatrice Dickens, Atlanta, Georgia.
Publisher: Heirloom Bible Publishers, 1964, Wichita, Kansas

Presented by Chas. & Lee Gallant, this 3rd day of Sept. 1967,
        Fayetteville, Tennessee.
"In Memory of your Husband Charles Herman Dickens."

FAMILY REGISTER:
Parents: Married July 25, 1928, Cookeville, Tenn.
Husband:
Charles Herman Dickens, born May 3, 1907 at Buffalo Valley, Tenn.,
    died September 3, 1967 (buried at Riverview Cem), Fayetteville,
    Tenn.
Wife:
Myrtle Beatrice Shearin, born March 29, 1913, Shelbyville, Tenn.

Beatrice Shearin Dicken's parents:
Father: Buford Edgar Shearin and
Mother: Mary Sue Hughson Shearin.

Charles Herman Dicken's parents:
Father: Leonard Forrest Dickens and
Mother: Loura Emma Steakley Dickens.   .

Children of Charles H. and M. Beatrice Dickens:
Son: Charles Shearin Dickens, born April 19, 1931, at Fayetteville, Tenn
Daughter: Peggy Jean Dickens, born July 9, 1933 at Fayetteville, Tenn.,
    and died July 14, 1943 at Fayetteville, Tenn.

Charles Shearin Dickens married Lucinda Riddle on June 9, 1953 at Nash-
    ville, Tenn., and divorced in 1966. They had one son, Paul Shear-
    in Dickens, born Mar 23, 1958 in Hartsville, Tenn.

Charles Shearin Dickens married Joanne Azar, Nov 23, 1966
Children:
John Charles Dickens, born Sept 26, 1968 at LaFallette, Tenn.
Joseph Scott Dickens, born Sept 30, 1970 at Atlanta, Georgia
Twins: Joanne Adele Dickens, born July 20, 1973 at Savannah, Ga.
       Jeanne Sue Dickens, born July 20, 1973 at Savannah, Ga.

M. Beatrice Dickens' Grandparents:
Father's side: William Thomas Shearin, born Feb 12, 1842, died Oct 13,
    1921. Louvenia Coffee Shearin, born June 12, 1845, died Sept 10,
    1897.
Mother's side: James Samuel Hughson, born Jan 22, 1857, died Sept 1, 1896.
    Myrtle Effie Hoover Hughson, born Sept 2, 1866, died June 23, 1946.

M. Beatrice Dicken's Great-Grandparents:
Father's side: James Fletcher Shearin, born 1818, died between 1860-70.
    Elizabeth Jane Hamble, born May 5, 1823, died Aug 28, 1862
Mother's side: James Hoover, born July 29, 1814, died Mar 4, 1894.
    Minerva Jane Winn Hoover, born June 4, 1844, died Sept 17, 1926.

M. Beatrice Dickens' Great-Great-Grandparents:
Father's side: Thomas Shearin, born Jan/Mar 26, 1749, died 1824/25.
    2nd wife: Sarah Mayfield Shearin, married Mar 21, 1810 in N.C.
Mother's side: Christopher Hoover, born 1776, d--
    Elizabeth Lotspeech Hoover, born 1776, d--

EDWARDS FAMILY RECORDS

In possession of Mr & Mrs James Edwards, Shelbyville, Tennessee

Lencil Andrew (Stripling) Edwards, born Jan 19, dec'd. Married Mary
    Jane Woodfin, born May 3,- died Oct 26, 1867
Their children:
Thomas, born Oct 31, 1809-died July 11, 1890
Minerva, born Oct 24, 1811- died Jan 8, 1900
Martin, born Sept 20, 1813- died..
Hannibal, born Mar 12, 1816- died Aug 26, 1826
John Woodfin, born Sept 21, 1818- died Sept 28, 1847
Narcissus, born Oct 27, 1820- died..
George Newton, born April 6, 1823- died Nov 18, 1903
Jane, born Mar 21, 1825- died Dec 20, 1910
Minus, born Jan 27, 1828- died Jan 7, 1915

Thomas Edwards (Judge), born 1747- died 1832, married Mary Ann McClana-
    han.
Children:
William, died unmarried
Peter, married Polly Solmon
Thomas, married Leah Ford
Lencil, married Miss Woodfin
John, married Mildred Earl
James, married Betsey Kindiech
Frances,

Thomas Edwards, born July 17, 1726, married Elizabeth Nicholas, Dec.
    1743- Settled in Orange Co., N.C.

Robert Thomas Edwards born 1690, married Isabel Downing, 1714
Children:
Robert, born 1716
Joshua, born 1718
William, born 1720
Thomas, born 1726
Lenard, born 1725
John, born 1727
Jacob, born 1729
Martha B., born 1731

Thomas John Edwards, born 1662
Children:
John, born 1683
Thomas B., born 1684
Hayden B., born 1687
Henry B., born 1688
Robert B., born 1690
Peter B., born 1701

William Edwards, (nothing known to date on him)

Richard Edwards, born 1533

Thomas Hall born 1669 died 1687, married Anne Metford of Bristol,
England, she was the widow of an English Surgeon named William Quick.
Thomas Hall paid Adrianson 1000 c_____ for New   about 402.00,
Anne left all her personal property to her husband, no real property.
She had been Thomas Edwards' executrix but produce no Will. Elizabeth
Hall, Thomas's daughter married Thomas Edwards, Ship Master of _____
Society, married in 1660, their son Robert born 1690.

The following is a copy of Mrs. Malissa May Edwards (Mrs P. R. Miller)
        made in 1924:
Great Grand father married in North Carolina, came to Rutherford Co.
        near Murfreesboro in 1810.
Brooklyn N. Y. Historical Sketches of the Edwards', about 1620, the bro-
thers: John, Thomas, Robert & William, sons of William and Grandsons of
Richard, came to America to settle land granted there for the Service
rendered to the King.

Record of my Great Great Grandfather:
Thomas Edward died 1832 (Judge was the ancestor who assisted in estab-
lishing American Independence while acting in the capacity of a Private
in the 4 South Carolina Regiment Artillery Commanded by Col. Bernard Bechman. His name appears upon the records of that organization with rewards
showing that he enlisted Nov 28, 1779.
His name in inscribed upon a Bronze Monument erected upon the Capital
grounds at Columbia, S. C., commemorating those who served in the different Wars of the United States. His name is also upon the base of a Monument to General Morgan and his men erected on the Public Square at
Spartanburg, S. C. His name is also registered in the Archives of Greenville, S. C., as a Soldier and a Statesman. Additional evidence shows
that Thomas Edwards was a member of the General Assembly of Greenville,
S. C., and continued to discharge his duties as a Legislator until some
time in 1779 when he later joined the Army about the first of Feb. 1780.
This Thomas Edward, Jr., settled in South Carolina on the South Tiger
River, some of his descendants still live on the South Tiger.
                                    ---Malissa May Edwards--
                                    (Mrs. P. R. Miller) 1924.
by Florence Gilmore, 1957

EDWARDS FAMILY TREE CHART:
1: Richard Edwards born in England, he had John, William, Robert and
        Thomas Edwards. The brothers came to America about 1620 for land
        grants.
2: Thomas Edwards, "Shipmaster," born 1639 in England and died 1771, he
        was married to Elizabeth Hall, 1660. Elizabeth Hall Edwards was
        the daughter of Thomas (H.) Hall, born 1614, died April 9, 1669,
        1st married in 1639 to a Welch girl,(Nothing else known of her).
        He married 2nd Alene Medford, died 1681, N. Y., ____ _____ of

England, Surgeon, Dr. G. Bristol.
Thomas Edwards, (2), had a son:
3: Robert Edwards, born 1662 & died 1774, married in 1685 to Margaret
   Curlein, born 1668 & died 1738.
   Robert Edwards, (3), had a son:
4: Thomas Edwards, born Oct 4, 1690, died Nov 2, 1781, he married on
   Mar 14, 1714 to Isabel Downing, born 1692 & died 1783 in Wales.
   Thomas Edwards, (4), had a son:
5: Thomas Edwards, born July 1723, died Jan 30, 1830, he married in
   Oct 1743 to Elizabeth Nichols(Margaret), born 1727 & died 1790.
   Thomas Edwards, (5), had a son:
6: Thomas Edwards, South Carolina, Judge, born 1747, died 1832, he
   married Mary Anne McClanahan (or Clanahan).
   Thomas Edwards, (6), had a son:
7: Lenciel Andrew "Stripling" Edwards, born Jan 19, 1783 & died May 6,
   1864, married Mary Woodfin, born April 3, 1790 & died Oct 1867.
   They came from Buncombe Co., N.C., to Rutherford Co., Tenn.,
   about 1810. They are buried in Woodfin Cemetery near Fosterville.
   (no markers).
   Lenciel Andrew Edwards, (7), had a son:
8: Thomas Edwards, born Oct 31, 1809, died July 11, 1890, married on
   June 11, 1841 in Rutherford Co., Tenn., by John D. Gilmore, Jr.,
   Esq., to Martha Jane Vaughan, born Jan 16, 1825, died Oct 12, 1906.
   Both buried in Woodfin Cemetery. (With markers).

JOHN TILLMAN, SR. BIBLE

In possession of Mr. Earl L. Philips, Phoenix, Arizona

MARRIAGES:
John Tillman, Sr. was married to Rachel P. Martin, Jan 17th, 1810.
William B. Sutton was married to Atlanta J. Armstrong, June 13th, 1828.
Barclay M. Tillman was married to Elizabeth F. Sutton, July 31st, 1849.
Charles M. Moore was married to Sophia Atlanta Tillman, December 31st,
   1889.
Henry A. Tillman was married to Annie Lee Capshaw, June the 30th, 1891.
Lewis A. Tillman was married to Sarah L. Peacock on June 16th, A.D.,
   1892. Sarah died April __ 1893.
_____ Aldrige Marshall   1900

BIRTHS:
John Tillman, Sr born Feb 5th, 1786
Rachel P. Tillman born 16th, 1789
William B. Sutton born Mar 9th, 1801
Atlanta J. Sutton born Aug 18th, 1805
Barclay M. Tillman born Oct 31st, 1825
Elizabeth F. Tillman born Dec 13th, 1830
William S. Tillman born July 7th, 1851

Sally Clay Tillman born Aug 20th, 1853
John Tillman, Jr., born Sept 3rd, 1855
Charles C. Tillman born May 14th, 1858
Henry A. Tillman born Dec 2nd 1860
Barclay M. Tillman, Jr. born May 9th 1863
Sophia Atalanta Tillman born Apr the 14th 1866
Lewis Abram Tillman born March the 27th A.D. 1869
Mary Elizabeth Tillman born Sept 21st A.D., 1871
An Infant daughter born 13th Oct, 1874

DEATHS:
John Tillman, Sr. died Oct 3rd, 1854
Rachel P. Tillman died Nov 9th, 1881
William B. Sutton died Nov 30th, 1833
Atlanta J. Sutton died July 1st, 1833
Sally Clay Tillman died Aug 11th, 1856
The Infant daughter lived only two days and died on the 15th Oct, 1874.
Mary Elizabeth Tillman died Sept 15, 1876
Henry A. Tillman(or, as he always signed his name) Henry A. Tillman
     died on Nov the 6th, 1892 in Shelbyville, Tenn.
Mrs. Elizabeth F. Tillman, wife of Barclay M. Tillman, died at her home
     in Shelbyville, Tenn., on 27th July 1893 at 12:15 p.m. aged: 63
     yrs., 7 mos., & 14 da.
Lewis Tillman, Sr. died at his residence in Bedford County, Tenn.,
     May 3rd, 1886.
Barclay M. Tillman died, Oct 2nd, 1901 at Auther City, Texas, was buried
     in Shelbyville by his wife.
(illegible)   died July 17, 1926
John Tillman died Nov 29, 1921 at (illegible)

MISCELLANEOUS:
Barclay M. Tillman's paternal grandfather was Lewis Tillman, who was a
native of Virginia, his paternal grandmother was Mary Tillman (formerly)
Mary Huff, also a native of Virginia. The former died in Ala., the
latter, at her son John's in Bedford Co., Tenn. His Maternal Grandfather
was Matt Martin, Sr. and his Maternal Grandmother was Sally Martin (Formerly Sally Clay) both natives of Virginia and both died in Bedford Co.,
Tennessee.
Elizabeth F. Tillman's paternal grandfather was John Sutton, her paternal
grandmother was Elizabeth Sutton (formerly Elizabeth Finley) both natives
of Virginia and both died in Bedford County, Tennessee. Her maternal
grandfather was the Dr. James L. Armstrong and her maternal grandmother
was Sophia Armstrong (formerly Sophia Smith), Dr. Armstrong was a native
of Virginia moved to Kentucky thence at early day to Tennessee, Mrs.
Armstrong was a native of (illegible). Dr. Armstrong was a medical
student graduated at Lexington, Kentucky, was a soldier in War of 1812
with Jackson, under Gen. Jackson. ____(illegible)_____ May 11, 1909
W. S. Tillman, at (illegible) May 11, 1909.

KELLER BIBLE

In possession of Klyne Jack Keller, Madison, Tennessee

William Hodge
John Keller was born September the 26th, 1782
Frances H. Keller was born November 18, 1794
Jacob Keller was born October 20th, 1797
John Keller was born September 26th, 1782
Ann Keller was born March 5th, 1785
Rachel Keller was born October the 3rd, 1787
Charlie Keller was borned May 11th, 1790
Joseph Keller was born October 10, 1792

DANIEL HOOSER BIBLE RECORD

In possession of Mr. Klyne Jack Keller, Madison, Tennessee
Publisher: Printed by D. Fanshaw for the American Bible Society,
          Instituted in New York in the year 1816
          1843

Daniel Hooser's Bible bought in the year of our Lord one thousand
eight hundred and forty five.
Price $1.25   Geo. M. Hooser
                  D. Hooser
NOTE: This Record was given to Mr. Klyne Jack Keller in May 1968, by a
      member of the Hooser family, Margaret Hooser Thomas.

MARRIAGES:
Daniel Hooser & Frances Kimbro was married August the 15th, 1830
John A. Couch & Sara Jane Hooser was married October 20th, 1853
Frances Hooser was born July the 11th, 1807(also on 1805 here)
Daniel Hooser was born June the 1st, 1807
George M. Hooser & Harriet V. Holt was married February the 4th, 1864.

BIRTHS:
Mary Ann Hooser was born August the 20th, 1831
George Marion Hooser was born November the 4th, 1832
Sarah Jane Hooser was born March the 1st, 1836
Rachel Lucinda and Harriet Luisa Hooser was born April the 1st, 1839
William Mitchell Hooser was born December the 18th, 1840
Martha Frances Hooser was born November the 12th, 1842
Eliza Almeda Hooser was born November the 3rd, 1844
Sefrona Alemander Hooser was born October the 9th, 1847
Virginia Ann Hooser was born March the 25th, 1850

DEATHS:
Rachel Lucinda Hooser departed this life October the 16th, 1841

Harriet Luisa departed this life May 31st, 1849
Mary Ann Hooser departed this life August 12th, 1856
Sarah Jane Couch departed this life May the 16th, 1863
Daniel Hooser departed this life April the 2nd, 1864
Frances Hooser departed this life May 6, 1885
William Mitchel Hooser departed this life Dec 15, 1907

Letters: This is a copy of a letter in the possession of Mr. R. L.
Couch, Jr., of Tullahoma, Tennessee. It was mailed to me by his father
Mr. R. L. Couch, Sr., in 1966. Mr. R. L. Couch, Sr.(Robert L.) passed
away in March 1967 and was buried on the 27th in the Rose Hill Memorial
Gardens at Tullahoma. He was a descendant probably a son of the Will
Couch of Tullahoma as mentioned in the letter which follows. Almeda
Couch's maiden name, Eliza Almeda Hooser, born Nov 3, 1844.

by- Klyne Jack Keller

Letter: Dated: Sept 16, 1927   •
The Couch Family
A sketch of the life of your Grandfather Couch and Family:
        Joseph and Catherine Patton Couch lived in a nice two story farm
home near Fairfield and Wartrace, Bedford County, Tennessee. Raised a
family of ten children, five sons and five daughters, namely: Elijah,
James Erwin, Reuben Calaway, John Archibald, and Dr. Robert Weight Couch.
Daughters to wit: Nancy Couch Stephens, Sarah Couch Cunningham, Margaret
Couch Payne, Mary Couch Hickerson, and Emily Couch Maupin. The Stephens,
Cunninghams and Hickersons are too numerous to mention but will give a
list of the sons, children. Elijah's: John and Arthur, who moved to
Arkansas and Elijah Patton (a Christian Preacher) who lives in Indiana
and their sister Mary C. Cortner, Sarah C. Thomas, Ruth C. Brantley and
Belle C. Cunningham of Bedford County.
        Reuben's Family comes next: Ruby Couch, Bell Buckle, Tenn., Lester
Couch and Gertrude Couch Dalby, Birmingham, Ala., next your Father's
Family: John Archibald Couch with whom you are acquainted, and Dr. R. W.
Couch's family. Robert L. Couch, Dallas, Texas. Will Couch, Tullahoma,
Tenn., Mary Couch Overall, Murfreesboro, Tennessee. Reuben Couch was a
Captain in the Federal Army and later one of the Legislators from Tenn-
essee made his home in Nashville, your grandfather, Joseph Couch was a
slave owner and a fine business man and had several brothers who moved
away from Tennessee in early days to Missouri, Kansas and perhaps other
places. Their names as they were called, Tommie, Jimmie, Ben, Isaac and
Calloway Couch, and maybe some others, so this accounts for the unknown
kin that we meet occasionally in life's journey.
        Joe Couch of Ellis County (Texas) was a first cousin of your
father and whose father raised him and were almost like brothers. His
wife was also a first cousin (Kizia Haynes) of your father on his mother's
side. They were grandparents of Jim Couch who lives here (Abilene, Texas).
Brother James Erwin Couch died in Alabama while a young man. I am the
only one living in the family except the many grandchildren.

Your Mother, Mrs. J. A. Couch (80 yrs)
Almeda Couch.

A Sketch of the lives of your Grandfather and Grandmother:
    Daniel and Frances Hooser:

       Daniel and Frances Kimbrough Hooser lived on a farm situated at
"Three Fork's" of Duck River near Shelbyville, Tennessee, Bedford
County, there a family of eight children, two sons and six daughters
grew to man and woman hood. George Marion Hooser, the eldest son was a
popular school teacher for that day, was loved and admired by all who
knew him for his gentle kind disposition. Married and left two sons, one
of them, George M., Jr., lives near Haley, Bedford County, Tenn., The
second son, William Mitchel Hooser was a successful farmer. Married a
very noted Lutheran preacher's daughter (old Billie Jenkins) raised one
son. Horace Hooser who was a teacher and banker, living at Haley, Tennessee. Your grandfather, Daniel Hooser, was never a very "big man" but
noted for the good things he did. My first memory, he was a Major in a
Militia Company stationed at Rowesville, Tennessee. The opulets he wore
on his shoulders, I thought were beautiful. He held the office of County
Trustee for several years. Then overseer on a negro plantation at the
sametime and when he was declining was made Magistrate until his death,
lived and died on the same place I mentioned above. His people were slave
owners but nothing was realized from them as they were set free. As you
are aware, I am the only one of the family living. Sister Martha Troxler
left no heirs at her death. Sister Terenia Williams left two daughters,
Mrs. Annie Clark and Virginia Mullins. One son Tom Williams all of whom
lived near Shelbyville, Tennessee. Sister Virginia Bomar passed away
in La., left two sons and a daughter there. My eldest Sister Mary Ann
died when a young lady. Sister Sarah Jane is the mother of George Couch
and Sarah Couch Parker. My father was Scotch-Irish descent and my mother
Dutch-German.

                          Your Mother, Mrs. J. A. Couch (83 yrs)
                          Mrs. Almeda Hooser Couch
                          Dated: Sept 17, 1927
                          Abilene, Texas

NOTE: The Sister refered to above as Terania Williams, the name in the
Hooser Bible is Sefrona Alexander or Alemander. John A. Couch married
Sarah Jane Hooser in 1853, she died in 1863, Bible Record. It is believed that he then married her Sister Eliza Almeda Hooser who was born
in 1844 but no Bible Record of this marriage. She is the one who wrote
this letter. The Hooser Bible spells the name Kimbro not Kimbrough.
                  by: Klyne Jack Keller, Madison, Tenn.

BLACK BIBLE

In possession of Mrs. Jo Isom (Black) Brown, Shelbyville, Tennessee
Copied by Mr. Klyne Jack Keller, Madison, Tennessee,July 8, 1975.

MARRIAGES:
James Black and Mary Baily was married January 3, 1808.
Sarah Black was married April 5th, 1832.
James M. Black married October 25, 1832.
Mary B. Black married February 12, 1835.
Susannah H. Black married February 2, 1837.

BIRTHS:
Robert Black, the father of James was born Aug 25, 1750
James Black, born January 13, 1782.
Mary, his wife, was born May 19, 1786.
John Black, born May 25, 1809.
James M. Black, born August 10, 1811.
Margaret F. Black, born July 30, 1813.
Sarah Black, born December 4, 1814
Mary B. Black, born April 10, 1817
Susannah H. Black born May 14, 1819
Martha L. R. Black, born May 29, 1821
John L. A. Black, born July 31, 1824
Elizabeth Black, born June 20, 1827
James Vaughan born April 7, 1833
Martha Abigail Black born Sept 17, 1833
David Vaughan born November 30, 1834
Mary E. Black born Nov. 13, 1835
James M. Walters born April 26, 1836

DEATHS:
Robert Black died October 16, 1820 (Father of J. B.)
Margaret Black died July 1782
Sarah Bailey died July 8th, 1833, in her 73rd year.
John Black, died June 5, 1811
Margaret F. Black, died August 10, 1813
Sarah Vaughan, died August 29, 1837
James Black, died May 31, 1853
Mary Black, died November 22, 1859
Mary Walters, died May 29, 1885.
Mary Nadley Black died January 23, 1885
James M. Black died October 15, 1900

BIRTHS:
Martha Abigail Black born September 17, 1833
Mary Elizabeth, born November 13, 1835
James Lawrence Black born December 31, 1839
William Harison Black born July 9, 1840
John White Black born November 2, 1842
Joseph Christopher Black, born January 31, 1845
Robert Scott Black, born May 24, 1847
Quincy Bailey Black, born November 18, 1849
Buckaniah Tailor Couch born March 3, 1847
Catherine Marthura Couch born May 15, 1849
Kenny Erwin Couch born Sept 25, 1851

Susan Catherine Black born December 20, 1851
Margret Caline Black born July 15, 1854
Jany June Black, departed this life September 2, 1857

MARRIAGES:
J. W. Black and Mary Ann Green were married January 30, 1866
Robert Black - Sarah Bailey
James Black - Mary Bailey
        &
Mary Black

FAMILY RECORDS
BIRTHS:
John W. Black born November 2, 1842
Mary A. Black, wife, born January 17, 1846
William W. Black born November 12, 1866
Florence M. Black born February 20, 1868
Robert Lee Black born January 8, 1870
Sallie Lula Black born April 4, 1872
John C. Black born January 29, 1874
James N. Black born June 28, 1876
Joseph R. Black born January 10, 1879
Edward M. Black born October 10, 1881
Mary E. Black born January 20, 1885
Susan Gertrude Black born December 13, 1886
Francis M. Black born September 12, 1888

DEATHS:
Florena M. Black died October 15, 1868
Mary Ann Black died January 19, 1913
John W. Black died October 27, 1917
Joseph R. Black died February 18, 1919
Susan Gertrude Black died February 26, 1921
Robert Lee Black died May 17, 1926
Mary E. Black died December 13, 1927
W. W. Black died October 10, 1940
Francis Marion Black died November 7, 1956

MARY PEARSON FLOYD BIBLE

In possession of Floyd Lee Moore, New Market, Alabama, in 1966.
Copied by Mr. Klyne Jack Keller, Madison, Tennessee, July 8, 1975.
Publisher: John E. Potter & Co., No. 617 Sansom Street, Philadelphia
        Purchased in 1876 for $8.00   Jayne Floyd Nov 9, 1903
The above was written in long hand in inside back cover.

MARRIAGES:
E. T. Floyd & Mary L. Pearson was married the 18th day of Nov 1869.

67

On Jan 19, 1896, E. E. Hart and Hester Floyd were united in marriage.
On March 17, 1898, John Ray and Orrie Floyd were united in marriage.
On March 31, 1898, Robert I. Keller and Ida Floyd were united in marriage.
On Dec 29, 1907, Wm. Ike Floyd & Inez Cunningham were united in marriage.
On June 19, 1910, A. L. Moore & Jayne Floyd were united in marriage.
On Jan 3, 1912, Jno. E. Floyd & Pearl Caples were united in marriage.
On May 18, 1913, Geo. W. Floyd & Nell Wiggins were united in marriage.

BIRTHS: . .
Orrie Floyd was born the 9th of September 1870, (died April 18, 1951)
John Ray born ___ __ 1860 (died _____ ___ 1948)
Hester Floyd was born August the 6th 1872 (died May 4, 1964)
Ed Hart born July 28, 1869 & died July 22, 1937.
Ida Floyd was born Aug 15th 1874 (died April 15, 1966)
Rob. Keller born Jan 19, 1876 & died July 28, 1957
Jane Floyd was born September the 10th 1876 & died April 15, 1966.
A. L. Moore born Sept 30, 1887 & died March 12, 1971
Sallie Floyd was born September 18th 1878 - died Oct 6th 1878
E. T. Floyd was born Oct 26th 1848 - died (Sat) Aug 27, 1887.
Mary L. Pearson was born Nov 18th 1850 - died Jan 17, 1940.
John E. Floyd was born Oct 13th 1879 (died Jan 22, 1955)
William Isaac Floyd was born January 17th 1882 (died Sept 20, 1974)
George Watson Floyd was born August 28th, 1884 (died Dec 1963 or Jan
    1974)
J. E. Pearson was born Apr 23, 1826 & died July 18, 1910.
Mrs. J. E. Pearson was born Apr 6, 1834 & died Sun. Aug 9, 1908.
Infant Son of John & Orrie Ray was born Nov 24, 1898 & died Nov 30, 1898.
Kline (should be Klyne) Jackson Keller was born Dec 30, 1898.
Clytus Ray Hart was born May 2nd 1900.
Thomas Earl Hart was born Jan 29, 1902, died May 21, 1916
Mary Lou Keller was born Mar 10, 1903
Wm. Isaac Floyd, Jr., was born June 29, 1910 (died Dec 11, 1969)
Margarette Long Floyd was born Mar 22, 1912.
Twin Sons were born to A. L. & Janye Floyd Moore, Sept 29, 1911
Twin Sons were born to A. L. & Janye Floyd Moore, June 24, 1913
(Floyd Lee Moore, one of the twins, born June 13, 1913).
Jewell Juanita Floyd was born Sept 7, 1914
Mildred Tressa Floyd was born Sept 5, 1915
Eugene Thomas Floyd was born Feb 12, 1914
Jane Ann Floyd was born Sept 23, 1915
John E. Floyd was born Aug 3, 1919 (died World War II, fighter Pilot)
Orrie Elizabeth Floyd was born Sept 9, 1927
Earl Thomas Moore was born April 28, 1918
Infant Sons of A. L. & Janye Floyd Moore died Sept 29, 1911.
Infant Son of A. L. & Janye Floyd Moore died June 27, 1913.

Parts in parenthesis were not in Bible but added after it was copied
from Old Bible- by Klyne Jack Keller, Feb 1967.

COUCH BIBLE RECORDS

By- Mr. Klyne Jack Keller, Madison, Tennessee
This Record was found in a trunk of Martha Couch Thomas, given to Mr.
Keller by Cenia Thomas Armstrong (Mrs. John Armstrong) in Chattanooga,
Tennessee.

BIRTHS:
James Couch, son of Joseph and Nancy Couch, his wife was borned April
      29 in the year of our Lord, 1789.
Abigail Couch, daughter of John Watson was born Dec 29th, 1798.
Magdalena Couch was borned Nov 24th, 1815.
J. E. Couch was born Sept 18, 1817. A.D.
Charity A. Couch was born July 14th A.D., 1819.
John W. Couch was born Sept 15 A.D., 1821.
Elisabeth J. Couch was born May 18 A.D., 1823.
Nancy C. Couch was born Nov 16 A.D., 1825.   ·
Rhoda C. Couch was born Dec 27 A.D., 1827.
Thomas F. Couch was born Jan 9, A.D., 1830.
Martha D. Couch was born December 27th A.D., 1831.
James Calvin Couch was born January 6th A.D., 1833.
Isaac A. Couch was born Jan 6th A.D., 1835.
Christopher C. Couch was born March 31st A.D., 1836.

MARRIAGES:
James Couch and Abigail Watson was married January 29th A.D., 1815.
Magdaleen Couch was married Oct the 25 A.D., 1832
Martin (?) Thomas and J. M. Black was married Oct 6, 1885

DEATHS:
John W. Couch died _____ A.D., 1822.
James Couch died A.D., June 8th 1837.
Abigail Couch died March the 25, 1843.
Charity Mills died Nov. 1853.
Magdaline Black, the wife of J. M. Black, departed this life, January
      23, 1885.
Martha T. Couch died April 13, 1913.

F. M. KELLER BIBLE

Furnished by Mr Klyne Jack Keller, Madison, Tennessee

F. M. Keller of Bedford Co., Tennessee and Lucinda Ayers of Bedford Co.,
      Tennessee, on Nov 14, 1867, at Mrs. Sallie Ayers, by Daniel
      Stephens.

MARRIAGES:
F. M. Keller and Lucinda Ayers was married Nov 14, 1867.

J. W. Simpson and Kittie Keller was married Jan 14, 1891.
J. Lane Keller and Ellen Ayers was married Dec 31, 1891.
Charley P. Keller and Edith Chilton was married Nov 10, 1897.
Robt. I. Keller and Ida Floyd was married Mar 31, 1898.
Klyne Jackson Keller and Louise Gray was married Jan 14, 1927.
Mary Loucinda Keller and J. C. Lorance was married June 25, 1937.

BIRTHS:
F. M. Keller was borned Feb 2, 1844.
Lucinda Keller was borned Dec 5, 1841.
Rhoda C. Keller was borned Nov 1, 1868.
Chas. P. Keller was borned Mar 7, 1870.
Joseph L. Keller was borned Aug 7, 1871.
Robt. I. Keller was borned Jan 19, 1876.
Ida Floyd Keller was borned Aug 15, 1874.
Klyne Jackson Keller was borned Dec 30, 1898.
Mary Lucinda Keller was borned Mar 10, 1903. ·
Faye Keller born July 9, 1940.
Jane Keller born Feb 9, 1932.
Louise Gray Keller, Nov 28, 1902.

DEATHS:
F. M. Keller died Dec 23, 1900.
Lucinda Keller died June 11, 1901.
J. L. Keller died Sept 4, 1944.
C. P. Keller died Mar 13, 1948.
Kittie Keller Simpson died Jan 13, 1951.
Faye Keller died June 5, 1943.
Robert I. Keller died July 28, 1957.
Ida Floyd Keller died April 15, 1966.
Mary Lucinda Keller Lorence died ------
Jane Keller died ------
Louise Gray Keller died April 28, 1972.

KINCAID BIBLE

In possession of Mrs. T. R. Marsh, Shelbyville, Tennessee
Publisher: Jasper Harding, No. 57, S. Third Street, Philadelphia, 1851

Samuel Ingram Kincaid was borned in the year of our Lord, October 9th,
    1825.
Margaret Lewis Kincaid was borned in the year of our Lord, July 11th,
    1825.
John Fulton Kincaid was borned in the year of our Lord, March 14th,
    1851.
Elisha Robbins Kincaid was borned in the year of our Lord, October
    3rd, 1852.
Edward Albert Kincaid was borned in the year of our Lord, June 19th,

1854.

James Thomas Kincaid was borned in the year of our Lord, March 25th,
1856.

John Fulton Kincaid died the 3rd day of May 1856. Aged: 5 years,
1 month, & 19 days.

DAVID H. BEASLEY BIBLE

In possession of R. A. Marsh, Shelbyville, Tennessee
Publisher: Missing.   Dated 1858

MARRIAGES:
David H. Beasley & Mary A. McGaugh married Dec 11, 1865.
W. T. Beasley & N. P. Meadows married Dec 25, 1892.
Michael Goodrum Marsh & Lelia Beasley married Dec 4, 1898
Richard A. Marsh & Blanche L. Mathis married Nov 28, 1918 at Huntsville,
Alabama.

BIRTHS:
David H. Beasley born Jan 25, 1843.
Mary A. Beasley born July 25, 1843.
W. T. Beasley born Nov 29, 1867.
A. Lelia Beasley born April 28, 1876.
Felix R. McGaugh born May 30, 1813
Susana McGaugh born May 27, 1813.
W. M. McGaugh born Oct 25, 1839.
Michael G. Marsh born Mar 17, 1871.
Richard A. Marsh born Sept 20, 1899.
Grady U. Marsh born Aug 26, 1900.
Adelbert H. Marsh born July 28, 1903.
John Beasley Marsh born Sept 1, 1911.

DEATHS:
Archibald Beasley died at Boonshill, Tenn., 1850, aged: 77 years.
Liberty Beasley, died at Delina, Tenn., 1879, aged 77 years.
D. H. Beasley died June 15, 1917. Aged 82 years.
F. R. McGaugh died July 25, 1897. Aged 84 years.
M. G. Marsh died Oct 11, 1962, aged 91 years.
Lelia Marsh died Sept 17, 1939, aged 63 years.

MARSH BIBLE

In possession of R. A. Marsh, Shelbyville, Tennessee
Publisher and Date missing from Bible.

Michael Marsh born July 26, 1800
Elizabeth Marsh born May 11, 1800
John William Marsh born Nov 11, 1835
Sarah Louisana Davis born Apr 2, 1848
Goodrum Davis born Sept 22, 1812
Henrietta Pryor born Jan 8, 1815
Michael Goodrum Marsh born Mar 17, 1871 in Bedford County, Tennessee
Anna Lelia Beasley born Apr 28, 1876 in Marshall Co., Tennessee
Richard Austin Marsh born Sept 20, 1899 in Marshall Co., Tennessee
Grady Urban Marsh born Aug 26, 1900 in Marshall Co., Tennessee
Adelbert Hall Marsh born July 28, 1903 in Marshall Co., Tennessee
Sarah Gladys Marsh born Sept 27, 1905 in Marshall Co., Tennessee
Mary Forest Marsh born June 27, 1908 in Huntsville, Alabama
John Beasley Marsh born Sept 1, 1911 in Huntsville, Alabama
John T. Mathews born Mar 13, 1876
Mary Lou Cantrell born June 22, 1876 in McMinnville, Tennessee
Blanche Leeann Mathews born Oct 19, 1901 in McMinnville, Tennessee
Allie Frances Mathews born Mar 1, 1903 in McMinnville, Tennessee
Timothy Richard Marsh born June 12, 1921 in Lincoln, Lincoln Co., Tenn.

MARRIAGES:
John William Marsh & Sarah L. Davis married Oct 29, 1868 in Bedford Co.,
    Tennessee
Goodrum Davis & Henrietta Pryor married Sept 14, 1834 in Rutherford Co.,
    Tennessee
Michael Goodrum Marsh & Lelia Beasley married Dec 4, 1898
Richard A. Marsh & Blanche Lee Mathews married Nov 28, 1918 in Huntsville,
    Alabama
Timothy Richard Marsh & Helen Joe Crawford married June 24, 1941 in
    Huntsville, Alabama
Marsha Joan Marsh & Arthur Ray Edwards married Feb 12, 1960, Shelbyville
Leslie Devons Marsh & Betty Jane Foster married Oct 4, 1968 in Hunts-
    ville, Alabama
Mary Lou Cantrell & John Mathews married July 9, 1897
Mary Lou Mathews & A. A. Flanders married Aug 6, 1908

DEATHS:
Michael Marsh died Aug 31, 1859, Bedford County, Tennessee
Elizabeth Marsh died Aug 22, 1875, Bedford County, Tennessee
John William Marsh died Oct 9, 1923, Lincoln County, Tennessee
Sarah L. Marsh died Sept 30, 1918, Lincoln County, Tennessee
Goodrum Davis died April 29, 1889, Bedford County, Tennessee
Henrietta Davis died Feb 18, 1866, Bedford County, Tennessee
Michael G. Marsh died Oct 11, 1962, Lakeland, Fla.(buried at Lincoln, Tenn)
Lelia Marsh died Sept 17, 1939, Lincoln County, Tennessee (buried at
    Lincoln Cemetery.
Adelbert Hall Marsh died Mar 31, 1956, Tyrone, Georgia
Sarah Gladys Marsh died Oct 14, 1910, Huntsville, Alabama
Mary Forest Marsh died Oct 14, 1910, Huntsville, Alabama
John Beasley Marsh died Sept 13, 1967, Lincoln County, Tennessee & buried
    at Lincoln, Tennessee.

Thomas B. Mathis died June 27, 1914, Johnson City TN.
John T. Mathews died Feb 4, 1904, McMinnville, Tennessee.
Mary Lou Flanders died Mar 26, 1941, Warren County, Tennessee.
Allie Frances East died Dec 10, 1924, Huntsville, Alabama.
Richard A. Marsh died July 2, 1980 at Shelbyville, TN. age 80yrs.
Blanche M. Marsh died Jan. 24, 1992 at Shelbyville, TN. age 90 yrs.

M. G. MARSH BIBLE

In possession of Grady Marsh, Fayetteville, Tennessee
Publisher and Date: Missing.

BIRTHS:
John William Marsh born Nov 11, 1835, son of Michael Marsh born July 26
        1800 and Sarah Louisiana Davis born April 2, 1848, daughter of
        Goodrum Davis born Sept 22, 1812, were married Oct 29, 1868.
The following are the children of this union:
Henrietta Elizabeth Marsh, Sept 3, 1869
Michael Goodrum Marsh, March 17, 1871
Archabald Patterson Marsh, August 6, 1872
Robert Algernon Marsh, January 17, 1874
James Benjamin Marsh, March 9, 1876
Mary Tennessee Marsh, December 31, 1877
George Washington Marsh, January 15, 1880
William Edward Marsh, January 24, 1882
Julia Valley Marsh, November 23, 1883
Annie Alabama Marsh, March 19, 1885
Laura Sue Marsh, January 11, 1887
John Landon Marsh, November 28, 1889
Sarah Florence & Clara Jane Marsh, Twins, Nov 27, 1891

The Marriage Ceremony for John W. Marsh and Sarah L. Davis was perfor-
med by Esq. J. M. H. Coleman, at the Home of Goodrum Davis, Bedford
County, Tennessee, about 7 miles west of Shelbyville. The six children
of this marriage were born at the old Michael Marsh home on the Lewisburg road, a mile or more westward of the mothers paternal home. The
eight younger children were born at the home of their parents in Lincoln County, Tennessee, about 3 miles south east of Petersburg, Tenn.

GAMBILL-TEMPLETON BIBLE

This Bible belonged to Lucy Templeton and Thomas Jefferson Gambill and
is now in the possession of Mrs. Avva Charles, Shelbyville, Tennessee.
Copied by Mrs. Thomas H. Brown, Columbia, Tennessee

BIRTHS:
Newton Templeton was born 20 December 1823

Telitha Templeton was born 3 January 1834

M A E Templeton was born 24 May 1851
Clary Jane Templeton was born 4 June 1856
Lucy Templeton was born 10 December 1858
William Pinkney Templeton was born 22 August 1861
Fany Bell Templeton was born 7 May 1864
Meedy Ann Templeton was born 5 January 1867
Addy Templeton was born 3 December 1869
JohnPeter Templeton was born 10 November 1872

Thos. J. Gambill born Dec. 14, 1852
Lucy Templeton Gambill born Dec. 10, 1858

Minnie Ella Gambill born Nov 17, 1877
Marvin Elmor Gambill born Oct 12, 1880
Joshua Cleveland Gambill born Feb 5, 1883
Newton Elgin Gambill born May 3, 1885
Nora Lee Gambill born Aug. 10, 1888
Addie Vera Gambill born Oct. 23, 1891
Avva Belle Gambill born Sept 13, 1894

MARRIAGES:
T. J. Gambill to Lucy Templeton Feb. 1877-28
Elgin Gambill to Carrie Simpson June 24, 1906
Avva Gambill to Ophni Charles Feb. 23, 1914
Cleve Gambill to Mary Hodge Nov. 10, 1914
Marvin Gambill to Lillian Gentry Apr. 27, 1915
Vera Gambill to Lewis Ellis July 14, 1920

DEATHS:
Clary Jane departed this life January 15, 1863
Mary Ann Elizabeth departed this life January 17, 1863
William Pinkney departed this life February 4, 1863
Telitha A. Templeton departed this life November 21st, 1879
Newton Templeton departed this life Feb. 11th, 1885

Minnie Gambill Oct. 16, 1879
Nora Lee Gambill Sept. 21, 1889
Lucy Gambill Aug. 7, 1909
T. J. Gambill Oct. 29, 1915
Marvin Gambill Feb. 17, 1934
Cleve Gambill Dec. 12, 1935
Vera Ellis Sept. 16, 1964
Elgin Gambill Aug. 4, 1972

ALLISON BIBLE

Copied from Bible Records of Mrs. Ben Barnes, Shelbyville, Tennessee
from: Maury County Cousins, Vol. 2, Maury County Tennessee Historical
    Society, Columbia, Tennessee
Copied by Mrs. Marvin Kinnard on Aug. 1970.

Robert Allison married Sarah Ogilvie and were among the earliest settlers
(by 1794) in Middle Tennessee. They came from Granville Co., N.C.
Children:
1: James Allison
2: Sallie Allison married Rev. James Williams, Methodist divine.
3: Bettie Allison married _____ Williams.
4: John Allison.
5: Robert Allison.
6: Kimbrow Allison, born 1 Jan. 1794, died 1 Jan. 1867.

Kimbrow Allison and Sarah Ogilvie were married at Allisona, Williamson
County, about 1822.
Children:
1: Richard S. Allison, born 10 Aug. 1825, died 23 April 1869.
2: Sally Allison, married _____ Whitaker.
3: Nancy Allison married B. F. Jarrell.
(Editors note: Sarah Ogilvie is shown on the copy submitted as being the
name of Robert Allison and Kimbrow Allison and copied this way.)

William Ogilvie married Nancy Phelps.
Children:
1: Sarah Ogilvie was born Jan. 1804, died 18 Nov. 1879, married
        Kimbrow Allison.
2: James Ogilvie, born 1805.
3: Annie Ogilvie married _____ Bullock.
4: Margaret Ogilvie married _____ Landis.
5: Nancy Ogilvie married _____ Wilson.
6: Tabitha Ogilvie married _____ Rushing.
7: Richard Ogilvie.

Richard S. Allison, son of Kimbrough and Sarah Ogilvie Allison, married
        Elvira A. Stegall.
Elvira A. Stegall was born 26 Aug. 1826, died 4 June 1903.
Children:
1: Sally Jane Allison, born July 1847, married E. D. Jones on 9 Oct. 1887.
2: Minnie Lucindy Allison, born 14 June 1849, married J. W. Chandler on
        31 July 1898.
3: James Kimbrow Allison, born 10 Sept. 1853, married Nannie Laura _____
        1890, died 12 May 1938.
4: Margaret Emma Allison, born 15 May 1856, died 6 Aug. 1876.
5: William R. Allison, born 3 Feb. 1858, died 13 July 1881.
6: Harris Allison, born 7 Oct. 1860, married 1887 Maggie Roberts, died
        13 May 1896.
7: Elvira Virginia Allison, born 15 Oct. 1863, died 1907.

8: Richard Duggan Allison, born 24 March 1868.

Richard Duggan Allison and Jennie B. Richman were married 10 Nov. 1910
Children:
1: Sarah Virginia Allison, born 9 June 1912. (Twin)
2: Cleopatra Allison, born 9 June 1912. (Twin)
3: Ruth Frances Allison, born 25 Oct. 1913.

Richard D. Allison married Myrtle Patterson as second wife, no children.
Jennie B. Allison, died 1916.
Richard D. Allison, died 14 March 1935.

RICH FAMILY RECORDS

This Record was sent to Mr. John T. Lane, Sept 12, 1950, by Mrs. Glenn
P. McPherson, Burlington, N.C.

Rich Family (German- Dutch)
Daniel Rich- Born Feb 25, 1801 (died 9-3-1867)
Barbara Clapp- Born Jan 12, 1804

Daniel Rich married Barbara Clapp, Sept 17, 1826.
To this union were born:
1: Mary A. Rich born July 9, 1827, she never married, died at the age of
      45, 8-15-1867
2: Emily E. Rich born March 5, 1829, married Hardie S. Rike Nov. 1, 1866,
      died 3-28-1921
3: Eliza Jane Rich born Oct 3, 1830, married William Anthony Jan. 1, 1850.
4: Henry M. Rich born Feb 18, 1833, 1st married Mary Jane Neese June 2,
      1859, 2nd marriage Unie C. Rike February 15, 1866.
5: Elizabeth Caroline Rich born Dec 28, 1834, 1st married Daniel E. Sharp
      May 17, 1855, 2nd marriage Mabe Ingle. (no date)
6: Barbara Harriett Rich born Oct 2, 1836, 1st married Peter Fogleman (no
      date), 2nd marriage Jerome Riggins Nov 28, 1868.
7: James R. Rich born May 29, 1838, died 6-11-1862. Returned from Civil
      War with fever and died.
8: Cornelia L. Rich born Aug 8, 1840, married Robert H. Anthony Feb 5,
      1865
9: Sarah Malinda Rich born Sept 3, 1842, married Ruphus Washington Ingle
      June 7th, 1866, died 3-28-1921. Born to this union:
      William Thomas Ingle, dead
      James Washington Ingle
      Alonzo Seymore Ingle, dead
      Ernest C. Ingle
      Benny Ingle

ErnestC. Ingle married Belle Clendenin, born to this union:
Prince Ernest Ingle, married Kate Whitesell

Lura Belle Ingle married Lawrence Jones
Koy Clendenin Ingle married Sue Ameck
Ruphus Clyde Ingle married Fannie Adams
Leta Marye Ingle married Glenn P. McPherson
Fred Dewitt Ingle married Ruth Isabell LaMar

10: Margaret T. Rich born Oct 26, 1844, married Thadeus Ingle May 27,
      1889.
11: Martha Francis Rich born March 15, 1848, married Caleb Tickle

DEATHS:
James R. Rich died June 11, 1862
Cornelia L. Rich Anthony died March 28, 1866
Mary A. Rich died August 15th, 1867
Daniel Rich died Sept 3, 1867
Barbara Harriett Riggins died March 29, 1892
Eliza Jane Anthony died March 28, 1921   •
Sara Malinda Rich Ingle died March 28, 1921 NOTE: Died 3 hours apart.
Martha Francis Tickle died Feb 5, 1934

CATHEY BIBLE

Mr. Calvin C. Sloan of·Charlotte, N. C., is the owner of probably the
oldest Cathey relic. This is an old family Bible which has been handed
down for generations in his family. His mother, Amanda Cathey Sloan en-
trusted it to his care; she having received it as the youngest daughter
of George Carruth Cathey (1815-1896) and his wife Nancy Allen Cathey
(1822-1896).
George Carruth Cathey was the oldest son of Henry Cathey (1770-1823) and
his wife Sarah Cathey (1773-1841).
Henry Cathey was the youngest son of George Cathey (1724-1801) and
Frances Henry Cathey (1724-1798).
George Cathey was the son of George Cathey, Sr. (---- - 1756?) and Jean
Cathey (1692-1777). The latter is the oldest Cathey whose records and
burial place have been located thus far, she is buried at Steele Creek
Presbyterian Church in Mecklenburg County, N. C.
The exact age of this Bible cannot be readily determined, as the fly-
leaf disclosing the printers date and name has been lost or destroyed.
However, the type printing is such that we are led to believe that it
was printed many years before the American Revolution, and undoubtedly
in England. The first notation written in the Family Record section of
the Old Bible states (Quote) "The above 10 children are the off-springs
of George Cathey and Frances Henry, alias, Cathey" (unquote).
These names were written in as follows:
" Josias Cathey, born May 15, 1749
Elizabeth Cathey, born May 15, 1752
Jean Cathey, born March 27, 1754
George Cathey, born March 10, 1756

Andrew Cathey, born February 24, 1758
Alexander Cathey, born September 11, 1759
Mary Cathey, born December 24, 1761
Frances Cathey, born December 26, 1763
John Cathey, born September 25, 1766
Henry Cathey, born February 9, 1770"

The page on which these names appear was undoubtedly recopied from a prior older page of the Bible, just a fragment of which still remains in it. Other pages contain entries on later generations.

This article was taken from the "Cathey Reunion" Paw Creek Presbyterian Church, Mecklenburg County, North Carolina, August 7, 1955.

LANE BIBLE

Zerox Copy given by Mr. John Thomas Lane, deceased, Shelbyville, Tennessee
Mr. John T. Lane died 1977.
Publisher: A. J. Holman & Co., Philadelphia

Presented to Robt. Henry Lane by his Mother Mrs F. M. Lane, Dec 25, 1903

FAMILY REGISTER,
BIRTHS:
Robert Henry Lane was born April 12, 1874
Mary E. Lane was born Sept 17, 1878
Mary Emma Lane was born Jan 31, 1876
Johnnie Jas. Lane was born July 24, 1901
Robert Henry Lane, Jr. was born April 28, 1904
Thomas Carl Lane was born Jan 1, 1910

MARRIAGES:
Robt. H. Lane was married to Mary E. Cannon. Oct 10, 1900
Robt. H. Lane was married to Emma Coats . Jan 1, 1902
Robt. H. Lane, Jr. married to Ruby Timmons Jany 30, 1927
Carl Thomas Lane was married to Lonnie Mai Gibson, Jan 13, 1940

DEATHS:
Mary E. Lane departed this life Aug 5, 1901, this closing out her brief
        life of only 22y, 10m, and 18 da.
Robert Henry Lane was born April 12, 1874 died March 19, 1913 aged 38
        years 11 months and 6 days.
Mary Emma Coats Lane was born Jan 31, 1876, Died July 9, 1950, aged
        74 years 5 months and 9 days.

WILLIAM McGUIRE BIBLE

Submitted by Nell Norvell, Hereford, Texas

William McGuire Born March 12th 1743
Mary McGuire his wife born Feby 17th 1762
Thomas McGuire born Aug 1st 1701
Polly McGuire born Dec 4th, 1783
Katie McGuire born 5th 1789
William McGuire born Nov 15th, 1794
Neely (Cornelius) McGuire born Oct 5th 1798
(Dr.) John McGuire born June 29th 1801
Bettie McGuire born July 22nd 1803

Sarah McGuire was born Oct 28th 1820
Synthia was born Sept 19th 1822
Issac Williams was born Aug 3rd 1824   .

Nathaniel G. Bryan born Aug 30th, 1806
Maryann McGuire his wife born July 5th 1807
James A. Bryan born Sept 1827 died Dec 5th 1827   .
Thos. W. Bryan born Aug 22nd 1828
T. W. Bryan born Sept 23rd 1827
W. J. Bryan born May 24th 1830

G. Bryan and Maryann McGuire were married Dec 24th 1826

TO WHOM IT MAY CONCERN:
        This is to certify that the attached list of names and dates
begining with William McGuire, was copied from the family Bible of
William McGuire by my brother Berry D. Shriver with the aid of our
Cousin Howard D. Henderson about 1908 to 1910. The Bible was then
in possession of a great aunt of ours "Tabby" West who had reached
an advanced age at the time and who lived near Wartrace in Bedford
County, Tennessee. After her death the Bible was lost-- at least we
have not been able to locate it.
        These records are from the files of my brother, Berry, now
deceased, and he discussed them with me and other members of the
family on numerous occasions, especially with my father and mother
who were familiar with most of the persons and events mentioned in
the record.
        This August 1, 1962   (Signed) Thos. A. Shriver
State of Tennessee
County of Davidson
Certified and subscribed before me this 1st day of August 1962
                                (signed) Glenn E. Frazier,
                                        Notary Public
                        Com. Exp. 5/7/63

JOHN SMITH ARNOLD BIBLE

The Bible was in the possession of Fannie Arnold Moore, at Manchester, Tennessee, in 1935 when it was copied by Frank C. Harmon, son of Jarusha Grady Arnold Harmon, on a visit there. Information in parenthesis was gathered from descendants of each, or from public records by Nell Taylor Norvell, Hereford, Texas.

Elijah Arnold married Sarah Smith, came to Bedford County, Tenn., from North Carolina. To them was born:
John Smith Arnold   married. Sallie McGuire
Sam Arnold married E.(Elizabeth) Madoris (Medaris)
Jarusha Arnold married E. (Edward Morris B.) Norvell
Elizabeth (Sarah E.) married   Wilhoit
William "Wid" (W.) Arnold married (P. A.) McAdams

William McGuire married (Mary) Fabra Ditto, lived in Bedford County, Tenn. To them was born:
Bettie (Elizabeth) McGuire married (Archibald) Pruitt
Cynthia McGuire married (Andrew E.) Mullins
William (Ditto) McGuire married (Killetta P.) Sharpe
Ben McGuire bachelor (died in Civil War)
John (A.) McGuire married (Irena Hoyt, bur. Hopkins Co., Ky.)
Fabra McGuire married (Dr. John B. R.) Snellings
Sarah S. ("Sallie" E.) McGuire married John Smith Arnold

John Smith Arnold born June 21, 1821 Bedford County, Tenn.(N. C.?)
          died June 10, 1900 near Manchester, Tenn.
Sarah S.(E.) McGuire born Dec 21, 1828 Bedford Co., Tenn.
          died Nov 5, 1911 near Manchester, Tenn.
(both are buried in Old Concord Cemetery, between Manchester and
          Tullahoma.), married Nov 30, 1843. To them was born:
Sarah E. Arnold born Nov 26, 1844, died in Texas, married Sept 9, 1866
          James D. Hardaway. (lived at Iowa Park, J. D. H. died at Zavala
          County, Texas, 1921)
Mary Arnold died age 15 months
Jarusha Grady Arnold born July 20, 1847, died Feb 9, 1936, married
          Thomas Jefferson Harmon Oct 29, 1868
Eligah W. (William) Arnold born Aug 6, 1849, died May (22), 1904,
          married Dec 24, 1874, Lucy F. Brown
Benjamin K. Arnold born Nov. 26, 1852, died (May 18, 1935), married
          24 Dec. 1874, Bettie Webb
Martha J. Arnold born May 25, 1855, died about 1905 (no children),
          married Jan. 2, 1890, G. W. Gunn
John W. Arnold born June 11, 1857, died   in Chattanooga, Tenn.,
          married Jan 6, 1879, Bettie Anderson
Mary "Mollie" D.(Ditto) Arnold born Dec 24, 1859, died 1934 (in
          Channing, Texas.), married A. L. (Lonnie) Johnson, Nov 12, 1878
Arch T. (Pruitt) Arnold born Feb 11, 1862, died (Apr. 22, 1915), Archer
          City, Texas, married Dec 24, 18(89) Angie (Elisey AngieLina)
          Penn.

Della (Adella) T. Arnold born Aug 29, 1864(5), died (Jan 25, 1943),
    near Byers, Texas, married Sept 4, 1884, J.(Joseph) Gilbert
    Roberts
Fannie Arnold born May 18, 1867, died (June 4, 1949, Miami, Fla.),
    married Nov 10, 1886, Troxel Harmon Moore
Samuel S. Arnold born Sept 4, 1868, died (before 1962), married Dec 10,
    1894, Annie Duncan
Robert A. Arnold born March 31, 1872, died (before 1962), married Nov
    19, 1894, Edna Duncan, cousin to Annie
Frank C. Arnold born June 5, 1876, died (July 28, 1969, Channing, Tex.,),
    married Nov 3, 1903, Cora Anderson

KELLER BIBLE

Zerox copy in possession of Nell Norvell. Original Bible believed to
be in the possession of Klyne Jack Keller of Madison, Tenn.
(information written across the bottom of a page of scripture)

    WILLIAM HODGE (with a great flurish)
John Keller was born September the 26, 1782 (each word marked thru)
frances A. Keller was born November 1, 8179

frances Keller was born november 1879 (marked through)
frances Keller was born november 7879

        The End of the Prophets.

Jacob Keller was born october the 20 1797
K   John Keller was born September the 2   (marked through)
(in a different hand writing)
John Keller was born September the 26 1782
ann Keller was born March the 5 1785
Rachel Keller wous born October th 3 1787
Charles Keller was born may th 17 1790
Joseph Keller was born october the ____ 1792
        this portion appears to have been wet

CANNON BIBLE RECORDS

Copied by Avalyn C. Rohwer, Mobile, Alabama, 9-10-1951 and copied from
Kinfolks by William C. Harlee, sent to Mr. John T. Lane, deceased.

Bible of William H. Cannon, wife Sarah Ann McTyre

81

Children of Henry and Mary Cannon:
William H. Cannon b. 25 April 1783
Jane Cannon, b 23 Aug. 1784. Departed this life 9 Aug 1793
Susanna Wilson Cannon, 26 Mch 1786. Departed this life 14 August 1793
Hugh E. Cannon, 4 Sept 1787
George James Cannon, 7 Feby 1789. Departed this life 23 August 1793
Elizabeth Cannon, 30 June 1790. Departed this life 20 June 1791
Mary Cannon 26 Nov 1791
Sarah Cannon 5 Oct 1793. Departed this life 2 Nov 1793
Robert Augustus Cannon 17 Feby 1795. Departed this life 23 Jany 1798
John Julius Cannon 19 Oct 1796. Departed this life 15 Sept 1822

Children of Henry Cannon and Susanna Cherry, widow of George Cherry.
They married 14 August 1798 by Rev. E. Pugh
Susan Marsella Cannon born 16 Jany 1800
Augustus Devan Cannon 31 Decm 1801. Departed this life 20 Oct 1817
Sarah Ann Cannon wife of Wm. H. Cannon departed this life 23 Sept 1824
William H. Cannon Senr departed this life 2 December 1843

DEATHS:
Children of Wm. H. & S. A. Cannon
Mary Erwin Cannon Dau of Wm. H. & Sarah Ann Cannon departed this life
        27th October 1820
Sarah Ann Cannon daughter of Wm. H. and Sarah Ann Cannon departed this
        life Thursday the 20 October 1823 half after ten at night
John J. Cannon departed this life 15th September 1822
Augustus D. Cannon departed this life 20 October 1817

BIRTHS:
Children of Wm. H. and S. A. Cannon (show that they could not have been
parents of Almon). They had a son: Wm. Henry Cannon born 28th July 1812.

MARRIAGES:
William H. Cannon and Sarah Ann McTyer married 13 May 1804
Hugh E. Cannon and Ann Muldrow married 5th October 1809

Cannon Family History from Kinfolks, by William C. Harlee:
        Progenitor of family was John Cannon, born in Charleston Dist.,
S. C., before the middle of the 18th Century and resided there until his
death before the close of the Revolution. His father's Christian name is
not preserved, but his descendants were told that he was Irish, and immigrated with the British settlers who colonized that portion of the State.
        John Cannon married in the section where he was born, a Miss
Allison. They had five children, Viz: Henry, George, John, Jane, and
Elizabeth.
        Henry Cannon married Mary Erwin and removed to Darlington Dist.
        George Cannon married Miss Williamson and had 5 children. His
four sons moved westward and were lost sight of. His daughter Sarah
married William Moye.
        John remained in Charleston, married twice, children by 1st marri-
age: John and Dolly, removed from Charleston and lost sight of (family

82

disgrace)

Eliz. Cannon, young child, kidnapped by Tories during the Revolutionary War. Later found, she had married a Hall and at birth of a son, she died. The father must have died also, as the child was carried to Georgetown, S. C., and was living with people uninterested in him. On learning of this Henry Cannon went and got him and adopted him and called him Rasha Cannon.

Rasha Cannon, 1st wife was Miss Melville, children: Thomas &Wm. R.
Rasha Cannon, 2nd wife Mary McIver, children: Sarah, Newton, Mary, Elizabeth, Melville, Robert, and Maria Mozelle.

WELLS BIBLE

In possession of Mrs. R. B. Fort, Jr., Shelbyville, Tennessee
Publisher: National Publishing Co., No. 724, 726 and 728 Cherry Street, 1886

BIRTHS:
John W. Wells was born May 15, 1848
Sarah Elizabeth Shoffner was born March 6, 1846
Margaret C. Jenkins was born Sept 9, 1847
Othneil D. Wells was born Jan 22, 1868
Willie S. Wells was born July 26, 1870
Mary S. Wells was born June 27, 1875
Thomas Emmett Wells was born Oct 23, 1878
Edgar Jenkins was born Aug 31, 1880
Ethel Wells was born Sept 17, 1882
Hubert John Wells was born Jan 12, 1885
Jennie Wells was born Jan 20, 1887
Annie P. Wells was born Sept 23, 1889
Mary Pepper Wells was born Aug 7, 1915
Norris Wesley McTaggart March 20, 1926

BIRTHS:
Children of Mary Pepper Wells and Robert Bridges Fort, Jr.:
Agatha Pepper Wells August 14, 1942
Robert Bridges Fort III, Sept 14, 1943
Bettie Frances Fort Aug 3, 1947
James Herbert Fort Aug 30, 1953
Emily Minatra Fort October 10, 1973, child of Faye and Robert Fort III
Susan Wells Fort July 13, 1976, child of Faye and Robert Fort III
Virginia Garvin Edwards July 8, 1975, child of Bettie and Van Edwards

DEATHS:
Sarah Elizabeth Wells died Sept 24, 1873
John Wesley Wells died July 11, 1894
Margaret C. Wells died April 23, 1907
Agatha Pepper Wells died Nov 20, 1915
Mary Wells Mullins died Oct 16, 1922

Thomas Emmett Wells died Jan 6, 1940
Herbert John Wells died Sept 5, 1952
Donald M. Street died July 23, 1949
Edgar Jenkins Wells died March 16, 1963
Ethel Wells Moore died Dec 31, 1966
Annie Wells Street died Nov 10, 1975
Jennie Wells McTaggart died Feb 18, 1977
Virginia S. Wells died March 21, 1966

MARRIAGES:
John W. Wells and Sara Elizabeth Shoffner was married Sept 2nd, 1866,
    by the Rev. Wm. Jenkins.
John W. Wells and Margaret C. Jenkins was married Sept 9, 1874 by
        Rev. A. J. King
Othneil D. Wells and Irma Fay was married October 3rd, 1888 by Rev. Bates
Willie S. Wells and Marie Angelico Dutreaux was married August 1899
Mary S. Wells and Joseph Mullins was married Dec 12, 1899 by Rev. Young
Ethel Wells and Hugh Lawson Moore was married October 19, 1905 by Rev.
        Taylor
Herbert J. Wells and Agatha Osborne Pepper was married December 10, 1913
    by Rev....
Herbert J. Wells & Virginia Seabright was married October 11, 1919 by
        Dr. Vance.
Mary Pepper Wells and R. B. Fort, Jr., married Nov 22, 1940, by Rev.
    Henry Sneed.
Annie Wells and Donald M. Street married June 5, 1915 by Rev Caldwell,
    New Orleans.
Jennie Wells and Ray S. McTaggart married July 5, 1925 by Rev. Armstrong
Martha Rees Street and George R. Gaines married June 9, 1949 by Rev.
    Henley.
Bettie Frances Fort and Van Everette Edwards married July 25, 1970, by
    Rev Butler and Rev. Giles, Winnsboro, S.C.
Robert Bridges Fort III and Brenda Faye Minatra married August 7, 1970,
    by Rev. Robins, in Columbia, Tenn.
James Herbert Fort and Pattye E. McGrew married August 23, 1970, by
    Rev. Dugger in Columbia, Tenn.

OSBORNE BIBLE

In possession of Mrs. R. B. Fort, Jr., Shelbyville, Tennessee
Publisher: Brattleboro Typagraphic Company, Incorporated, October 26,
        1836, Brattleboro, Vt.   1838

Names:	Births:	Deaths:
Gabriel G. Osborne	March 20, 1803	May 21, 1879
Nancy Osborne	Dec 26, 1802	Nov 4th, 1860
The above married Dec 3, 1822		

Their Children:	Births:	Deaths:
William J. Osborne	Oct 20, 1823	Dec 1896
Henry Phillip Osborne	March 30, 1825	August 29th, 1846, M.D.
Mary G. Osborne	June 28, 1827	Oct 9, 1827
Rep G. Osborne	July 25, 1828	July 10, 1831
Ann E. Osborne	Jan 30, 1831	August 5, 1831
Margaret Osborne	Oct 26, 1837	June 10, 1873
Gabriel Glen Osborne	April 9, 1835	August 5, 1864
Nancy J.. Osborne, Jr.	Sept 14, 1837	Jan 19th, 1861
Sarah V. Osborne	Jan 1, 1840	Sept 10th, 1864
Martha G. Osborne	April 24, 1842	Nov 1887
James Samuel Osborne	Jan 9, 1845	July 16, 1845
Lucy Nance Osborne	Sept 6, 1846	
Sophia E. Osborne	Feb 21, 1849	Oct 3, 1850

Gabriel G. Osborne	March 20, 1803	May 21, 1879
Nancy Osborne	Dec 26, 1802	Nov 4th, 1860
The above married Dec 3, 1822		
Their Children:		
William J. Osborne	Oct 20, 1823	Dec 1896
Henry Philip Osborne	March 30, 1825	August 29, 1846, M.D.
		age: 21-4-29
Mary Osborne	June 28, 1827	Oct 9, 1827

MARRIAGES:

Margaret H. Osborne	August 7, 1849
William J. Osborne	Sept 4, 1849
G. G. Osborne, Jr.	May 16, 1861
Nancy J. Osborne, Jr.	Nov 29, 1854
Lucy N. Osborne	Sept 3, 1867

Names:	Births:	Deaths:
Henry Philip Osborne	August 11, 1850	
Rachel Ann Scruggs	August 14, 1850	
Henry P. Scruggs	May 2, 1852	1888
John F. Scruggs	13 Nov, 1853	
G. G. Osborne, 3rd.	May 18, 1852	
Mary Ann Osborne	Aug 5th, 1854	
Clement N.B. Osborne	May 3rd, 1856	
Nancy Jones Osborne	June 27, 1858	June 2, 1859
Wm. J. Osborne, 2nd	June 3, 1860	
Susan Paul Osborne	Jan 20, 1863	
Margaret M.T.Osborne	June 15th, 1865	
Elizabeth V.M.Osborne	June 23, 1867	
John F. Osborne	Jan 4, 1870	

TURRENTINE BIBLE

Taken from: "The Turrentine Family" by George R. Turrentine
Records From Old Bibles
From a Bible in the possession of the Carolyn Smith Lamb Family:

James Turrentine, Sr. born January 9, 1770
James Turrentine & Katherine Clower his wife, were married September
    19th A.D. 1793
Katherine (alias Clower) Turrentine was born A.D. January 4, 1775
James Turrentine, Sr. died September 7, 1831. Age 61 years.
D. C. Turrentine (Daniel Clower) and Caroline E. Lucy, his wife, were
    married A.D. December 3, 1838
Caroline E. Lucy, wife of Daniel Clower Turrentine, was born March 19,
    1822.
William Turrentine born June 4, 1794
William Turrentine and Priscilla were married June 8, 1815
Samuel Turrentine born April 7, 1796
Samuel Turrentine & Mary Ann Harvey ...
George Turrentine born April 28, 1798
Elizabeth Turrentine born --- 22, 1812
Nancy Turrentine born August 29, 1815
Thomas Clower Turrentine born December 4, 1817
Joseph T. Turrentine born January 26, 1821
Francis L. Turrentine born June 28, 1805
Morgan C. Turrentine born September 17, 1800
Belinda Turrentine died September 19, 1817
Priscilla Turrentine died September 22, 1824--29th year of her life
Lucy Jones Turrentine died December 15, 1831

Bible in the possession of the Carolyn Smith Lamb Family:
Daniel C. Turrentine and Caroline E. Lucy were married December 3, 1837
Rodolphus O. Randall and Josephine L. Turrentine were married February
    22, 1860
Joshua L. Turrentine and Christine E. Gibbs were married March 21, 1877
Virginia Adelaide Turrentine and A. Harris were married November 8, 1876
Minnie E. Turrentine (Mary Ellen) and Newton N. Polk were married Novem-
    ber 15, 1882
Lillie A. Turrentine and J. J. Anshutz were married July 1884
George E. Turrentine and Minnie Mitchell were married August 1889
James L. Turrentine and Maggie E. Wacasar were married December 1, 1868
Daniel Clower Turrentine was born October 18, 1807
Caroline Elizabeth Lucy was born March 19, 1822
Ann Catherine Turrentine was born December 17, 1838
William Adolphus Tarpley Turrentine was born August 30, 1840
Louisa Josephine Turrentine was born September 10, 1842
Virginia Adelaide Turrentine was born October 18, 1844
James Lafferty Turrentine was born August 15, 1846
Caroline Leonora Turrentine was born June 2nd, 1848
Joshua Lucy Turrentine was born December 20, 1849
Samuel Morgan Turrentine was born July 28, 1851

Lillie Ann Turrentine was born October 8, 1853
Daniel Clarke Turrentine was born June 18, 1855
George Edward Turrentine was born April 17, 1857
Mary Ellen Turrentine (Minnie) was born May 13, 1859
Albert Forney Turrentine was born November 7, 1861
Leila Irene Turrentine was born February 22, 1865
Ann C. Turrentine died January 5, 1839
William A. T. Turrentine died July 18, 1862
Leila Irene Turrentine died September 25, 1873
Caroline E. Lucy Turrentine died July 18, 1881
Daniel Clower Turrentine died September 11, 1883
Samuel Morgan Turrentine died October 1882
George E. Turrentine died April 16, 1891
Mary Ellen T. Polk (Minnie) died January 8, 1896

From Bible in the possession of F. W. Park Family:
George S. Turrintine born September 1st, 1820
Samuel Turrintine born March 2nd, 1823
Phebe Turrintine born March 11th, 1825
Sarah J. Turrintine born February 25th, 1829
Mary Elvira Turrintine born November 3rd, 1831
Wilson E. Turrintine born March 29th, 1834
Nancy Elizabeth Turrintine born October 15th, 1836
Eleanor Turrintine born March 7th, 1839
Zerelda Turrintine born January 15th, 1830
Mary F. Turrintine born February 21st, 1848
Margaret Turrintine born February 6th, 1849
Archelus Turrintine born January 16th, 1851
Nancy E. Turrintine born January 19th, 1853
George S. Turrintine born December 16th, 1854
Sarah C. Turrintine born August 21st, 1859
John H. Turrintine born May 18th, 1862
George S. Turrinine died June 19th, 1864
George S. Turrintine and wife Mylinda C. Hamilton married September
    9th, 1844
George S. Turrintine and wife Zerelda Bradshaw married December 10th,
    1846
Jane F. Turrintine born August 25th, 1842
Phebe Smith died April 3rd, 1830
Daniel Turrintine born December 5th, 1827, died December 30th, 1827 (son
    of Archelus and Margaret Turrintine)
John E. Smith died December 13th, 1840 (son of George and Phebe Smith)
George Smith was born in the year 1763 and died November 1842.
Samuel A. Turrintine died November 13th, 1845
Nancy E. Turrintine died November 12th, 1846
Melinda C. Turrintine died May 12th, 1845
Margaret Turrintine wife of A. Turrintine died October 4th, 1855
A. Turrintine died February 12th, 1885
James F. Turrintine died year 1861, son of Archelus Turrintine
Phebe Steel died October 23rd, 1910

T. J. G. Steel born December 5th, 1819, died January 30th, 1889
James W. Walker born September 16th, 1866
A. T. Walker born April 6th, 1869
James Stewart born January 29th, 1871
Sarah Turrintine died September 6th, 1835

From an Old Bible Record in the possession of the Heirs of William R. Turrentine:
Elizabeth Turrentine, daughter of Alexr. and Deborah was born January
    29, 1759

Martha	April 6, 1761
Sam'l	August 3, 1763
Jean	April 4, 1766
Daniel	November 4, 1769
Alex'dr	September 12, 1772
James	July 26, 1774
Mary	March 17, 1777

Asael Moore was born February 23, 1783

From the Anderson Family Bible:
Edmund Anderson was born March 15th A.D. 1813
Nancy Anderson was born July A.D. 1813
Permilia Anderson was born February 17th A.D.1835
John T. Anderson was born April 12th A.D. 1836
James A. Anderson was born March 11th A.D. 1838
Rachele Anderson was born August 20th A.D. 1839
Warner P. Anderson was born July 23rd A.D. 1812
Claiborne W. Anderson was born June 10th A.D. 1844
Robert S. Anderson was born Nov 12th, A.D. 1848
Mary E. Anderson was born Feb 9th A.D. 1853
Louisa Anderson was born July 15th 1852
Chester C. Anderson was born August 7th A.D. 1875
Mollie E. Anderson was born August 9th A.D. 1878
Nora Anderson was born April 20th 1881
Permelia Anderson }
John T. Anderson   }   Received the ordinance of Baptism Previously to
James A. Anderson }   the present date, This October 22nd A.D. 1850
Rachel Anderson   }
Warner P. Anderson Baptised October 22nd A.D. 1850
Claiborne W. Anderson Baptised October 22nd A.D. 1850
Robert S. Anderson Baptised October 22nd A.D. 1850
Mary E. Anderson Baptised June 17th 1855
Chester C. Anderson Baptised Sept. 29th 1885
Mollie E. Anderson Baptised Sept. 29th 1885
Nora Anderson Baptised Sept. 29th 1885
Edmund Anderson & Nancy Turrentine was married February 20th A.D. 1834
Warner P. Anderson and Louisa Sandusky was married October 25th A.D.
    1874

Edmund Anderson died on the 11th of August 1863
Claiborne W. Anderson died Nov 5, 1870
James A. Anderson died Apr. 26th A.D. 1875
John T. Anderson died May 10, 1911
Nancy Anderson died May 4th A.D. 1876
Mary E. Anderson died July 4th A.D. 1878
Permelia Mangis died July 25th A.D. 1878
Robert S. Anderson died Feb. 16th A.D. 1915
Rachel Weldin died Nov. 2, 1924
Warner P. Anderson died April 16, 1927
Louisa Anderson died May·24, 1934
Mollie E. Anderson Bell died May 16, 1951, 11:15 P.M.
Chester C. Anderson died August 13, 1955, 3:10 P.M.
Nora Anderson Hemphill died Sept. 30, 1963- 8 A.M.

From Samuel and Mary Bryant Turrentine's Family Bible which is in the
possession of the Lillian McMannen Fitzgerald Family:
James Turrentine was born Jany. 9th, 1770
Sarah Turrentine was born Jany. 11th, 1772
Samuel Turrentine was born Sept. 13th, 1774
Lydia Turrentine was born Feby. 9th, 1776
Susanna Turrentine was born July 24th, 1779
Nancy Turrentine was born Sept. 11, 1782
Absolom Turrentine was born Nov. 15th, 1784
Daniel Turrentine was born Octo. 3, 1788
Mary Jane Turrentine was born March 5, 1835
Samuel Wilson Turrentine was born June the 10th, 1837
Harrison Turrentine was born September the 7th, 1840
Salena Ann Turrentine was born September the 20th, 1843
Mary Turrentine Dec'd. June the 6th day 1828
Liddia Turrentine died August the 6th day 1827
Samuel Turrentine deceased November the 5th, 1845
Absolom Turrentine deceased August the 13th, 1856
Fannie Turrentine deceas. May 28th, 1874
Samuel W. Turrentine died September 18th A.D. 1873

From an Old Bible belonging to the Wilson Family:
Thomas Wilson was born January 11th, 1759
Ann Wilson was born January 11th, 1790
Elizabeth Wilson was born April 9th, 1791
Charles Wilson was born November 6th, 1793
John Wood Wilson was born January 3rd, 1796
Robert Wilson was born April 21st, 1798
Josiah Wilson was born May 9th, 1800
Faney Wilson was born June 8th, 1803
Anderson Wilson was born April 14th, 1806
Caleb Wilson was born December 9th, 1809
Thomas Wilson departed this life July 11th, 1829
Jane.Wilson departed this life January 10th, 1851

Elizabeth Latta departed this life February 13th, 1854

NOTE: Photostatic copies of the above records are on file in the
Turrentine Archives, Mrs. Viva Moore, Archivist.

ARNOLD BIBLE RECORDS

Submitted by Mabel Clare Arnold, as written in 1896.
Copied by Miss Mary V. Bass and Helen C. Marsh, Wartrace, Tenn.

Mabel Clare Arnold, Nat. No. 18193, Shelbyville, Tennessee, Shelby
Chapter, Number 10, Descendant of Captain Thomas Arnold.
Application examined and approved January 28th, 1897.
                              Abbie W. Scudder, Chapter Regent
Examined and approved   2-2-1897
                              Mary Jane Smith Seymour
                              Registrar General
Accepted by the National Board of Management, Feb 4, 1897
                              Charlotte Emerson Main
                              Recording Secretary General
Mabel Clare Arnold born in the town of Wartrace, County of Bedford,
State of Tennessee, daughter of James Arnold and Nannie Francis, grand-
daughter of Thomas Martin Arnold and Nancy Johnson, Great-granddaughter
of James Arnold and Margaret Bagley, Great-great-granddaughter of Samuel
Arnold and Miss Wright, Great-great-great-granddaughter of Capt. Thomas
Arnold and Miss Wiche.

    Capt. Thomas Arnold was assigned to Col. Lewis Nicolas "Regiment
of Invalids," which was made up entirely of officers. He was a member of
this Regiment until 1783. He was entitled under Act of Congress, August
14th, 1776 to half-pay, Commutation and bounty lands.

ARNOLD BIBLE

Publisher: Wm. Garretson & Co., Columbus, Ohio; Galesburg, Ill.; Nash-
           ville, Tenn.; Houston, Texas; San Francisco, Cal.
           Bradley, Garretson & Co., 66 North Fourth Street,
           Philadelphia, Pa.   1874

This Certifies that the Rite of Holy Matrimony was celebrated between
James Arnold of Shelbyville, Tenn., and Nannie Francis of Shelbyville,
Tenn. on Jan 6th, 1870 at Shelbyville, Tennessee. By Rev. Wm. Halsell
C. P. M.

MARRIAGES:
James Arnold & Nannie Francis were married in Shelbyville, Tenn., Jan
     6th, 1870 by Rev. Wm. Halsell.
Hugh Turney Arnold and Matchie Willingham of Macon, Ga., were married
     Feb 16th, 1898, by Rev. Kline.

Katherine Louise Arnold & William Millard Stancell of Jackson, N.C.,
    married in Wartrace, Tenn., May 1st 1901, by Rev. B. McNatt.
Mabel Clare Arnold & Frederick Smartt married in Wartrace, Oct 18th, 1905,
    Ceremony by Rev. G. L. Boles.

BIRTHS:
James Arnold, Born near Shelbyville, Tenn., Oct 25th, 1843.
Nannie Francis Arnold, Born at Wartrace, Tenn., April 8th, 1848.
Thomas Francis Arnold, Born at Shelbyville, Tenn., June 7th, 1871.
Hugh Turney Arnold Born Wartrace, Tenn., May 17th, 1874.
Mabel Clare Arnold Born at Wartrace, Tenn., February 22nd, 1876.
    "Centennial Baby" Born on Washington's Birthday.
Katherine Louise Arnold Born at Wartrace, Tenn., April 14th, 1881.

DEATHS:
Thos. Francis Arnold Died May 30th, 1895, age 23 years- 11 months &
    23 days, at Wartrace, Tenn.
Hugh Turney Arnold Died May 18th 1912, age 38 years, 1 day at Wartrace,
    Tenn.
Both children having died in infancys, he is survived by his wife
Nannie Francis Arnold died in Wartrace, Tenn., Mch 11th, 1913- age
    64 yrs and 11 mos.
James Arnold died in Wartrace, Tenn., July 29th, 1915- age 71 years,
    9 mos.
Mabel Arnold Smartt died December 28, 1946, age 70.

FAMILY HISTORY: A Record of important events.
Hugh Turney Arnold was married to Matchie Willingham, daughter of
Thomas and Fannie Willingham near Macon, Ga. (at Dunbar), on Feb 16th,
1898 by Rev. Cline. Taking a trip to St. Augustine & Jacksonville, Fla.,
returning to Wartrace on Feb 21st to meet many relatives.
    Born to Hugh & Matchie Arnold, June 28th 1899, a son in Ga.,
named Thomas Francis, died in Waverly, Tenn., August 24th, 1899, buried
in Wartrace, Tenn.
    Born to Hugh & Matchie Arnold, a daughter, Winnifred Willingham,
April 16th, 1901, birth place Ga.
Winifred Willingham Arnold died Feb 3rd, 1902, buried in Byron, Ga., near
Dunbar, Ga., their home.
    Born to Katherine Arnold Stancell and William Stancell, a son,
James Arnold, Feb 13th, 1902 at Wartrace, Tenn., married.
    Born to Katherine Arnold Stancell and Wm. M. Stancell, a daughter,
Katherine Louise Stancell, Newport News, Va., Jany 17, 1909.
    Drothy Stancell, daughter of Janes A. Stancell born Feb 12th,
1921, Washington, D.C.
    Katherine Stancell married Robert Rudy- Sept 1931
    Bobby Rudy their son Sept 29th 1935.

NEWSPAPER OBIT:
Thomas Francis Arnold died at his father's home, Mr James Arnold, on
    Thursday May 30th, 1895, at 9:30 A.M., aged 22 years, 11 months
    and 24 days. Funeral Services were conducted by Rev. O.C.Peyton,

at the Baptist Church, Friday May 31st, at 10 o'clock A.M., buried in Hollywood Cemetery. 10 years a member of the Baptist Church. Parents, sisters, brother and friends mourn.

NEWSPAPER OBIT: Wartrace, Tennessee
Mrs. Nannie Francis Arnold, 64, wife of James Arnold of this place, died last night. The summons came without warning after she had retired for the night. Apoplexy was the cause of her death. She was the daughter of Judge Hugh Francis of Winchester, Tenn. She is survived by her husband, two daughters- Mrs F. W. Smartt, Wartrace, Tenn., and Mrs·William M. Stancell, Washington, D.C., two brothers and one sister. Funeral conducted by Rev. C. H. Bailey.
Another Obit:
Died March 11, 1913 at the Family home in Wartrace. She was born April 8, 1848. Member of Presbyterian Church. She was married Jan 6, 1870 to Jas. Arnold. Four children born to them, two sons and two daughters. Thomas Francis, a noble, godly young man, died in 1895. Hugh Turney, the other son, died May 18, 1912.

NOTICE:
"Written on the sudden death of Miss Mary Alice Francis, which occured Aug 31st, 1865 at Jacksonville, Ala."

NOTE: On back of Bible Picture:
"Great-grandfather Miller Francis married Hannah Henry."
Grandfather Hugh Francis

NEWSPAPER OBIT: Wartrace, Tenn.
Oliver P. Cunningham departed this life Saturday morning November 18th, at 9:15. He had been sick for two weeks with fever, pneumonia developed.

WEDDING ANNOUNCEMENT:
Mr & Mrs James Arnold announce the marriage of their daughter Katherine Louise to Mr William Millard Stancell on Wednesday May the first, nineteen hundred and one, Wartrace, Tennessee.

NEWSPAPER CLIPPING:
"6 more Tennessean's on Duty with the Armed Forces of the United States in the War Zones:
"R. C. Stanfill, Jr., son of Mr & Mrs R. C. Stanfill of near Savannah, is with the Navy in the Hawaiian Area."
"Arthur Bowling, son of Irving Bowling of Hickory Point near Clarksville, is aboard a Battleship in the Pacific Fleet."
"Robert James, son of Mr & Mrs Ben James of Hickory Point near Clarksville, is stationed on the same Vessel as Bowling."
"Alvin C. York, namesake but no relation of the Hero of World War No. 1, is with the Army in the War Zone. His home is in Coffee County."
"Sam K. Lynch, Jr., son of Mr & Mrs Sam K. Lynch of Lebanon, is with the Navy Air Corps in the Atlantic War Zone."

"Richard S. Davis, son of Mr & Mrs Scott Davis of Bedford County, is in the signal corps of the Army in the Atlantic War Zone."

WEDDING ANNOUNCEMENT:

Mr & Mrs James Arnold announce the engagement of their daughter Mabel Clare, to Mr Frederick William Smartt. Marriage to be Wednesday October 18.

PICTURE: Pasted in Arnold Bible:

Description of a Newspaper picture pasted in Arnold Bible, of Mr. James Arnold.

" He was a very handsome man, greying hair and a mustashe and whiskers greying, (not to long whiskers). He had a pair of wire glasses on. Dressed is a dark suit with vest with white shirt & string black bow-tie."

NEWSPAPER OBIT: Mrs. Mabel Smartt of Wartrace, died Saturday. Dec 28, 1946.

Mrs Mabel Smartt, 70, died Saturday at 8 P.M. in a Nashville Hospital, were held at 2:30 P.M. Sunday at Wartrace Baptist Church, conducted by the Rev. James Harney, Pastor. Burial was in Hollywood Cemetery. She suffered a stroke recently. She was born in Bedford County Tennessee, daughter of the late James and Nannie Frances Arnold. She was a member of the Wartrace Baptist Church since childhood. She was church organist for a number of years.

ITEMS WRITTEN ON BACK OF BIBLE PICTURES IN BIBLE:

Great-great-great-grandfather Thomas Arnold of Virginia married a Miss Wich or Wight. There were 18 of the Wich children called the "Immortal eighteen". He served as Captain in Revolutionary War and when he retired, joined "The Regiment of Invalids".
Great-great-grandfather, Samuel Arnold married Miss Elizabeth Wright. He was from Virginia and his wife also-- They had 8 children: James, Eliza, Elisha, Daniel, John, Thomas, William and Elizabeth. He moved to Hamptonville, N. C., served in Revolutionary War and made guns.
Great-grandfather, James Arnold had six brothers: Elijah, Elisha, Daniel, John, Thomas and William. He had one sister named Elizabeth, who married John Parks of North Carolina. He married Margaret Bagley, his second wife, who came from North Carolina, Surrey County. She had one sister, Martha Bagley, who married a Cunningham. She had four brothers: John, Thomas, Edward and _____.
They had nine children: James, Oliver, Thomas Martin, Louisa, Elizabeth, Lucinda, Martha Ann, Sophia M., and Lamyra. (James Arnold's first wife was Hannah, born of S.C.) He moved to Bedford County, Tennessee. Children born in Tennessee.
Grandfather, Thomas M. Arnold of Tennessee, married Nancy Ann Jackson. They had four children: James Arnold, Joseph Arnold, Arabella, Margaret E. Arnold.

93

Grandfather Arnold had two brothers: Oliver and James, and six sisters: Louisa, Elizabeth, Lucinda, Martha Ann, Sophia M. and Lamyra.

Grandmother Arnold had five sisters: Millie, Rebecca, Cynthia, Rury, Sophia and one brother Joe.

Grandmother's Sisters:	Married:
Nancy Johnson	T. M. Arnold
Millie Johnson	Jas. Foster
Rebecca Johnson	Dr. White
Cynthia Johnson	___ Dozier
Rury Johnson	_____McMurray
Sophia Johnson	_____ Jarrett
Brother Joe Johnson	Miss McLean

My Grandfathers & his brothers & Sisters:	Married:
James Arnold	Mrs' Mary Vance Fogleman
Oliver P. Arnold	Miss Rachel Tarver
Thomas M. Arnold	Nancy Ann Johnson
Louisa Arnold	_____ Gray
Elizabeth Arnold	Robert Petty
Lucinda Arnold	_____ Cunningham
Martha Ann Arnold	Charles Hickerson
Sophia M. Arnold	Stephen Chitwood
Lamyra Arnold	Unmarried
My Father: (children of Thomas M. Arnold)	
James Arnold	Nannie Francis
Joseph Arnold	Bettie Davidson
Arabella Arnold	Harrison Dyer
Margaret Elizabeth Arnold	Isaac White

James Arnold's Children:

James Arnold married Nannie Francis. They had 4 children: Thomas F., Hugh Turney, Mabel Clare and Katie.

Written by Mabel Clare Arnold, 1896

OBIT NOTICE: I. H. White, Died Sept 26, 1916. Aged: 64 years

SISTERS OF GRANDMA NANCY

Nancy Wortham married William Buchanan

Mother of:	Married:
Catherine M. Buchanan	Hugh Francis
Mary E. Buchanan	Wilson Brazelton
Sarah C. Buchanan	Tazewell W. Newman
Jane Buchanan	James Anderson
Amanda Buchanan	Nathan Greene, Sr.
(William Sidney Green, son of Judge Nathan Green)	

FRANCIS KIN

Brothers and Sisters of Grandpa Hugh Francis

Susan M. Francis   James D. Porter

BUCHANAN:

Great-great Grandfather William Buchanan married Catherine McCaleb.
They probably live in Pa. Their son
William Buchanan, my great-grandfather, was born (died in 1876) in
Lancaster Co., in 1785. He married in Wilson Co.--later Maury Co.
Nancy Wortham born 1796 of N.C., He had two sons, George and James &
7 girls.

     James Buchanan married Margaret Blackwell, Tenn.

     George Buchanan married Virginia White, Franklin, Tenn.

     Amanda Buchanan married Dr. Sidney Green, son of Supreme
          Court Judge of Tenn., Nathan Green, brother of Judge
          Green of Lebanon.

     Catherine Buchanan married Col. Hugh Francis who was a mail
          agent of Southern Confederacy for a while.

     Elizabeth died in infancy.

     Mary married Wilson Brazelton.

     Sarah married Col. Tazwell Newman, U.S.Senator from Tenn.

     Jane married James Anderson.

     William, the father of these was related (a second cousin) to
          President Buchanan. He had one sister Betsy who married
          Mr. Frost, who owned Frost Iron Works in N.C.

     William had three brothers, James who lived in Florida, Archi-
          bald who lived in Greenville (or Greensboro), Ala. &
          George.

WORTHAM:

My great-grandmother Buchanan was Nancy Heath Wortham. She died in
     1876. A daughter of William Wortham of Maury Co., Tenn. (who
     moved to). Her mother was Miss Irene Sims. Nancy Heath Wortham
     two sisters who married Johnsons. Another married a Craddock.
     Jane married a Logan. Nancy had three brothers William, Zach-
     ariah and Robert. Nancy's father had four brothers, Heath, Tom,
     Duke and Robert. These five brothers conjointly weighed over
     1000 lbs & all lived in Maury Co., Tenn.

My great-great-grandfather Wortham's mother's name was Heath. Worthams
     came from Mecklenburg Co., N. C.

                    written by Mabel Clare Arnold, grand-
                    daughter of Hugh Francis.

Another page:
     Mr & Mrs James Arnold announces the marriage of their daughter
     Katherine Louise to Mr William Millard Stancell on Wednesday,
     May the first nineteen hundred and one, Wartrace, Tennessee.

STANCELL-ARNOLD

     On Wednesday morning, Tennessee lost to North Carolina one of
     her fairest young women when Prof. William Millard Stancell of

Jackson, N.C., was united in marriage to Miss Katheryn Arnold at the home of the Bride.Rev. B. McNatt, while surrounded by immediate relatives of the contributing parties, spoke the impressive words which united two souls and two hearts which are ever to think and beat in unity and love. Miss Arnold is the youngest daughter of Mr and Mrs Jas. Arnold and is a womanly little woman, whose charms are many and whose sunny disposition will always brighten the home she left us to adore. Prof. Stancell, whose home is Jackson, N.C., was formerly connected with Brandon Training School here and is a true type of a Southern Gentleman. He is highly educated, refined and cultured and this bespeakes for them a happy future. They left on the noon train for Raleigh, N.C., after which they will go to Jackson, Newport News, and places of interest before returning to their future home in Cobbs, N.C. The Tribune wishes for them that their life may be a bright and sunny as the May morn of their union.

....Bride's home Wednesday at 11 o'clock.... Rev. L. B. McNatt of Tullahoma.

.... Relatives ... only a few invited friends and the Brandon School Faculty of which Prof. Stancell was a member a year ago.

..... A dainty little valentine reached the home of Mr and Mrs James Arnold on Thursday evening at six o'clock... delighted grandparents.... fond and loving parents, Mr and Mrs Wm. Stancell. May little James Arnold Stancell live long and grow up....

FRANCIS KIN:

Margin Note: Brothers Sisters of Grandpa Hugh Francis:
Susan M. Francis married James D. Porter, Missionary to Brazil
Teresa H. Francis married Hopkins L. Turner, U.S.Senator
Malinda W. Francis married John H. Woodward
Mary E. Francis married Joseph Carter
Elizabeth Francis married Wm. Griffith
Margaret Francis married Wm. Givens
Woodson Francis married Sallie Newell
Hugh Francis married Catherine M. Buchanan
John Francis married Mattie E. Grant
Dr. James Francis married Amy Montgomery
Joseph Francis (New York I met him there), Died unmarried
William Francis, Died in Texas

Sons of Hugh & Catherine (Margin note: Children of Hugh Francis)
Joseph H. Francis married Mary E. Grant
Hugh Francis married 1st Sallie Woodward, 2nd Margaret Smith
James Francis married Mattie Manier
Bettie Francis married Harvey Wilson
Nannie Francis married James Arnold
Turner Francis, Died in 1864. Killed in the Battle of Resaca, Ga.
Mary Francis, buried in Jacksonville, Ala.

George Francis, buried in Jacksonville, Ala.
Katie Francis, buried in Winchester
Willie Francis, buried in Winchester
Miller & Hannah, buried in Winchester

Margin Note: Miller Francis, father of Hugh, married a Henry, cousin
        of Patrick.

Brothers of Grandma Francis --- Catherine Buchanan (written by Nannie
        Francis Arnold)

James & George Buchanan Brothers of my Mother.

James Buchanan married Margaret Blackwell
George Buchanan married Virginia White

James had three boys, William, Robert & Jimmie

George had one child, named Hugh, died in infancy

Mabel Arnold   1897

FRANCIS

Children of Joseph Francis and Mary Francis, son of Hugh Francis.
Lonnie Francis,Unmarried, died in New York City
Katherine Francis married Harry Bostwick, Erie, Pa.
Grant Francis, died in New York City
Mary Francis, unmarried, still living, 1938
Hugh Francis, died in New Jersey, family in Nashville
Joe Francis, died

Children of Hugh Francis who married Sallie Woodward first:
Sallie Francis
Willie Francis

Hugh one son by second wife Margaret Smith:
Hugh

Children of James Francis who married Mattie Manier has:
None- died in Jefferson, Texas

Children of Bettie Francis who married Harvey Wilson: died in Calif.
John, George, Mamie, Foster, Kate, Hugh, Joe, Miller & J. C. Wilson

Children of Nannie Francis who married James Arnold- died in Wartrace
Thomas, died; Hugh, died; Mabel & Kate still living in 1908 Jan 6th.

The other brothers & sisters died unmarried.

FUNERAL NOTICES:
>   Died at Wartrace, May 30, '95, at 9:30 a.m., Thos. Francis
>   Arnold, aged 22 years, 11 months, 24 days. Funeral services
>   conducted by Rev. C. C. Peyton, at the Baptist Church, Friday,
>   May 31st at 10 o'clock, a.m. Burial at Holly Wood Cemetery.
>   Pall Bearers:

R. L. Davis   P. A. Murphy
A. S. Justice   A. B. Blackman
W. K. Pruett   M. G. Plumlee
>   Wartrace, Tenn., May 30th, 1895

FUNERAL NOTICE:
>   Born July 9, 1820
>   Died Mch 29, 1902
The friends and acquaintances are invited to attend the funeral of
>   Mrs. Lucinda Cunningham
at the Baptist Church, Tuesday, April 1st, 9 a.m. Services by Rev.
G. L. Boles, assisted by Rev. Jerome Winford.
>   Pall Bearers:

C. B. Murphey   A.M. Young
J. E. Justice   G. A. Cortner
R. M. Cleveland   B. I. Hall
Interment at Holly Wood Cemetery, Wartrace, Tenn.

OBIT:
In Loving Remenberance of I. H. White, Died Sept 26, 1916 Aged 64 yrs.

FUNERAL NOTICE:
Died at his residence in this City July 29th, 1915, James Arnold,
Funeral services at 11 o'clock to-day from his late residence.
Rev. C. H. Bailey in Charge. Interment at Hollywood Cemetery.
>   Pall Bearers:

R. M. Cleveland   J. W. Holt
G. W. Clark   B. E. Rushing
J. A. Cunningham   J. E. Russell
>   Wartrace, Tenn. July 30, 1915

NEWSPAPER CLIPPING: Wartrace, Tenn. Oct 18. (1905) (SPECIAL)
>   This morning at 8 o'clock Frederick William Smartt and Miss
>   Mabel Clare Arnold were married at the residence of the bride's
>   parents and left immediately on an extended bridal tour North.
>   Many costly and valuable presents were recieved although no
>   invitations were sent out. They will be at the residence of
>   Mr and Mrs James Arnold for the winter upon their return.
>   This morning at 11 o'clock, at the residence of the bride's
>   mother, Mrs. B. W. Blanton, Miss Lula Blanton and E. R. Hill,
>   of Augusta, Ga. were married. After the ceremony refreshments
>   were served. The couple left on the noon train for the groom's
>   home in Augusta. Mrs. Hill comes of a wealthy and prominent
>   family, and Mr. Hill is an attorney for the Georgia Railway.
>   The presents were many and costly.

NOTICE: Wartrace

> Mr and Mrs James Arnold announce the engagement and approach-
> ing marriage of their daughter, Mabel Clare, to Mr. Frederick
> William Smartt, the wedding to be quietly solemnized at the
> home of the bride, Wednesday, October 18. Miss Arnold is
> widely known and a representative of a prominent and wealthy
> Middle Tennessee Family. She is a charming, cultured young
> woman, a graduate of Boscobel College, and has a large circle
> of friends in Nashville. Mr. Smartt is a young man who is pop-
> ular and widely known as one of the leading druggists at this
> place, Bell Buckle and Dechard, and admired for his business
> ability and sterling qualities.

INDEX to obituaries from James Arnold Family Bible (pasted in back)

> Mrs. Sallie Woodard, in this place Monday, 17th inst., at 1
> o'clock a.m., of dropsy, wife of Mr. Hugh Francis, aged about
> 27 years....Burial in Rose Hill Cemetery.

> Sallie, the wife of Hugh Francis... by a Friend.

> Francis, In this place, last Sunday, Mrs. Sallie, wife of Hugh
> Francis, aged about twenty-six years. Member of the Presbyter-
> ian Church.

> Thomas F. Arnold, death, at his home in Wartrace, on May 30,
> son of Mr. James Arnold of that place....about 23 years old.

> Mrs. Catherine M. Francis died ...advanced age, at 3 o'clock
> p.m., Tuesday, May 10, 1904, at the residence, in Fayetteville,
> of her son Hugh Francis, aged 86 years. Native of Winchester...
> After funeral service at the residence by Rev L. R. Hogan and
> Geo. A. Morgan, the remains were taken to Winchester for burial.

> Mrs. Francis, mother of Mrs. James Arnold, who died Tuesday at
> the home of her son Hugh Francis at Fayetteville. Her remains
> were carried to Winchester for interment on Wednesday.

> Col. Hugh Francis, Sr. died at his residence in Winchester last
> Sunday morning. (aged 61 years). Col Francis was for several
> years a resident of Shelbyville, and by his uniform, courte-
> ous and dignified bearing won the esteem and respect of our whole
> community, and his many warm friends will be deeply saddened by
> the news of his death (in ink: died 1876).

> Thomas F. Arnold, eldest son of James and Nannie F. Arnold died
> at Wartrace, Tenn., on May 30, 1895, aged 23 years.Baptised into
> the fellowship of Wartrace Baptist Church by Bro. Wm. Huff some
> twelve years ago..... death of Tommy Arnold.......

> Miss Willie Francis, daughter of Dr. J. O.(C?) Francis.

Arnold- Mrs. Rachel Tarver Vallotton Arnold, widow of the late
O. P. Arnold, Sr., died at her home near Wartrace, Tenn., on
Friday, April 3d, 1896. She was born in Richmond County, near
Augusta, Ga., on January 30th, 1819..... Member of the Wartrace
Baptist Church..... O. C. P.

OBITS: Pasted in front of Arnold Bible.
Thomas Francis Arnold, son of James and Nannie Francis Arnold,
died at the home of his parents, at this place (Wartrace) on
the morning of Thursday last, May 30th, aged: 23 years....

Thomas Francis Arnold.... died at his father's home, Mr. Jas.
Arnold, on May 30th, 1895, at 9:30 a.m., Aged 22 years, 11
months, and 24 days. Services by Rev. O. C. Peyton, at the
Baptist Church, Friday May 31st, at 10 o'clock a.m., and laid
to rest in Hollywood Cemetery.

Little Winifred Willingham Arnold
From the home of her parents Mr and Mrs. Hugh Arnold at Dunbar,
Ga., on the morning of the 3rd of February..... little Winifred
Arnold.... after weeks of suffering...

(Wartrace)
Mrs. Nannie Francis Arnold, 64, wife of James Arnold of this
place...Apoplexy was cause of her death. She was the daughter of
Judge Hugh Francis of Winchester, Tenn. She is survived by Husband and two daughters-- Mrs. F. W. Smartt, Wartrace, Tenn., and
Mrs. William M. Stancell, Washington, D.C.; two brothers and one
sister. Funeral services by Rev. C. H. Bailey.

James Arnold (Special to the Banner). Wartrace, Tenn., July 30.
Mr. James Arnold, one of the community's oldest citizens, died
suddenly at his home Thursday afternoon of heart failure. The
deceased was widely known in business circles, having entered
the mercantile business here with his brother, J. O. Arnold,
in 1871, and continued for 38 years... Member of the Baptist
Church and was 72 years old. Two daughters survive him. Services
by Rev. C. H. Bailey and Rev. L. B. Jarmon.

ARNOLD- sister Nannie Francis Arnold, wife of Bro. Jas. Arnold
died at the family home in Wartrace, March 11, 1913. She was the
daughter of the late Judge Francis. She was born April 8, 1848.
United with the Presbyterian Church, later with the Baptist
Church at Wartrace. She was married to Jas. Arnold, Jan 6, 1870.
Four Children... Thomas Francis died in 1895... Hugh Turney.. died
May 18, 1912, his wife who was Miss Matchie Willingham, survives
him. She (Nannie) is survived by her husband and two daughters.

Hugh Arnold, friends of Mr and Mrs. Jas. Arnold... learn of the
death of their only surviving son, Hugh Arnold, who had lived in
Montgomery, Alabama for the past 12 years. He came to Wartrace

a few days ago, but died Saturday afternoon of heart failure.
He was 38 years old Friday. Survived by his wife...Services
by Rev. L. B. Jarmon. Burial in Hollywood Cemetery.

WILLIAM JENNINGS BIBLE

Files of Helen C. Marsh, from National Archives, Washington, D.C.
   WILLIAM JENNINGS No..W.27144

John B. Smoot was born March 4th 1795

John B. Smoot and Salley H. Jennings was married December 30th 1820

John B. Smoot Departed this life July 12th 1840
Sarah W. Smoot Departed this life January 12th, 1842

William Jennings departed this life July 17th 1840

William Jennings was born February 26, 1761
Polly Kidd was born November 2nd 1770

William Jennings and Poley Kidd was married January 18th 1787

1st: Martin Jennings was born November 4th 1787
2nd: Nancy Jennings was born September 4th 1790
3rd: Elizabeth Jennings was born January 1, 1892
4th: Allen Jennings was born December 8th 1794
5th: Nancy Alen was born March 14th 1796
6th: William K. Jennings was born July 19th 1798
7th: Salley Jennings was born Feb. 10th 1801
8th: Webb Jennings was born May 11th 1802
9th: William Calvin Jennings was born June 20th 1805
10th: Robert Jennings was born April 18th 1808
11th: Lucreecy Jennings was born May 12th 1810
12th: Sophy Jennings was born 27th May 1812, departed this life June
      6, 1812
13th: James W. Jennings was born December 31, 1813

James W. Jennings & Mary Bevel was married August 4th 1836

WILLIAMS BIBLE

Taken from: "History of the Harris Family of Tennessee" by Harris
      Family Reunion Association 1973

MARRIAGES:

James Harris and Nancy Thompson was married June 29th 1797 in Union
  City, South Carolina.

David Williams and Sarah Turrentine Harris was married Sept 6th 1836
  in Bedford County. Said Sarah Turrentine Harris is the Great-
  great-granddaughter of John Harris who immigrated to America
  in Company with William Penn and assisted him in the setling
  of Pennsylvania. He gave the land in which Harrisburg the Capital stands.

HARRIS FAMILY RECORDS

Taken from: "History of the Harris Family of Tennessee"
            by Harris Family Reunion Association 1973.

(1) John Harris, born in Rowan Co., N.C.
(2) James Harris, son of James & Hannah Stapleton Harris, born
     2-10-1777, Rowan Co., N.C., died 11-3-1863 in Bedford County,
     Tennessee, married 6-28-1797 in Union County, S. C., to Ann
     (Nancy) Thompson, born 10-29-1780 in Union County, S. C., died
     10-1-1869 in Bedford County, Tennessee. 8 Children:
     1: James Stapleton Harris
     2: Ann Wallace (Nancy) Harris
     3: John Thompson Harris
     4: Hiram Harris
     5: Elizabeth (Betsy) Harris
     6: Elvira Harris
     7: Sarah Turrentine Harris
     8: Almedia Jane (Babe) Harris
(3) Margaret (Peggy) Harris, born 12-21-1781 in Rowan County, N. C.,
     died 6-13-1868 in Bedford County, Tennessee, married James Gra-
     ham IV of Rowan County, N.C., 3-25-1801. Had 7 children, later
     4 born in Bedford County, Tennessee: Henry F. Graham, James
     Graham,V., Nicholas Graham, Mary Graham, William Graham, Nancy
     Graham, Edward J. Graham.
(4) Elizabeth Harris, born in N.C., married Abraham Trott
(5) Nicholas Harris, born North Carolina.
(6) Polly Harris, born North Carolina.
(7) Hiram Harris, born 1814 in Rowan County, N.C., moved to Bedford
     County, Tennessee about 1825/30, later to Marshall County, Tenn.
(8) James Stapleton Harris, born in N.C.
(9) Ann Wallace (Nancy) Harris, born Rowan County, N.C., 2-8-1801,
     died 12-30-1902 in Bedford County, Tennessee, married 10-5-1821
     to Hartwell Freeman, born Rowan County, N.C., 1-1-1798, died
     1-8-1871 Hickory Hill M.E. Church Cemetery, Bedford County, Tenn.
     Had 8 children.
(10) John Thompson Harris, born Rowan County, N.C., 7-6-1804 & died 10-
     13-1864 in Bedford County, Tenn., married 1st: 8-30-1827 to

Gillie Perry Orr, born 1805, died 1828, daughter of David &
Jane Orr of Sumner County, Tenn., They had one child: Martha
Gillie Ann Harris; 2nd marriage to Sarah Brown, born 3-9-1806
of Williamson County, Tennessee, died 2-15-1856, they had 9
children; married 3rd. to Catherine Bass Wallis of Eagleville,
Williamson County, Tenn, born 8-13-1824, died 7-4-1912. They
had 4 children.

(11) Hiram Harris, born 10-20-1806, Rowan County, N.C., died 1889 in
Marshall County, Tenn., married 1828 Jane Porter Johnson. 10
children.

(12) Elizabeth (Betsy) Harris, born 6-5-1809, Bedford County, Tennessee,
died 3-?-1885, married John Jackson Lentz, born 1808 in Bedford
County, Tenn., died 1848, buried in Crowell's Chapel Cemetery.
3 children.

(13) Elvira Harris, born 9-23-1813 in Bedford County, Tennessee, died
10-?-1875, grave unmarked in Burns Cemetery, Bedford County,
Tenn., married 1829 to Wilson Turrentine, born 1804 N.C., M. E.
Preacher, died 12-5-1898, buried in Willow Mount Cemetery. 9
children.

(14) Sarah Turrentine Harris, born in Bedford County, Tenn., 12-1-1816,
died 10-4-1910, married 9-6-1836 David Williams, born 3-?-1815,
died 9-?-1887, both buried in Harris-Williams Cemetery, Bedford
County, Tenn., 10 children.

(15) Almedia Jane Harris, born Bedford County, Tenn., 6-10-1818, died
184? in West Tennessee, married 184? to John Hill. 1 son, James.

(16) Henry F. Graham, born Rowan County, N.C., 180?

(17) James Graham,V, born Rowan County, N.C., 180?, came with parents
James IV & Peggy Harris   to Tennessee 1809, married about
1849 to Louise Anne Jones.

(18) Nicholas Graham, born Rowan County, N. C. 1809, came to Bedford
County, Tenn., with parents shortly thereafter.

(19) Mary Graham, born Bedford County, Tennessee 181?.

(20) William Graham, born Bedford County, Tennessee 181?.

(21) Nancy Graham, born Bedford County, Tennessee 181?.

(22) Edward J. Graham, born Bedford County, Tennessee 181?.

(23) James Hartwell Graham, born Bedford County, Tennessee 1822

(24) Celia Ann Freeman, born Bedford County, Tennessee 2-29-1824, died
8-8-1901, buried in Hickory Hill M. E. Church Cemetery, unmarked.

(25) Elizabeth Rebecca Freeman, born Bedford County, Tennessee 12-11-
1825, died in Georgia, married William Miller of Rutherford on
12-12-1844.

(26) Mary Neil Freeman, born Bedford County, Tennessee 6-20-1829, died
5-15-1883, married 1-27-1856 to John Wesley Hester, born 2-8-1825,
died 11-28-1910, both buried at Ransom Cemetery at Rover.

(27) Robert Bailey Freeman, born Bedford County, Tennessee 9-18-1831,
died 2-2-1892.

(28) Elvira Jane Freeman, born 5-20-1833 Unionville, Bedford County, Tennessee, died 5-13-1900 Bedford Co., Tenn., married 4-5-1857 James
M. Kirby, born 8-30-1830, died 8-7-1864 Raleigh, N.C.

Martha Gillie Ann Harris born Bedford County, Tenn., 9-2-1828, died
8-28-1869, left motherless when 18 days old, married 1-27-1848
to Michael F. Williams, born 10-12-1820 and died 2-18-1900,
Buried at Hickory Hill M. E. Church Cemetery.

William Harris, born 18??, married Nannie Bryant, born 18??. Both
buried in Harris Cemetery, Bedford County, Tennessee.

Benj. Franklin Lentz, 1839, died 1924, married 1865 Nancy Jane Ray, 1845,
died 1940, both buried at Crowell Chapel.

William James Turrentine, 3-1-1837 Bedford Co., Tenn., died 3-8-1898
Bedford County, Tennessee, married 11-23-1858 to Mary Thompson,
born 9-14-1840 Bedford County, Tenn., died 9-25-1915 Bedford Co.,
Tennessee

Sarah Jane Turrentine, 1-27-1840 Bedford Co., 'Tenn., died 188?, Bedford
or Marshall County, Tennessee, married Joseph Pulaski Logan Neil,
born 10-9-1835 Bedford Co., Tenn., died 8-21-1903 in Mo., buried
in Willow Mount. (Bedford County, Tennessee)

WHEELHOUSE BIBLE

In possession of Mrs. Gladys Eley Harper, Unionville, Tennessee

Joshua Thomas Wheelhouse was born the 26th December 1824
Parthena Primrose consort of Thomas Wheelhouse was born 22nd of October
1826.
Joshua T. & Parthena married 23 of December 1847

Mary Elizabeth child of the above born 23 October 1848
Miles Calvin was born 21 of December 1850
Sarah Ann Loucinda Wheelhouse was born May the 18th 1854
William Thomas Wheelhouse was born August 17th 1856
Manda Louisa Wheelhouse was born Sept 21 1859
Collumbus Grant Wheelhouse was born Oct. 4th 1863
Clamenza Anetah Wheelhouse was born January the 8 1866
Parthena Wheelhouse was born July 11, 1870

MARRIAGES:
Joshua Thomas Wheelhouse and Parthena Primrose was married December
23rd 1847
James Allen Puckett and Mary Elizabeth Wheelhouse was married.
Miles Calvin Wheelhouse and Sarah Elisebeth Cook were married Dec. 25th,
1872.
Joshua Thomas Wheelhouse and Mrs. Roberta Francis Smith were married
Jan 12th 1874

DEATHS:
Sarah Ann Lucinda second daughter of J. T. Wheelhouse died March 24th
      1856.
Parthena wife of J. T. Wheelhouse died July 12th 1871
James Allen Puckett died August 3rd 1879

Wheelhouse Family Register
Copied by Mrs. Gladys Eley Harper, Unionville, Tennessee

Joshua Thomas Wheelhouse was born December 26, 1824.
Roberta Frances Wheelhouse was born Oct 28, 1847, married Jan 12, 1874.
Laura Wheelhouse was born Mar 23, 1876.
Alla Wheelhouse was born Aug 6, 1877.
Beta Wheelhouse was born Sept 20, 1879.
Mattie Wheelhouse was born August 29, 1881.
Isaac Wheelhouse was born Oct 21, 1883.
Lila Wheelhouse was born Apr 7, 1886.
Edna & Evie Wheelhouse was born May 31, 1889.

Levi G. W. Smith was born (first husband of Roberta Frances, nee Turner)
      Wheelhouse.
Mary Frances Smith was born Dec 28, 1867.
Amanda Virginia Smith was born Oct 4, 1869.
Levi Temple Madison Smith was born Apr 4, 1871.

DEATHS:
Joshua Thomas Wheelhouse died Sept 10, 1904.
Isaac Wheelhouse died Feb 28, 1885.
Lilah Wheelhouse died Dec 10, 1886.
Beta Wheelhouse died Oct 27, 1891.
Edna Wheelhouse died Aug 29, 1898.
Mattie Wheelhouse Neal died Jan 23, 1919.
Roberta Frances Wheelhouse died May 11, 1927.
Laura Wheelhouse Cook died May 12, 1960.
Alla Wheelhouse Haynes died Dec 9, 1956.

Levi G. W. Smith died Nov 2, 1870.
Mary F. Smith Webb died Apr 29, 1893.
Amanda V. Smith died Mar 16, 1890 (She was called Patsy).

MARRIAGES:
Laura Wheelhouse & C. B. Cook were married Oct 11, 1896.
Mattie Wheelhouse & S. M. Neal were married Dec 26, 1900.
Alla Wheelhouse & Thomas H. Haynes were married Dec 29, 1907.
Evie Wheelhouse & W. A. Eley were married Dec 25, 1910.

NOTE: Joshua Thomas Wheelhouse was son of Dennis Wheelhouse and his wife
      Mary Ann Browder Wheelhouse. (See Dennis Wheelhouse's Will, dated
      August 26th, 1868 and proven Jany 6, 1869) The Wheelhouses came
      to Bedford County from Sussex County, Virginia about 1834 when
      Joshua Thomas (My Mother's father) was a little boy. They sold

their land in Sussex County, Va., in 1833.

Copied by Gladys (Eley) Harper from the Family Bible Register, which
is owned by: Mrs. Evie (Wheelhouse) Eley this 6th day of September, 1975.

ELEY BIBLE

Eley Family Record, copied by Gladys (Eley) Harper from a Photostat of
Bible belonging to Mrs. Margie A. Fain of Boulder Creek, Calif., and
combined with a photostat of the Family Record belonging to Mrs Marion
Rozear of Panama City, Fla.

Notations when they are combined:
Eliza J. Eley, Sr. was a Rowland before marriage, (full name: Eliza Jane
Rowland).
J. A. Eley's name was Josiah Auguston Eley.
Jemima Mary Ann Eley (nee Corlett), 1st wife of Josiah Auguston Eley.
Mary Ann Catherine Eley (nee Winsett), 3rd wife of Josiah Auguston Eley.
Mary Margie Anna Kingston, 2nd wife of Josiah Eley.
Saphronia (nee Drumright) Barbour, fourth wife of Josiah Auguston Eley.

Josiah Eley, born 1809, married Mary Williams as his second wife. She
was daughter of Robert Williams (born 1773) and his wife Mary
(born 1790). Robert and Mary Williams are buried in the Davis
Family Cemetery in 9th district of Bedford County right on
Rutherford County Line. I do not know where Josiah Eley and his
wife Mary Williams Eley are buried. They lived in Marshall Co.,
when they died.

FRANCIS MARION ELEY BIBLE

Copied by Mrs. Gladys Eley Harper, Unionville, Tennessee

Francis Marion Eley & his wife Harriet Catherine Mangrum Eley

F. M. Eley and H. C. Mangrum was mared in the year of our Lord August
1875 (26th).

Jesse Lee Eley was born in the year of our Lord September the 23, 1877.
John Frank Eley was born in the year of our Lord 3 day of January 1878.
Wilum (William) Anderson Eley was born in the year of our Lord July
18, 1884.

Mary Eley died in the year of our Lord July 7, 1889 (She was Mary Williams,

106

daughter of Robert Williams & his wife Mary).
John Franklin Eley died Dec the 11th 1897 (Buried in Davis Cemetery).
M. F. Eley died in the year of our Lord September 7, 1899.
Harriet Catherine Eley died in the year of our Lord Dec 24th, 1920.
Frances Marion Eley died in the year of our Lord March 11, 1922.
William Anderson Eley died Feb 28, 1961.

BIRTHS:
Josiah Eley, Sr. was born A.D. May the 25th 1809.
Eliza J. Eley, Sr. was born A.D. December 1st 1822.
J. A. Eley, Sr. was born A.D. October 17th 1847.
Jemima M. A. Eley was born A.D. July 20th 1837 (1st wife of J. A. Eley)
Mary M. A. Eley was born A.D. April 1st 1858.
Mary A. C. Eley was born A.D. February 14th 1867.
Eliza J. Eley, Jr. was born A.D. December 5th 1867.
Sarah R. E. Eley was born A.D. February 4th 1869.
Auguston B. Eley was born A.D. May 19th 1870. '
James W. Eley was born A.D. August 22nd 1871.
Melvina L. Eley was born A.D. June 10th 1873
Irene Eley was born A.D. February 7th 1875.
Joseph A. Eley was born A.D. January 26th 1876.
Frank S. and Fannie Eley, twins, was born A.D. June 11th 1877
Mary A. Eley, still born, was born A.D. July 28th 1880
John W. Eley was born June 16th 1883.
Grover C. Eley was born A.D. June 2nd 1886.
Thomas H. Eley was born A.D. Jan 29th 1888.

DEATHS:
Josiah Eley, Sr. departed this life A.D. August 27th 1870.
Eliza J. Eley, Sr. departed this life A.D. May 26th 1849.
Jemima M. A. Eley departed this life A.D. March 22nd 1882.
Mary M. A. Eley departed this life A.D. July 7th 1884.
Mary A. C. Eley departed this life A.D. October 3, 1888.
Josiah Auguston Eley died July 21, 1899 aged 51 yrs, 9 mo, 4 days.
Eliza J. Eley, Jr. departed this life A.D. September 17th 1868.
Sarah R. E. Eley departed this life A.D. July 25th 1869.
Auguston B. Eley departed this life A.D. February 22nd 1871.
Irene Eley departed this life A.D. July 26th 1875.
Joseph A. Eley departed this life A.D. June 18th 1876.
Frank S. Eley departed this life A.D. August 5th 1877.
Fannie Eley departed this life A.D. August 8th 1877.
Grover C. Eley departed this life A.D. December 30, 1886.
Sophronia Eley departed this life A.D. March 6th 1931.

MARRIAGES:
J. A. Eley and Jemima M. A. Eley was married A. D. 1866 December 30th
    on Sunday.
J. A. Eley and Mary M. A. Eley was married A.D. July 23rd 1882 on Sunday.
J. A. Eley and Mary A. C. Eley was married A.D. July 3rd 1885 on Friday.
Josiah Eley and Eliza J. Eley was married A.D. November the 17th 1846
    on Tuesday night.

James W. Eley and Kizzie M. Drumright were married A.D. December 25, 1889 on Wednesday night.

B. F. Lane and Melvina L. Eley were married A.D. December 26, 1889 on Wednesday night.

J. A. Eley and Saphronia Eley were married A.D. March 16th 1890 on Sunday night.

Henry O. Wells and Hattie Lee Barbour were married Wednesday April 11th 1894.

COOP BIBLE

In possession of Mrs. Walton Woodfin, Bell Buckle Tennessee
Publisher: American Tract Society, 150 Nassau Street, New York

G. W. Coop and Laura Harris were married Nov 4, 1880
Horatio Coop and Lillian Kittrell were married Wed. Apr 18, 1906.
George W. Coop, Jr. and Helene Hummel were married Sunday Sept 30, 1928.
Walton Woodfin & Laura Kittrell Coop were married July 10th Saturday 1937.

BIRTHS:
G. W. Coop, born 1846, Dec 16.
L. H. Coop, born June 11th, 1858.
Horatio Coop Jr. born Aug 19th 1881
Corrie M. Coop, born Apr 29, 1883

Son & Daughter of G. W. & L. Coop

Robt. Geo. Coop, born Tues Apr. 9, 1907.
George W. Coop, born Mar. 28, 1908
Laura Kittrell Coop born July 5, 1910.
Sons & Daughter of Horatio & Lillian Coop.

Lillian F. Kittrell Coop borned June 5, 1885
Walton Chunn Woodfin, Jr. Sat. Aug. 4, 1945, son of Laura Kittrell & Walton Woodfin.

DEATHS:
Corrie M. Coop, Died Aug 12, 1897
Robt. Geo. Coop, Died May 6, 1907.
Horatio E. Coop, Died Sept 24, 1910.
George W. Coop, Died July 17, 1923.
Laura H. Coop, Died Feb 2, 1925.
Lillian Kittrell Coop Whitsett died Sunday May 16, 1948
Walton Chunn Woodfin died Monday December 13, 1954

ENOCHS BIBLE

In possession of Mrs. Mevolene Mabee, Raus, Bedford County, Tennessee.
Publisher: B. F. Johnson & Co., Richmond, Va.   1886

FAMILY RECORDS
MARRIAGES:
David L. Enochs and Martha A. E. Daniel was married Aug the 11, 1842.

BIRTHS:
David L. Enochs, Feb the 8 in the year of our Lord, 1819.
Martha A. E. Enochs, born January 31 in the year of our Lord, 1818.
Margaret A. L. Enochs was born Dec the 19 in the year of our Lord, 1843.
George Washington Enochs was born Sept..(rest of record torn away)......

BIRTHS:
J. H. Enochs born in the year of our Lord Jan 5, 1850.
Stephen W. J. Enochs was born in the year of our Lord Oct 24th, 1854.
Ferdinand Smith
Petway Enochs

DEATHS:
Stephen W. J. Enochs departed this life March 20, 1859.
Sarah M. L. Enochs departed this life August 19, 1860.
Elsie S. Enochs was born June 23, 1879.

MARRIAGES:
J. E. Enochs & Sena Daniel was married December 28th, 1871.
Nannie M. Rogers & J. E. M. Enochs was married July 20th, 1876.
NOTE:*These late entries were made by Lant Wood in Feb 1972, at the age
       of 91 years (Feb 28, 1972)*

BIRTHS:
James E. M. Enochs was born January 1848, * born Jan 3rd, died July 5.
Sena Enochs was born * 1st wife, Sena Daniel, daughter of Calloway
       Daniel & 2nd wife, Mrs. Vanzant (Matilda). * Sena died July
       20th 1875.
Nannie M.(*Rogers) Enochs was born Dec 13th, 1855.
*2nd wife, daughter of Geo. Rogers & wife Polly Awalt, departed this life
       April 17, 1926.
Dorah B.(Bell) Enochs, daughter of James & Sena (*Daniel) Enochs, was
       born Jan 8th 1873.   * Died 1964.
Sena E. Enochs (*Stephens) Daughter of James & Nannie Enochs was born
       June 23rd 1879.   * Died Sept 1965.
Mary E. Enochs daughter of James & Nannie Enochs was born March 19th,
    . 1885.
* Dora Enochs married W. B. Stephens, 1891
* The mother of one daughter Carmie
* Scena Elsie Enochs was married to W. H. Sparks. 1912.
* One daughter Born to them Aug 1916.
* She now Mr Louis G. Akin of Franklin, Tenn.

* Mary Elma Enochs married Lant Wood born Oct 13th, 1917.
* Now Mrs. Morgan McDowell, 1941
* Feb 28, 1972.

DEATHS:
1st Sena Daniel Enochs wife of J. E. M. Enochs, departed this life
        January 7th, 1875.
2nd Nannie M. Rogers Enochs wife of J. E. M. Enochs, departed this life
        May 17, 1926.
*Dora, daughter of J. E. M. and Sena Daniel Enochs, born Jan 8th 1873
        and 1964.
* Scena Elsie, daughter of J. E. M. and Nancy Rogers Enochs, born Jan
        23, 1879 died Sept 1965.

Stephen M. Dance, Grandfather was born Mch 8, 1788 and departed this
        life August 23, 1853.
Sarah wife of Stephen M. Dance. Born March 5, 1793 and departed this life
        June the 8, 1863.
* Martha Dance born Jan 13, 1818, died July 20, 1876
J. T. S. Dance was born Jan 28, 1822 and departed this life July 3rd,
        1897.
J. W. M. Dance was born May 1826 and departed this life Nov. 1903.
S. E. H. Dance was born Mch 30, 1834 & departed this life Mch 20, 1900.
Susan Finetta (*Landers) Dance wife of J. T. S. Dance was born August
        5th, 1828 & departed this life April 19, 1900.
* I Helped dig Mrs. Finetta Dance grave April 19, 1900.- Lant Wood.

Father of D. L. Enochs & Mother
Isaac Enochs was born Nov 1st 1776 and departed this life, July 20, 1853.
Sarah Enochs wife of Isaac Enochs was born April 2nd 1779
G. A. J. Enochs was born Mch 1st 1812, and departed this life May 18th
        1886 at 6 o'clock in the morning.
Polly M. Enochs was born Dec 14th 1814.
Rebecca Enochs was born April 5th 1818.
* Dora L. Enochs born Feb 8, 1820 died June 4, 1894.
Sally S. Enochs was born Oct 16, 1821.
Jane T. Enochs was born Mch 1823.

Miss M. A. E. Dance & L. L. Enochs was married in the year of our Lord
        1842.
Mrs. M. A. E. Enochs was born Jan 13, 1818.
D. L. Enochs was born Feb 8, 1820.
Mrs. M. A. E. Enochs died August 29, 1876.
D. L. Enochs died June 4th 1894.

* The Family of David L. and Mollie Dance Enoch
M. A. L. Enochs was born Dec 19, 1843 (* died March 17, 1918)
* His wife Elizabeth Lucas
G. W. F. Enochs was born Sept 15, 1846/7
* His wife Fannie Sullivan.

J. E. M. Enochs was born Jan 3, 1848
* First wife Scena Daniel daughter of Calloway died July 5, 1925
* 2nd wife Nancy M. Rogers daughter of Geo. Rogers & Polly Awalt
* Born Dec 11, 1855, died April 17, 1926
J. H. Enochs was born Jan 5, 1850
* Was never married & died July 31, 1925.
F. P. Enochs was born July 14, 1857
* Wife was Fannie Lavan, died 1938
Stephen W. I Enochs was born Oct 24th 1854 and departed this life
       Mch 20, 1859.
Sarah M. L. Enochs was born August 1860 and departed this life August
       19th 1860
Dr. M. A. L. Enochs departed this life March 17, 1918
G. W. F. Enochs departed this life Aug 1919
J. E. M. Enochs (*born Jan 3, 1848) departed this life July 5, 1925.
J. H. Enochs (*born Jan 5, 1850) departed this life July 31, 1925
*NOTE: The remainder is from Mr. Lant Wood:
F. P. Enochs born July 14th 1857 died April 17, 1938
Their children & Families:
1st Dorah B. Enochs, daughter of J. E. M. Enochs and Scena Daniel Enochs
       born Jan 8, 1873 died 1964.
2nd Scena Elsie Enochs, daughter of J. E. M. Enochs and Nancy Rogers
       Enochs, born Jan 23, 1879 died 1965.
3rd Mary Elma Enochs, daughter of J. E. M. & Nancy Rogers Enochs,
       born Mar 19, 1885.

Seperate page:
Dora Bell (Enochs) born 1-8-1873, Died Oct 7, 1964, married 1891, Dec 8.
       (Book 3, page 324, Moore County, Tenn.)
William "Willie" Barnett Stephens born May 5, 1867, died Sept 2, 1927
one daughter:
Carmie Stephens, born 1-31-1895, married Oct 27, 1912 to Thomas Chapel
       Couser March 12, 1891, died May 8, 1948. 2 girls:
       Mevolene Lenoir Couser, born 8-2-1913, married 12-26-1946 to
       Charles Aaron Mabee, born 12-24-1918.
       Thelma Colleen Couser, born April 5, 1931, died June 10, 1948.

SMITH BIBLE

In possession of Mrs. Gladys Eley Harper, Unionville, Tennessee
Publisher: American Bible Society, New York   1871

Family Record
BIRTHS:
Mary Francis Smith was born December the 28, 1867
Amanda Virginia Smith was born Oct the 4, 1869
Levi Temple Maderson (Anderson) Smith was born April the 4, 1871

111

Mattie Wheelhouse was born August 29, 1881
Isaac Wheelhouse was born October 21, 1883
Lilah Wheelhouse was born April 7, 1886
Edna and Eva Wheelhouse was born May 31, 1889.
Edna Wheelhouse died Aug 29, 1898.

MARRIAGES:
C. B. Cook and Laura Wheelhouse was married Oct 11, 1896
S. M. Neal and Mattie Wheelhouse was married Dec 26, 1900

DEATHS:
Levi G. W. Smith departed this life November the 2 1870
Mary Francis Smith died April 29, 1893.
Amanda Virginia Smith died March 16, 1890.
Isaac Wheelhouse died Feb 28, 1885
Lilah Wheelhouse died Dec 10, 1886
Beta Wheelhouse died Oct 27, 1891.

Seperate page:
A Prayer for Old Age
to Mrs R. F. Wheelhouse from Mrs H. C. Turner, written by Miss Nora B.
    Williams.
"O Most Merciful God, cast me not in the time of old age; forsake me not
if my strength faileth. May my hoary head be found in righteousness. Pre-
serve my mind from dotage and imbecility, and my body from protracted
disease and excruciating pain. Deliver me from despondency in my declining years, and enable me to bear with patience whatever may be Thy Holy
will. I humbly ask that my reason may be continued to the last and that
I may be so comforted and supported that I may leave my testimony in
favor of the reality of religion and of Thy faithulness in fulfilling
Thy gracious promises. And, when my spirit leaves this clay tenement,
Lord Jesus, receive it! Send some of the blessed angels to convay any
inexperienced soul to the mansions which Thy love has prepared; and O,
May I have an abundant entrance ministered unto me into the Kingdom of
our Lord and Saviour, Jesus Christ." (written prior to 27 Dec 1907)
                                written by- Miss Nora B. Williams.
Miss Nora B. Williams later married Mr. L. V. McLean and lived in
Oklahoma City, Oklahoma.

WILLIAMS BIBLE

In possession of Mr. H. Young Williams, Unionville, Tennessee
Publisher: Missing.

MARRIAGES:

BIRTHS:
M. M. Williams was born April the 15 1827.

Sarah Ann Williams was born November 25, 1834.
Charles Franklin Williams was born February the fifth 1855.
John Enoch Williams was born February the fifth 1856
Mary Elizabeth Williams was born September the 14th, 1857.
Marildy Jane was born August the 28th day in 1859.
William Thomas Williams was born February 2nd 1861.
George Peyton Williams was born November 5th, 1862.
James Henry Williams was born April 13th, 1864.
Eva Frances Williams was born December 21st, 1865.
Emit Madison was born May 29th 1867.
Lewis Cooper Williams was born December the 16th, 1868.
Mattie M. Williams was born July the 11th, 1870.
Samuel B.(Bell) Williams was born August the 25th, 1872
Sarah Annie Williams was born March the 22, 1874.
Robert Tune Williams was born August the 16, 1876.
Jarman Whitman Williams born November 9th, 1878.

WELCH BIBLE

Contributed by Mrs Mary F. Dunn, Henderson, Texas
Publisher: J. R. Lippincott & Company, Philadelphia 1860

MARRIAGES:
Robert W. Welch and Mary A. Nelson was married Oct the 1st A.D. 1839.

BIRTHS:
Robert W. Welch was born the 17th of September A.D. 1812.
Mary A. "wife of R. W. Welch" was born Jan 20th A.D. 1817.
Sarah E. Welch was born the 28th of March A.D. 1840.
Amanda T. Welch was born 14th of April A.D. 1853.
Nancy M. Welch was born August 3rd A.D. 1845.
Buena Vistar Welch was born 12th July A.D. 1847.
Helen W. Welch was born Oct 27th A.D. 1849.
Dorothy A. Welch was born Feb 1st A.D. 1852.
Margaret J. Welch was born Jany 22nd A.D. 1854.
Rosetta W. Welch was born April 5th A.D. 1858.

BIRTHS:
Mary A. V. Welch was born April 1st A.D. 1859.
Rebecca P. Welch was born July 8th A.D. 1860.

DEATHS:
Mary A. V. Welch departed this life August 30th 1867, aged 9 years,
     4 months, 16 days.
Amanda T. Welch departed this life September 27th 1867, aged 24 years,
     5 months, 13 days.
Nancy M. Crow Died Aug 21, 1916.

FAMILY RECORDS:

John Nelson, born about 1783, died 15 Aug 1830 in Bedford County, Tenn., Holland Cemetery, married 1 March 1808 in Jefferson County, Tenn., to Elizabeth Mansfield, born about 1787 (Tenn Census), died after 1862 in Rusk County, Texas.
Children:
1: Andrew M. Nelson, born about 1809, Jefferson County, Tenn., died 1836 at Alamo, Texas.
2: Daughter, _____, married _____ Holland, her son: Thomas Blakemore Holland, who married Buena Vista Welch.
3: Rebecca B. Nelson, born about 1812, Jefferson County, Tenn., married John W. Nelson, her 1st cousin.
4: Mary Ann (Polly Anna) Nelson, born 20 Jan 1817 in Jefferson County, Tenn., died 6 May 1895 in Rusk County, Texas.
5: Elizabeth (Betty) Vina Nelson, born 10 Apr 1821, in Jefferson County, Tenn., died in Ellis County, Texas, married _____ Dandridge.
6: John McCampbell Nelson, born 28 Nov 1825 Jefferson County, Tenn., C.S.A., died 26 Apr 1893 in Globe, Arizona.
7: Nancy M. Nelson, born 7 Sept 1827, died 16 Sept 1889 in Rusk County, Texas, married James Little.
8: Amanda C. Nelson, born about 1828 in Bedford County, Tenn., died 27 June 1916 in Clarendon, Texas, married to William D. Little.
There was a Luther Nelson, Ellis Co., Texas, who may have been a son, who had a daughter, Maude.

Robert W. Welch, born 17 Sept 1819, N.C., died Spring of 1902 in Rusk County, Texas at Welch Springs, buried at Pine Grove Cemetery. He married 1st: 1st Oct 1839 in Bedford County, Tenn., to Mary Ann "Polly Anna" Nelson, daughter of John and Elizabeth Mansfield Nelson, born 20 Jan 1817 in Jefferson County, Tenn., died 6 May 1895 in Rusk County, Texas, Welch Springs, buried in Pine Grove Cemetery. They had:
1: Sarah Elizabeth, born 28 Mar 1841 in Bedford County, Tenn., died 9 Jan 1884, married 21 Sept 1862 to Benjamin F. Jones.
2: Amanda T., born 14 Apr 1843 in Bedford County, Tenn., died 27 Sept 1867, married 17 Aug 1865 to Gustavus A. W. Treadwell.
3: Nancy Malinda, born 3 Aug 1845 in Bedford County, Tenn., died 21 Aug 1916, married 9 Sept 1869 to John M. Crow.
4: Beuna Vista, born 12 July 1847 in Bedford County, Tenn., died 1 Nov 1881, married 25 Dec 1871 to Thomas Blakemore Holland.
5: Helen W., born 27 Oct 1849 in Bedford County, Tenn., died 1884, married 1 Oct 1870 to Jesse Knight.
6: Dorothy Ann, born 1 Feb 1852 in Rusk County, Texas, Welch Springs, died 1915, married to Andrew Cannon.
7: Margaret Jane, born 22 Jan 1854 in Rusk County, Texas, died 20 July 1926, married 15 Sept 1875 to Dr. Timothy Deason.
8: Rosetta Washington, born 4 April 1856 in Rusk County, Texas, died 18 May 1929, married 10 Dec 1882 to James Henry Jennings
9: Mary Alice Virginia, born 14 April 1858 in Rusk County, Texas,

died 30 Aug 1867, unmarried.

10: Rebecca P., born 9 July 1860 in Rusk County, Texas, died about 1920, married 18 Oct 1877 to George A. Brock.

JONES BIBLE

In possession of Mrs. James Edwards, Shelbyville, Tennessee
Publisher: American Bible Society, New York, Instituted in the year 1816
          New York   1844

MARRIAGES:
M. C. Jones and Frances Melson was married the 24th dau of January 1838
T. P. Jones and Miss Mary E. Harrison was married the 14 day of Aprile
      1864.
W. R. Jones and Miss Joannah Harrison was married the 18 day of March
      1864.

BIRTHS:
Milinday Elender Jones was bornd the 13th day of November 1838
Rebecker Elizabeth Jones was bornd the 16th day of Aprile 1840
Thomas Jackson Jones was bornd the 2nd day of November 1842
William Robert Jones was bornd the 17th day of February 1845
Brint Calvin Jones was bornd the 9th day of August 1847
Peter Riley Jones was bornd the 22nd day of Aprile 1851

George W. Jones was bornd the nineteenth of March 1854
James Mines Jones was bornd the 22nd of Oct 1857
Marthey Eveline Jones was bornd the 30th day of June 1862

DEATHS:
Rebecker E. Jones died the 27th day of September 1842
Peter Riley Jones Departed this life August the 26th 1855
Bryant Calvin Jones departed this life the 2nd day of September 1869
M. C. Jones Departed this life the 26 day of June 1873

PHILLIPS BIBLE

Photocopy in possession of Mrs. Carlysle Langley, Sr., Shelbyville, Tenn.
Publisher: Jesper Harding, No. 57 South Third Street, Philadelphia 1848
          J. Harding, Printer

MARRIAGES:
Martha Ann Phillips, daughter of Jesse & Elizabeth Phillips married on
      the 14th of August 1851.
Marrgarett Jane Phillips married on the 5th of September 1854.

Mathew James Phillips married on the 10th of January 1855
Malinda J. Phillips married Jany 24th 1861
Meriea Jane Phillips born May 22th 1867
Tennessee Phillips born April 15th 1870
Cathrine E. Phillips was born September the 11, 1872
Samuel H. Phillips was born the 21 Oct 1875

BIRTHS:
Emily W. Phillips was born on the 17 of February 1823
Martha Ann Phillips born September 17, 1824
Thomas G. Phillips born on the 24th of March 1826
Martha T. Phillips born June 29th 1828
Margarett Jane Phillips born June 19th 1832.
Joseph G. Phillips Born Nov 2nd 1858
Emily E. A. Phillips born June 15th 1860
Caldona M. Phillips born September 19th 1861
Margarett M. Phillips born March 23, 1864
John G____ Phillips born ___ 20, 1866

DEATHS:
George W. Phillips died October 15th 1840
Thomas G. Phillips died August 26th, 1833
Emily W. Phillips died on the 9th of October 1855 A.D.
Elizabeth Phillips died June 28th 1859
Jesse Phillips died March 17th 1861
William T. Phillips died Feby 2nd 1857
Adolphus J. Phillips died November the 2, 1870
Mary M. Phillips born March 23, 1864
John G. Phillips born Feb 20, 1866
Tennie Phillips died March 30, 1898
Amanda Phillips died Oct 11, 1900
Mary M. Phillips died May the 23, 1901
Mathew James Phillips died November the 29, 1908
Elizabeth Brown died Oct 6th 1933
John Phillips & Flonnie Thompson married Feb 7, 1892
Bettie Phillips & G. W. Brown married Oct 12, 1893
Kate Phillips & Will Nance married Dec 1, 1897
Sam Phillips & Della Turner married May 25, 1899
Meck (America Jane) Phillips & John Adams married Jan 23, 1901

BARRINGER BIBLE

In possession of Mrs Gust E. Johnson, Shelbyville, Tennessee
Publisher: American Tract Society, 150 Nassau Street, New York

Front Back of Bible: Daniel Laurens Barringer
                       Born-Oct 1st 1788
                       Died-Oct   1852

MYERS BIBLE

In possession of Mrs. Gust E. Johnson, Shelbyville, Tennessee
Publisher: Brattleboro' Typographic Co., Incorporated October 26, 1836,
          Brattleboro, Vt.   1841

Hugh B. Myers, Nov 13, 1876

Row Blakemore

MYERS BIBLE

In possession of Mrs. Gust E. Johnson, Shelbyville, Tennessee
Publisher: Union Publishing Co., 335 Wabash Ave., Chicago

Front page: Aug 26th 1874

MARRIAGES:
Thos. R. Myers and Anne E. W. Blackmore were married at the Blakemore
        house in Shelbyville, by the Rev. T. H. Henson on June 13th, 1871

Hu B. Myers and Rebecca Lipscomb were married in Moore Memorial Church,
        Nashville on the ___ day of ___ 190_.
Paul B. Myers and Florence Hunter were married in Memphis, Tenn., on
        the ___ day of ___ 190_.
Ethel Myers and Dr. Thomas (Fletcher) Bates were married on the ___
        day of July 1914.

MYERS BIBLE

In possession of Mrs. Gust E. Johnson, Shelbyville, Tennessee
Publisher: J. A. Wilmore & Co., New York   1891

Grandparents:
Father's Father: Died   Where
Abram Myers, born 1798Flauvanna Co., Va., 12 May 1849, Trigg Co., Ky.
Father's Mother:
Martha Little Talbot, Dec 5, 1799(44),Person Co., N.C.,
                              died 1883 Bedford Co., Tenn.
Mother's Father:
J. U. Blakemore, June 17, 1811 Lee Co., Va.,
                              died Feb 1, (17) 1878 Bedford Co.
Mother's Mother:
Gaither (?) A. Barringer, Feb 17, 1824, Raleigh, N.C.,
                              died Jan 21, 1873, Bedford Co., Tn.

117

PARENTS:
Father:
Thos. R. Myers, June 17, 1840 Bedford County, Tenn., Jan 15, 1919,
     Shelbyville, Tennessee
Mother:
Anne E. W. Blakemore, Dec 30, 1848, Bedford Co., Tenn., Oct 30, 1936
     Bedford County, Tennessee

Children:
1: Henry Myers, born May 17, 1873 Bedford County, Tennessee, died 1873.
2: Hu B. Myers, born Nov 13, 1876 Bedford Co., Tenn., married Rebecca
     Lipscomb
3: Paul B. Myers, born Mar 22, 1879 Bedford Co., Tenn., married Florence
     Hunter, died Sept 1918.
4: Ethel Myers, born Dec 22, 1884 Bedford Co., Tenn., married July 21,
     1914 to Thomas Fletcher Bates
5: Thos. R. Myers, Jr., born April 1, 1887 Bedford County, Tenn.,
     died Oct 21, 1888.

OBIT:
Anne Eliza Wadsworth Myers, wife of Thos. R. Myers, Born October the
     thirtieth, eighteen hundred and forty-eight; Died October the
     thirtieth, Nineteen Hundred and Six....Burial in Willow Mount,
     Shelbyville, Tennessee.
     Pall Bearers: O. Cowan   H. L. Dayton
                    N. P. Evans   R. W. Clark
                    D. G. Shapard   W. P. Cooper
     Shelbyville, Tennessee November 1st 1906

NEWSPAPER OBIT:
Death of Mrs. T. R. Myers.
          Mrs Annie E. Myers, wife of Hon. Thomas R. Myers, died at her
     home here at 11 o'clock, on Tuesday last. aged 58 years. She
     was the daughter of Dr. A. and Mrs Gartha Blakemore, both of
     whom died here some years ago and was granddaughter of Hon.
     Daniel L. Barringer who served in Congress for many years and
     who was subsequently speaker of one of the houses of the Tenn-
     essee General Assembly. Mrs. Myers was born in Shelbyville, here
     grew to womanhood, and here became the wife of Mr. Myers. She was
     very highly accomplished and justly ranked as one of the most
     brilliant women in the state, although ill for several days, her
     death was somewhat sudden and entirely unexpected. Hence is a
     heavy shock to all Shelbyville and especially so to her family
     and kindred. Mrs. Myers had been a member of the M. E. Church
     South since her girlhood and was a strong believer in the doct-
     rines of that denomination. She stood high in the social and in-
     tellectual circles, not only here but with those throughout the
     state and in other states. She was devoted to her family and
     other relatives and to the friends her death is an irreparable
     lost. We are sincerely sorry to hear her death and tender warmly
     sympathies to the bereaved husband and family.

FUNERAL NOTICE:
John W. Frierson, Born August 21st, 1876; Died July 9th, 1898, aged 21
    years, 10 months and 18 days. The friends and acquaintances of
    John W. Frierson are invited to attend his funeral at the Pres-
    byterian Church at 4:30 o'clock to-morrow afternoon, Sunday July
    10, 1898. Services conducted by Revs. R. C. Anderson and A. M.
    Trawick, Jr. Burial at Willow Mount Cemetery.
    Pall Bearers: Arthur L. Landers   Garrett Stewart
                   Henry W. Woosley   Nat. L. Burton
                   Claude V. Houston   W. H. Morford
    Shelbyville, Tennessee, July 9, 1898.

FUNERAL NOTICE:
Entered into reat at 5 o'clock, A. M., October 2d, 1896, Mrs. Felicia C.
    Frierson. Friends and acquaintances are invited to attend her
    funeral to-morrow, Saturday, at 2 P. M. Services at her late
    residence, conducted by Rev. W. C. Clark. Burial at Willow Mount
    Cemetery.   Shelbyville, Tennessee, Oct. 2d, 1896.

FUNERAL NOTICE:
Mrs. Lucy Swift Frierson was born Sept. 1st 1843- Died in Shelbyville,
    Tennessee, Oct. 7th, 1892, age forty-nine years and twenty-four
    days. Funeral Services from the Presbyterian Church to-day at
    11 o'clock, Saturday, Oct 8th, 1892, by Rev. W. C. Clark, Assist-
    ed by Rev. T. F. Bates.   Shelbyville, Tennessee, Oct 8th, 1892.

FUNERAL NOTICE:
Robert S. Miller--- Born July 23rd, 1835. Died at his home in Shelbyville
    at 10 o'clock A.M., September 3rd, 1896. Services at the M. E.
    Church, South, Friday evening at 3 o'clock, conducted by Revs.
    T. F. Bates and J. E. Wasson.
    Pall Bearers: R. N. Hutton   M. L. Allison
                   W. G. Hight   R. E. Ayers
                   R. W. Clark   E. Shapard
    Honorary Pall Bearers:
                   J. S. Nowlin   G. W. Moody
                   Jno. W. Thompson   R. L. Singleton
                   H. C. Whiteside   J. S. Gillis
    Shelbyville, Tennessee, September 3rd, 1896.

FUNERAL NOTICE:
Robert Brank Davidson. Born March 12th, 1817. Died October 3rd, 1900.
    The relatives and friends are requested to attend his funeral
    at the Presbyterian Church at 10 o'clock a.m., Friday, October
    5th, 1900. Services by Rev. R. C. Anderson. Burial at the Old
    Cemetery.
    Pall Bearers: Dr. J. S. Nowlin   O. Cowan
                   N. P. Evans   T. H. Woods
                   C. S. Ivie   W. S. Bearden
    Shelbyville, Tennessee, October 4th, 1900.

FUNERAL NOTICE:
J. A. Blakemore was born March 27, 1858; died in Charleston, West Va.,
    March 12, 1906. The friends and acquaintances of the family are
    invited to attend his funeral at the home of his brother, Thos.
    R. Myers, at 2:30 o'clock, March 14, 1906. Services by Rev. J. B.
    Erwin, assisted by Rev. W. S. Taylor.
    Pall Bearers: Chas. S. Ivie   H. L. Dayton
                   M. C. Webb   W. S. Bomar
                   Chas. J. Thompson T. C. Lipscomb
    Shelbyville, Tennessee, March 14, 1906.

NOTE: There is a Picture of George Floyd of Flat Creek, inside this
    Bible. "A Tennessee Boy who recently died in the Army in
    Phillippines."

MALLARD BIBLE

Copy by Mrs. Amie C. McGrew, Shelbyville, Tennessee
Publisher: Collins Stereotype Edition, Published by Charles Ewer,
    Boston   1812
NOTE: Grace Mallard Long, who remembers seeing the Bible many times
    when she was a child, says it originally belonged to Thornton
    Mallard. She also·says that it once had other pages of Family
    information.

(Thornton) was born the 13th of October 1769
(Elisabeth) was born the 22nd December 1769
(John) their eldest son was born the 4th September 1789
(George) was born the 6th March 1791
Sarah was born the 29th October 1794
Eldridge was born the 26th September 1797
Richard was born the 4 September 1800
Deborah was born the 8th February 1802
William was born the 29th May 1804
James was born the 29th April 1806
Joseph was born the 21st March 1809
Rebecca was born the 22nd February 1811
Alfred was born the 4th October 1813.

John Mallard Shot by the British at Orleans the 28th and died the 29
    of December 1814 in the 25th year of his age.

William died the 11th August 1806 in the 3rd year of his age.
James died the 11th March 1829 in the 23rd year of his age.
Thornton Mallard died July 13th 1842 in the 73rd year of his age.
Elizabeth Mallard died November 20th 1845 in the 76th year of her age.
Alfred Mallard died July 17th 1854 in the 41 year of his age.
George Franklin Mallard died the 12th of June 187?.

Deborah died Oct 8th 1844.

On page opposite 536:
George Franklin Mallard was born Sept 28, 1840.
Mary Jane Mallard was born March 1, 1842.
Eldridge Thornton Aug 13th 1843.
Martha Ann Nov 7th 1844
Eliza June 23rd 1846
Sarah Christina Jan 8, 1848
Samuel Bell, May 21st, 1850
Susan Elizabeth, Oct 30th, 1851
Hariett Tennessee, March 21st, 1853

George F. Mallard died June 12, 1859
Mary Jane died Aug 13th, 1865
Sarah Mallard died Jan 1895   Grandma.

Piece of paper pinned to page 536:
S. B. Mallard was born May 21st 1850
Fannie B. Mallard was born was born May 15th 1848
Hattie T. Mallard was born Oct 6th 1874
Mary Edna Mallard was born Aug 18, 1882
Marvin M.(S.) Mallard was born May 8, 1884
Grace M. Mallard was born Feb 20, 1887
Clara Bell Mallard was born Aug 21st 1888

Clara Bell Mallard died Sept 16, 1889
S. B. Mallard & Fannie B. Harris were married Sept 22, 1881
Alfred T. Mallard was born Sept 18, 1890

CLEMENT CANNON, JR. BIBLE

Copy by Mrs. Amie C. McGrew, Shelbyville, Tennessee
Publisher: Jesper Harding, Philadelphia   1854
        The original owner of this Bible was Clement Cannon, Jr., Bedford
        County, Tennessee. The present owner is Miss Sara Cooper.

FAMILY RECORD:
Clement Cannon, Jr., was born April 1st 1823
Mary S. Yell   January 2, 1823
Sarah Blythe Cannon   January 21, 1847
Archibald Yell Cannon   Oct 21, 1850
Sarah B. Cannon   May 4, 1852
Archibald Yell Cannon   February 10th, 1856
John Scott Cannon &
Samuel Clement Cannon were born July 8th, 1858
Cora Yell Cannon born 23 August 1865
Clement Cannon born Sept 26, 1887

Daughter of Samuel Cannon....

MARRIAGES, WHEN AND WHERE:
Clement Cannon, Jr., & Mary S. Yell married April 7, 1846.
Alexander Byers and Sallie B. Cannon married July 4, 1872.
Samuel Clement Cannon and Minnie Lewis Wood married Sept 6, 1886.

DEATHS, WHEN AND WHERE:
Sarah B. Cannon died 6th March 1847,(aged 2 years, 1 mos, 13 days.)
(The date on her tombstone is 1849, and this date tallies with the age
       in parentheses)   · .
Archibald Y. Cannon died March 31, 1852.
Archibald Yell Cannon died March 22, 1862.
Clement Cannon died August 23, 1866.
Sallie B. Byers died Sept 5, 1872.
Mary Y. Cannon died Jan 22, 1891.
John S. Cannon died May 22, 1894.
Samuel C. Cannon died July 4th, 1894.
Cora Y. Cannon died Nov 26, 1955, Chatanooga, aged 90 years. Buried at
       Fairfield.

JACKSON LILE BIBLE

From the files of Helen C. Marsh, From the National Archives,
       Washington, D. C.   JACKSON LILE   W.116 B.L.Wt. 26662-160

Jackson Lile was born December 10th day A.D. 1761
Elizabeth Hester was born November 1st A.D.1774
Jackson Lile & Elizabeth Hester was married July 18th day 1793

James Hester Lile first child of Jackson & Elizabeth Lile was born
       October 12th day A.D. 1794
Benjamin Lile was born March 17th day A.D. 1797
Sally Lile was born September 4th day A.D. 1798
William Lile was born September 25th day A.D. 1800
Rebecca Lile was born July 8th day A.D. 1803
Nancy Lile was born March 7th day 1810
Clary Lile was born August 29th day 1812
Elizabeth Lile was born the 9th May 1814
Jackson Lile was born March 2nd day 1816

Sally Lile was married 23 Jan 1816
James H. Lile was married 7th Nov 1816
Wm. Lile was married 29 Aug 1820
Rebeca Lile was married 29 Oct 1821
Benjamin Lile was married 5th Sep 1822
Jackson Lile was married 25 Dec 1834
Elizabeth Lile was married 2nd April 1835.

\.

WILLIAM TEAGUE BIBLE

Files of Helen C. Marsh, From National Archives, Washington, D.C.
WILLIAM TEAGUE W.208

William Teague was born the 23rd of November in the year of our Lord,
1761 A.D.
Elizabeth Teague was born the 22nd of June in the year of our Lord,
1768

John Teague, son of the above parents was born the 21st of June in the
year of our Lord 1786 A.D.
Rebecca Teague was born the 13th of May A.D. 1788
Margaret Teague was born the 5th of Feby A.D. 1790
Sarah Teague was born the 1st of February A.D. 1792
James Teague was born the 2nd of Feby A.D. 1794

GSA RECORD:
William Teague died 23 Sept 1848 in Wilson County, Tennessee.
Elizabeth Teague was living 24th April 1849 in Wilson County, Tenn.,
age 81 years.
They were married 3rd July 1785 in Lawrence County, South Carolina.

THOMAS ALDRICH SIKES BIBLE

Files of Helen C. Marsh, From National Archives, Washington, D. C.
THOMAS ALDRICH SIKES W.991

Thomas A. Sikes born abt 1760 Virginia, died Sept 5, 1835
married 13 Oct 1783 to Sarah

Elisabeth An Sikes was born September the 5, 1785
Jese Sikes was born October the 13, 1787
Susanna Sikes was born April the 10, 1789
Rebecker Sikes was born September the 16, 1791
Jonas Sikes was born July the 3, 1793
Nancy Sikes was born July the 3, 1795
John and Mary Sikes was born August the 25, 1797
Robert Sikes was born October the 16, 1799
Anna Johns West was born July the 25, 1809

Nancy Lowe was born December the 14, 1796
William Lowe was born October the 1, 1798

MARTIN SHOFNER FAMILY RECORDS

Ref: DAR # 272410, The DAR 1941-42 year book, page 101-102.

Martin Shofner, born December 3, 1758 in Orange Co., N.C., died in
      Bedford County Tennessee September 30, 1838. Married July 7,
      1780 in Duplin County, N.C., to Catherine Cook.
Catherine Cook born May 27, 1762 & died June 14, 1823.

Children:
1: Margaret Shofner, married Philip Burrow
2: Tessey Shofner, married Adam Euless
3: John Shofner, married Amelia Shoffner, 2nd to Miss Beams
4: Christian Shofner, married Elizabeth Jennings
5: Eva Shofner, married William Holt
6: Fred Shofner, married _____ Coble
7: Austin Shofner, born Aug 12, 1801, died Oct 18, 1852, married
      Katherine _____, born April 21, 1798, died Oct 10, 1875
8: Dorotha Shofner, married Adam Euless

CAPT. CHRISTOPHER SHAW FAMILY RECORD

Ref: Texas DAR, page 1907

Christopher Shaw, born in Edgefield Dist., S. C., on October 25, 1765
      and died in Bedford County Tennessee on February 22, 1832,
      married Mary Butler in Edgefield Dist., S. C., in 1808, She was
      born 1779 & died 1861 in Bedford County, Tennessee.

Children:
1: Thomas Lewis Shaw
2: David William Shaw, married Elizabeth Cunningham
3: Christopher George*
4: Washington Brooks Shaw, married 1st Sophia Armstrong & 2nd Martha
      Keyser.
5: Robert Charles Shaw
6: Cotesworth Pinckney Shaw, born April 17, 1817, married Sarah Ann
      Morris
*C. G. W. B. Shaw & Martha Shaw
  Oct 29, 1811   born   1811 Pa.
  Oct 6, 1852   died   buried in Shaw Cemetery, Bedford Co.,
                              Tennessee, near Fairfield, Tenn. Eds.

NOTE: On child No. 2: David A. J. B. Shaw, son of C. & Mary Shaw, died
     Jan 3, 1826, aged 16 years, 5 months & 18 days. (New Hope Church
     Cemetery, Fairfield, Tennessee, Bedford County)

SAMUEL SARRETT BIBLE

Files of Helen C. Marsh, National Archives, Washington, D.C.
    SAMUEL SARRETT No. W.5981

Samuel Sarrett born about 1754, died April 1st, 1821, married Nancy,
    24th May 1792 on the Line of Person and Caswell County, N.C.

BIBLE RECORD:
Joseph Sarrett, son of Samuel Sarrett and Nancy Sarrett, was born
    June the 3rd, 1793 .
James Sarrett, November 15th, 1794
Samuel G. Sarrett, was born April 1st, 1796
Hiram M. Sarrett born Sept. the 2nd, 1800

Also mentions a Nephew: Wilson Sarrett of Davidson County, Tennessee.
    Sept 7, 1818.

ANTHONY REAGOR FAMILY RECORD

Ref: DAR Lineage Reference

Anthony Reagor born 1760, died Sept 7, 1824 in Bedford County, Tennessee,
    married Margaret Shook, born 1766 and died Sept 18, 1838.

Children:
1: William Reagor, born Aug 10, 1790 in Knox County, Tenn.
2: John Reagor, born Jan 3, 1792 in Knox County, Tenn.
3: Mary Magdalene Reagor, born Dec 9, 1793, died Bedford County, Tenn.,
    on Nov 22, 1856, married 1811 to David Floyd, born June 19, 1786,
    and died Dec 18, 1856. Buried in Shook Cemetery. 9 children.
4: Jacob Reagor, born Oct 10, 1795, died young.
5: Anthony Wayne Reagor, born June 18, 1797, died June 8, 1846, married
    Rhoda Boone Dec 10, 1820, Rhoda Boone Reagor was born Nov 17,
    1803 and died April 23, 1846. Both buried in Shook Cemetery, Bed-
    ford County, Tennessee.

JAMES PATTON FAMILY RECORD

Ref: DAR # 490632   Certificate # 4842 Military Service of N. C.,
                     Morgan Dictrict.

James Patton born Feb 20, 1764 Buncombe Co., N.C., died Aug 9, 1827 in
    Bedford County, Tennessee, married Aug 3, 1784 in Buncombe Co.,
    N.C. to Sarah Cunningham, born Dec 12, 1765 in Buncombe Co., N.C.,

125

died Aug 13, 1825 in Bedford County, Tennessee.

Children:
1: Margaret, born Oct 5, 1785, married William Hannah
2: Rhoda, born Mar 12, 1787, married Thomas Couch
3: Jane, born Mar 14, 1789, married Joseph Erwin(Irwine)
4: Sarah, born Mar 27, 1791, married Joseph Haynes
5: Thomas, born Mar 11, 1793, died in infancy
6: Elizabeth, born Nov 30, 1794, married Robert Haynes
7: Katherine, born July 10, 1796, died Mar 10, 1886, married Nov 4,
    1813 to Joseph Couch .
8: Magdaline, born Dec 16, 1797, married Robert Waite
9: James Erwin, born Apr 5, 1799, married 1st Mary Cowser, 2nd Mrs.
    Mary Snead
10: Abigail, born Dec 11, 1800, married Jacob Anderson
11: Mary, born Apr 10, 1802, married Enoch Haynes
12: Nancy Ann, born Aug 8, 1803, married Rev. Silas Morrison
13: Humphrey, born July 21, 1805, died in infancy
14: Keziah, born Feb 24, 1809, married _____ Hanceford, 2nd _____
    Davidson.

TEMPLETON BIBLE

Taken from: Lincoln County Tennessee Bible Records, by Tucker & Waller.
    Vol. 4.
Bible in possession of John D. Templeton, Shelbyville, Tennessee

John H. Templeton was born March 27th, 1812
Avus Whitty Cashion was born August 6th, 1817

Sarah Emaline Templeton, daughter of John H. & A. W. Templeton, was born
    Sept 6th, 1838
James Palis Templeton, son of John H. & A. W. Templeton, was born Feb
    19th, 1840
Mary Elizabeth Templeton, daughter of John H. & A. W. Templeton, was
    born Nov 26th, 1842
Robert Henry, son of J. H. Templeton was born March the 1, 1845
Wm. Eden was born Aprile the 10, 1847, the son of John H. & A. W.
    Templeton
Andrew J. Christian was borned Oct the 22, 1840 this the 17 day of
    Jan 1858
NOTE: (Neighbor. Pencil entry)
NOTE: Here follows same information as first six above, except middle
    initials are used instead of full middle names.
Abner W. M. Templeton was born March 17th, 1850
Nancy J. Templeton was born Oct 2, 1852
John Rufus Templeton was born August 22nd 1859
James Palis Templeton, son of John & A. W. Templeton was borned

february the 19, 1840
James H. Templeton was born April 27, the year 1821
John H. Templeton & Avus Whitty Cashion was married Nov 9, 1837
John W. Lenord and Sarah E. Templeton was married february the 5, 1855
James A. Michael was bornd October the 9th 1865
Avus E. Michael was borned february the 10th 1868
Josy Ann Michael was born April the 8th 1871
John F. Michael was born October 16th, 1873

Sarah Templeton died August 18th 1840
Robert Templeton died Oct __, 1816
James Cashion died Oct 15, 1831
James P. Templeton, son of J. H. & A. W. Templeton died Feb 26th, 1859
J. H. Templeton died Dec 2nd 1877
Avus W. Templeton died July 2nd 1881
Mary Cashion died May 6, 1826

JOEL VANNOY BIBLE

In possession of Mrs Marie Arnold, Richmond, Texas
Copied at Miss Mary V. Bass, Wartrace, Tennessee

FAMILY RECORD OF MRS. MARIE ARNOLD:
Andrew Vannoy, born Nov 4, 1783 & died Jan 25, 1869 in Shelbyville,
    Bedford County, Tennessee. He married first: Nov 30, 1809 in
    Wilkes Co., N.C.; to Elizabeth Dogan, born about 1787 & died
    Aug 31, 1819. He married second: Jan 7, 1821 to Jane McMichael,
    she probably died Shelbyville, Tenn., date: Feb 15, 1872.
Andrew Vannoy was a devout member of the Baptist Church, a gifted School-
    teacher and Clerk of the Bedford County Tennessee Court for many
    years. Andrew had two other brothers: one named Nathaniel. They
    were the sons of Joel Vannoy & Mary Reese, his wife. Their first
    three (3) sons were born in Wilkes Co., N.C. A Son, Andrew, was
    born Aug 30, 1812, Bedford County, Tenn.
The three brothers went to Nacogdoches Co., Texas. The Vannoy's were
    Dutch. 3 of the Vannoys went to Anderson Co., Texas & several
    went to Pike Co., Missouri.
Mr. John B. Foster, born 1852, a great grandson of Nathaniel Vannoy,
    Andrew's brother, stated in his application for membership into
    the "Sons of the American Revolution"- Andrew was granted bounty
    land for War Service, it was near Murfreesboro, Rutherford Co.,
    Tenn., his wife was Susanna Sheppard. Nathaniel Vannoy was a
    Revolutionary Soldier, buried in Greenville, S. C. His grave is
    marked with a Revolutionary War Marker. He was living with his
    daughter Sarah Cleveland.

VANNOY BIBLE
Joel Vannoy was born February 23rd A.D. 1777

127

Mary (Reese) Vannoy his wife was born 7th December A.D. 1781
John Vannoy, a son was born Nov 25th, 1801
Jesse Vannoy, son was born Oct 1st 1803
Isaac R. Vannoy Born April 14th, 1809
Andrew Vannoy Born August 30th, 1812
Eliza Ann Vannoy Born Sept 17th, 1814
Nealy (Cornealous Peter) Vannoy Born May 15th, 1817
Sarah Jane Vannoy Born April 27th, 1820

NOTE: Written into Record:
> Joel Vannoy was born in Wilkes Co., N.C., on Lewis Fork Creek,
> farm of his Father Nathaniel Vannoy, adjoining those of Robert
> Cleveland, brother of Benjamin Cleveland of Kings Mt. Fame,
> Jeremiah Cleveland, son of Robert Cleveland, married Sarah,
> daughter of Nathaniel Vannoy. Capt. Andrew Vannoy lived in Bed-
> ford County, Tenn., too, (A Uncle of Joel Vannoy) Rev. Soldier of
> Kings Mt.

MARRIAGES:
Bennett Smith and Mary Ann Susan Vannoy, on 21st February 1843
George M. Gaut to Mary Jane Smith, July 15th, 1863
Andrew J. Hamilton to Altha Pauline Smith, December 19th, 1866
Egbert V. Smith to Allice M. Moore, Decr 18th A.D. 1873
Robert B. Smith to Eugene Camron, February 5, 1885
R. L. Smith to Kate Smith, July 1902
Sam Malone to Addie Pauline Smith, Feb 8, 1912

DEATHS:
Camaro Augustus Smith, on the 8 of June 1853 of Flux.
Samuel Jarrett Smith on the 24 of September A.D., of conjestion of
    Bowells
Samuel Smith (Father of Bennett Smith) died 27 May 1856, aged 90 years,
    8 months, 29 days.
Mary Smith (Mary Jarret), mother of Bennett Smith, died 8 of April 1862,
    aged 86 years, 10 months & 16 days.

SMITH BIBLE

In possession of Mrs. Marie Arnold, Richmond, Texas

MARRIAGES:
Bennett Smith to Mary S. Vannoy, 28th February 1843.
George M. Gaut to Mary Jane Smith, 15 July 1863.
Andrew J. Hamilton to Altha Pauline Smith on 19th December 1866.
Egbert Vannoy Smith to Missouri A. Moore, December 18th, 1873.
Robert B. Smith married to Eugena Cameron, February 5, 1885.

BIRTHS:
Mary Anne Susan Vannoy born May 31, 1823
Joel Vannoy, Jr., born April 27, 1825.
Joel Vannoy, Senr. and Mary Reese was married 16 Oct 16th 1800

DEATHS:
Mary Vannoy on 21st November 1835, sick 9 months.
Joel Vannoy Sr on 8th February 1840
Nealy P. Vannoy on 30th March 1842

MARRIAGES:
Bennett Smith to Mary S. Vannoy 28 February 1843
George M. Gaut to Mary Jane Smith, 15 July 1863
Andrew J. Hamilton to Altha Pauline Smith on 19th December 1866.
Egbert Vannoy Smith to Missouri A. Moore, December 18th 1873.
Robert B. Smith maried to Eugena Cameron, February 5, 1885

DEATHS:
Camaro Augustus, Sen. died on the 8th of June 1853 of Flux.
Samuel T. Smith died on the 24 of September A.D. 1866 of conjestion of
    Bowells.
Altha P. More, nee Smith, on 17 December, died 1896 in San Antonio, Texas
Mary Susan Smith on January 28, 1898, 74 yrs, 8 mo old.
Bennett Smith, Dec 8th 1904.
Altha P. Hamilton, Oct 1915, Madill, Okla.
Mary Jane Gaut, died April 5, 1926, age 81 years, 2 mos & 5 days.
Egbert V. Smith, died Jan 2, 1927, 75 years, 2 mos & 24 days.

OBITS: From Newspaper clippings:
Mrs Mary Susan Smith, wife of Bennet Smith, died Jan 28, 1898, at an
advanced age of 74 years, 7 months and 28 days. She was born in Bedford
County, Tenn., May 31, 1823. She moved to Macogdoches County, Texas, in
1842, and was married to Bennet Smith Feb 21, 1843. She moved to Hill
County in 1869, and settled near Woodbury, where she resided until her
death. Unto them were born six children. She leaves a devoted husband,
aged 91, quite a number of grand children, two sons and two daughters
to mourn her loss, namely, Messers. R. B. and E. V. Smith, of this Community, Mrs Altha Hamilton of Peoria and Mrs. Jane Gaut of Smith Co.,
Texas.

ITEM: Nov 11, 1904   Hillsboro, Texas (Saturday)
    Judge Bennett Smith of Woodbury, ten miles northwest of Hillsboro,
who is 98 years of age and voted for Andrew Jackson, was at the polls
last Tuesday and voted for the Democratic Party. Judge Smith was born in
Buncombe County, N. C., Sept 25, 1806 and voted for Jackson in 1824 and
has continued to vote the Democratic Ticket ever since.
    The Judge moved to Texas in 1839, when Texas was a Republic, and
is well acquainted with frontier life.
    He was County Judge of Rusk County four years. He lived in East
Texas thirty-four years and then moved to Hill County in 1867 and has
resided in the County ever since. His wife was born in 1823 and died in

1898. The Judge is in the best of health and lively for one 98 years of age. He is the father of six children.

OBIT: JUDGE BENNETT SMITH
Died, at 11 o'clock on December 8th, 1904. Judge Bennett Smith, aged 98 years, two months and fourteen days. He was buried at Woodbury by the side of his wife who died a few years ago.

Notwithstanding his great age, Judge Smith's faculties, both mental and physical were all well preserved till the last.

Bennett Smith was born in Buncombe County, N. C., September 25, 1806, where he grew to manhood, from which place he emigrated to Georgia, where he spent nine years of his life and from there he came to Nacogdoches County, in 1839, which County then comprised a good portion of Eastern Texas, where he located was finally organized into Rusk County, and there he remained 39 years. In 1869, he came to Hill County and settled near Woodbury where he spent the last 35 years of his life.

Bro. Smith was perhaps the oldest Mason in Texas. He was a member of the Methodist E. Church, South.

JOHNSON BIBLE

Copied at Miss Mary V. Bass, Wartrace, Tennessee

This Certifies that W. M. Johnson of Shelbyville, State of Tennessee and Margaret Louise Roper of Greenville, State of South Carolina, were by me united in Holy Matrimony according to the Ordinance of God and the Laws of the State of Tennessee, Normandy, on the 15 day of May in the Place of our Lord 1861.   Signed: Nath Sphere

Father of W. M. Johnson was Major J. M. Johnson.
Mother of W. M. Johnson was Malinda Greene Johnson.

Children of W. M. Johnson and Margaret Louise Roper Johnson:
Alice E. Johnson born May 12, 1864
Ada Florence Johnson born Feb 29, 1868
Hattie May Johnson born Nov 29, 1871
James Arthur Johnson born July 29, 1875
Sarah Malinda Johnson born Jan 19, 1879
Earl Conquest Johnson born April 19 1882
Grover Cleveland Johnson born March 22, 1885

MARRIAGES:
Ada Florence Johnson married Oct 9, 1892
Hattie May Johnson married Oct 9, 1892
Sarah Malinda Johnson married Oct 24, 1894
James Arthur Johnson married June 1896
Earl Conquest Johnson married Jan 12, 1907

Birthday of Margaret Louise Roper, August 6, 1846
Birthday of W. M. Johnson was Sept 25, 1842

DEATHS:
Grover Cleveland Johnson died June 18, 1911
Hattie May Johnson Bradshaw died June 25, 1911
Alice E. Johnson died Sept 22, 1868
Ada Florence Johnson Corbin died Nov 24, 1938
Sarah Malinda Johnson Criswell died .....
Earl Conquest Johnson died ......
James Arthur Johnson died :...
W. M. Johnson died March 4, 1922
Margaret Louise Roper Johnson died Jan 12, 1929
W. M. Johnson died March 4, 1922 and is buried in the Wilson Cemetery,
      East of Eaton, Tenn., He was married to Margaret Louise Roper,
      April 30, 1861.

DOZIER BIBLE

In possession of Mrs. Betty J. Cravy, Columbus, Georgia.

MARRIAGES:
Zachariah Dozier and Cyntha Ann Johnson were married April 3rd, 1828.
W. M. Dozier and N. C. Talley was married 12 Nove 1868.
Charlie N. Cowden & Ada M. Dozier was married the 7 Aug 1886.

BIRTHS:
Zachariah Dozier was born July 12th, 1800
Cyntha Ann Johnson wife of Zachariah Dozier was born Dec 21st, 1808
Joseph Thomas Dozier was born Feb 8th 1829.
Mary Evens Dozier was born Oct 26, 1830.
Arabella Dozier was born Nov 5th 1832
Sarah Ann Dozier was born Jan 1st 1839
Paul Dozier was born Nov 22nd 1840
William Talley was born August 10, 1814
Elizabeth A. Talley was born Oct the 10th, 1817
_____ __ _____ was born Nov 27, 1871
Donie Latita Neill was born the 25th of Aug 1881
William M. Dozier was born December 15, 1834
Narcissa C. Talley was born October 8, 1847
Ada May Dozier was born September 7, 1869
Infant Son was born June 26, 1871
William Zachariah Dozier was born May 18th 1877
Mary D. Cowder was born Fryday 16th of December 1887
William Eugene Cowden was born the 5th, Fryday Nov 188_(7)
John Cowden was born Saturday the 11th of April 1890
Raith Cowden was born July 20th, 1901.
Mildred Cowden was born December 16th, 1904

DEATHS:
Infant Son dide July - 1871
W. M. Dozier died Nov 24, 1902, Monday Morning 9 o'clock.
Ada Dozier Cowder dide June 23rd, 1918
Charlie Norris Cowden died Thursday night at 11 o'clock April 20th, 1933
William M. Dozier died October 30th, 1955
Mother dide the 28 of Nov. 1882
My Father dide the 31st of March 1885

Mother, Narcissa C. Talley Dozier, died Saturday morning at 3 o'clock
Aug 11th, 1934.

Zachariah Dozier died Feb 20th, 1870
Cyntha Ann Johnson Dozier died Sunday July 5th, 1885
Joseph T. Dozier died Sept 26th, 1863

HOOSER BIBLE

In possession of Miss Edmund Hooser, Wartrace, Tennessee
Publisher: Missing

MARRIAGES:
Daniel Hooser & Frances Kimbro was married August 15th, 1830
John A. Couch & Sarah Jane Hooser was married October 20, 1853
Frances Hooser was born July the 11th, 1807
Daniel Hooser was born June the 1st, 1807
George M. Hooser and Harriet V. Holt was married February the 4th, 1864

BIRTHS:
Mary Ann Hooser was born August 20th, 1831
George Marion Hooser was born November the 4th, 1832
Sarah Jane Hooser was born March the 1st, 1836
Rachel Lucinda and Harriet Luisa Hooser was born April 1st, 1839
William Mitchell Hooser was born December the 18th, 1840
Martha Frances Hooser was born November the 12th, 1842
Eliza Almeda Hooser was born November the 3rd, 1844
Sepronia Alexander Hooser was born October the 9th, 1847
Virginia Ann Hooser was born March the 25, 1850

DEATHS:
Rachel Lucinda Hooser departed this life October the 16th, 1841
Harriet Luisa departed this life May 31st, 1849
Mary Ann Hooser departed this life August 12th, 1856
Sarah Jane Couch Departed this life May the 16th, 1863
Daniel Hooser Departed this life April the 2nd, 1864

Seperate page: Frances Hooser Departed this life May 6, 1885
William Mitchell Hooser departed this life Dec 15, 1907

JOHN BENTON McNATT BIBLE

In possession of Mrs Noel Paisley Chittam, Jr., Elkmont, Alabama
Copied from Lincoln County Tennessee Bible Records, Vol. 1.

J. B. (John Benton) McNatt of Lincoln County, Tennessee and A. E.
(Annie) Raby of Lincoln County, Tennessee, were united in Holy Matri-
mony 3rd of January 1869 at Residence of Rev. Green Nichols. Witness:
J. R. Raby·and John Gill.

MARRIAGES:
J. E. Bartlett and M. E. (Etta) McNatt united in marriage 6th of August
    1890.
E. Warren and S. T. McNatt united in marriage 17th September 1893.
J. B. McNatt and Nancy I. Brown united in marriage 17th October 1893.
J. B. (John Birgie) McNatt and Yullar Bedwell united in marriage 7th
    January 1894.
J. B. (John Benton) McNatt and J. M. E. (Dolly) Seagraves united in
    marriage 25th January 1897.
Clarence McNatt and Leona Boyd united in marriage 22nd December 1897.

BIRTHS: ·
Leona (Boyd) McNatt borned 8th May 1891
Nancy I. McNatt borned 7th September 1851
J. B. (John Benton) McNatt borned 14th February 1848
A. E. (Annie) McNatt borned 12th September 1848
L. T. (Tennie) McNatt borned 5th November 1869
M. E. (Etta) McNatt borned 21st December 1871
J. B. (John Birgie) McNatt borned 20th April 1874
S. E. (Lizzie) McNatt borned 7th February 1876
D. C. McNatt borned 7th September 1878
Cora McNatt borned 20th July 1881
W. O. (Will) McNatt borned 18th August 1883
G. A. (Annie) McNatt borned 5th December 1885
Clarence McNatt borned 17th January 1888
Florence McNatt borned 17th January 1888
Nelly M. McNatt borned 1st February 1890
B. A. Brown borned 15th August 1871

DEATHS:
D. C. McNatt departed this life 4th April 1880
John McNatt departed this life 22nd June 1880
Mary McNatt departed this life 1st March 1902
Elizabeth Raby McNatt departed this life 31st May 1887
E. B. (Ept Birgie) Raby departed this life 24th February 1895
A. E. (Annie) McNatt departed this life 4th March 1892
Nancy McNatt departed this life 11th May 1896
Yullar McNatt departed this life 5th March 1895
L. T. (Tennie) Prosser departed this life 14th March 1902
Lisan McNatt departed this life 18th March 1912
Willie McNatt departed this life 6th November 1912

JOHN BENTON McNATT BIBLE

In possession of Mrs Noel Paisley Chittam, Jr., Elkmont, Alabama
Copied from Lincoln County Tennessee Bible Records, Vol. 1.

J. B. (John Benton) McNatt of Lincoln County, Tennessee and A. E.
(Annie) Raby of Lincoln County, Tennessee, were united in Holy Matri-
mony 3rd of January 1869 at Residence of Rev. Green Nichols. Witness:
J. R. Raby and John Gill.

MARRIAGES:
J. E. Bartlett and M. E. (Etta) McNatt united in marriage 6th of August
    1890.
E. Warren and S. T. McNatt united in marriage 17th September 1893.
J. B. McNatt and Nancy I. Brown united in marriage 17th October 1893.
J. B. (John Birgie) McNatt and Yullar Bedwell united in marriage 7th
    January 1894.
J. B. (John Benton) McNatt and J. M. E. (Dolly) Seagraves united in
    marriage 25th January 1897.
Clarence McNatt and Leona Boyd united in marriage 22nd December 1897.

BIRTHS:
Leona (Boyd) McNatt borned 8th May 1891
Nancy I. McNatt borned 7th September 1851
J. B. (John Benton) McNatt borned 14th February 1848
A. E. (Annie) McNatt borned 12th September 1848
L. T. (Tennie) McNatt borned 5th November 1869
M. E. (Etta) McNatt borned 21st December 1871
J. B. (John Birgie) McNatt borned 20th April 1874
S. E. (Lizzie) McNatt borned 7th February 1876
D. C. McNatt borned 7th September 1878
Cora McNatt borned 20th July 1881
W. O. (Will) McNatt borned 18th August 1883
G. A. (Annie) McNatt borned 5th December 1885
Clarence McNatt borned 17th January 1888
Florence McNatt borned 17th January 1888
Nelly M. McNatt borned 1st February 1890
B. A. Brown borned 15th August 1871

DEATHS:
D. C. McNatt departed this life 4th April 1880
John McNatt departed this life 22nd June 1880
Mary McNatt departed this life 1st March 1902
Elizabeth Raby McNatt departed this life 31st May 1887
E. B. (Ept Birgie) Raby departed this life 24th February 1895
A. E. (Annie) McNatt departed this life 4th March 1892
Nancy McNatt departed this life 11th May 1896
Yullar McNatt departed this life 5th March 1895
L. T. (Tennie) Prosser departed this life 14th March 1902
Lisan McNatt departed this life 18th March 1912
Willie McNatt departed this life 6th November 1912

Frances Ann Bayley Brown was born May 1, 1850
Martha J. Brown was born Jan 14, 1852
Sarah Malissa Brown was born Nov 12, 1853
John Franklin Brown was born March 31, 1855
William Davidson Brown was born March 31, 1855
Nancy Matilda Brown was born Jan 19, 1857
Margaret Jane Brown was born Dec 4, 1859

Humphrey·Cunningham was born April 13, 1777
Margaret Patton was born June 12, 1780
G. W. Cunningham was born Oct 22, 1802
T. P. Cunningham was born Jan 13, 1805
T. P. Cunningham was born June 23, 1806
James E. Cunningham was born Feb 8, 1809
J. W. C. Cunningham was born March 27, 1812
W. N. Cunningham was born Dec 13, 1814
H. L. D. Cunningham was born Dec 29, 1819
J. A. Cunningham was born March 6, 1822
Caye F. Cunningham was born Feb 27, 1824

SLAVES:
Allen, son of Harriet was born March 23, 1846
Merriah,   do   do was born December 1848

Louisa Jane Brown was born June 26, 1850
James Rutledge Roberts was born June 9, 1867
Jesse Mourton was born Nov 5, 1873
Pleasant Lee Brown was born Jan 25, 1872
John Thomas Brown was born Dec 2, 1874
Julia Delk was born Dec 30, 1882
John Delk was born Feb 12, 1888

DEATHS:
Margaret H. Brown died June 30, 1842
Jennett Brown died Aug 13, 1852
Louisy Jane Brown died July 13, 1870
R. R. Roberts died Jan 9, 1870
William D. Brown died Sept 29, 1873
America P. Roberts died Jan 30, 1875
Marthy J.Brown died March 6, 1878
Humphry Cunningham died Aug 15, 1836
Margaret Patton Cunningham died Feb 3, 1847
Nancy M. Brown died Dec 5, 1878
John F. Brown died Dec 7, 1879
Margaret M. Brown died Oct 27, 1888
W. D. Welch died March 7, 1921
NOTE: Mrs. William T. Cleek, Julia Delk Cleek, is a grand-daughter of
     Frederick Brown. She is 90 years old in 1973)

WOMACK FAMILY RECORDS

Taken from: Genealogy of Michael Womack, by Miss Virginia Buxton

Michael Womack, born 1794 in Virginia & migrated to Bedford County, Tenn.
with his parents. He was one of the 23 who enlisted in War of 1812 from
Bedford County, Tennessee, under Capt. Barrett, West Tennessee Militia,
at N.O., Jan 8, 1815., After War, he returned to Tennessee and married,
1815 in Bedford County, Tennessee, to Sarah Jones, daughter of Charles
& Rebecca Norman Jones, who had removed from Union County, S. C.
Children:
1: Charles W. Womack, born Dec 8, 1816 in Bedford County, Tenn.,
   died Aug 4, 1888.
2: Mariah H. Womack, born 1818 Bedford County, Tennessee & died
   Nov 27, 1886 Howard County, Ark.
3: John W. Womack, born 1822 Bedford County, Tennessee, died 1857
   Howard County, Ark.
4: Tacy Womack, born 1823 Bedford County, Tennessee, died Dec 27,
   1879 in Howard County, Ark.
5: Nancy Womack, born Mar 6, 1825 Bedford County, Tennessee, died
   Apr 25, 1915 in Howard County, Ark.
6: Katie A. Womack, born Sept 13, 1827 Bedford County, Tennessee,
   & died Apr 1, 1897 in Howard County, Ark.
7: David Dickins Womack, born Dec 7, 1829 Bedford County, Tenn.,
   died Mar 6, 1898.
8: Wade H. Womack, born 1832 Bedford County, Tenn., died 1863,
   in C.S.A.
9: Frances Jane (Fannie) Womack, born Mar 23, 1835 Bedford County,
   Tenn., died Feb 2, 1915 in Stephens, Ark.

NORMAN BIBLE

In possession of Mrs. James A. Thomas, Morrow, Georgia
Taken from: "The River Counties", by Garrett, Vol 2.

Robert Norman, was born 1777 in N.C., died 10 Oct 1855, age 78 years,
    in Perry County, Tennessee, married 28 Dec 1816 to Martha "Pat-
    sey" Coffee, born 1795 in Georgia, died 7 Feb 1852. He was a
    native of N.C., as were his parents. After his father's death,
    his mother, Nellie Norman came with Robert to Tennessee. He
    served in War of 1812, drafted in Bedford County, Tennessee,
    mustered at Nashville 12 Oct 1814, and in service nine months;
    honorably discharged at Nashville 12 July 1815. On 6 Feb 1851
    in Marshall County, Tennessee, he applied for Pension or Land
    Bounty, at the age of 74 years. He served under Capt. Andrew
    Patterson in the 1st Regiment of Tennessee Militia. His Bounty
    Land Warrant No. 32052-80-55 was signed by A. H. Gutherie of
    Linden, Tennessee. He will be found on 1850 Census of Marshall

County, Tennessee.

On 17 May 1856, William A. Norman, son of Robert, applied from Perry County, Tenn., for rights (Land) in behalf of a minor son of Robert Norman, deceased...... the minor was Robert Porter Norman. These papers said Robert Norman married 28 Dec 1816 to Martha Coffee (Coffey?) and that Robert Norman died 10 Oct 1855. Martha, his wife, died 7 Feb 1852. Bible Records were in File.

Children of Robert Norman:

1: Thomas N. Norman, born 25 Dec 1817, died 14 July 1862, married Maria Phillips.

2: James C. Norman, born 18 April 1818 in Bedford County, Tenn., married (1) Mary "Polly" Grammer; married (2) Sarah J. Gibson.

3: Mary Jane Norman, born 26 Sept 1819, died 30 Aug 1852, married James Shelton Butler, born 17 Dec 1810, died 19 Sept 1890.

4: Eliza E. Norman, born 29 Nov 1821, married 11 April 1839 to William Noblett. (He vouched that he had known Robert Norman for about 18 years and was present when Robert Norman died in Perry County).

5: William Allen Norman, born 4 Aug 1823 in Maury Co., Tenn., died 24 Oct 1895; married 30 Dec 1849 to Mary Ann Gibson, born 6 Oct 1829, died 20 March 1879.

6: Elizabeth P. Norman, born 29 Dec 1827, married _____ Craig.

7: Martha Ann Norman, born 26 Oct 1829, married A. Hugh Gutherie.

8: Robert Porter Norman, born 16 March 1836, died 20 Nov 1900; married Mary Lucretia Phillips, born 3 July 1840, died 1925.

James C. Norman, son of Robert Norman, born 18 April 1818 in Bedford Co., Tenn., died in Benton County. He was married (1) to Mary Grammer, born in Bedford Co., Tenn., and they were the parents of four children. He married (2) about 1851 to Sarah J. Gibson, daughter of John M. and Martha (Harper) Gibson of Tennessee, and they had ten children. This family migrated in 1854 to Missouri and lived in Greene County until 1877, then moved to Benton County, Arkansas. They were members of Cumberland Presbyterian Church at Springfield. Records of this family will be found in "History of Arkansas" by Goodspeed Publishing Co., Chicago, pages 874 and 875.

Children of James C. Norman by first marriage:

1: Nancy A. Norman	6: George F. Norman
2: John M. Norman	7: James Mc. Norman
3: Infant	8: Amanda H. Norman, married Carl.
4: Infant	9: Dora Norman, married Sciprey
5: Infant	10: Infant (Infants were all deceased at time of Goodspeed Biography)

Mary Jane Norman, daughter of Robert Norman, born 26 Sept 1819, died 30 Aug 1853, married in Lawrence Co., Tenn., to James Shelton Butler, born 17 Dec 1810 in Bedford Co., Tenn., died 19 Sept 1889 in Prairie Grove, Ark., son of David Butler who married in 1802 to Rebecca Milliken.(They were on 1820 Census of Bedford County, Tenn). After the death of Mary Jane, James S. Butler married (2) in 1854 to Jane Hannah (Nixon) Kirkpatrick, born 1827, died 1906. There

were four children by his marriage to Mary Jane Norman, and one
by Jane. James S. and Hannah Jane are buried at Prairie Grove
Cemetery.

James Shelton Butler moved to Greene Co., Missouri, in 1857 to Brook-
line Township and in 1862 moved to Evansville, Washington Co.,
Ark., He was a member of the Vineyard Missionary Baptist Church,
organized 14 Dec 1867 in Fayetteville. An old newspaper at Prairie
Grove gives an account of his daughter Martha helping to bury a
Mr Borden after Battle of Prairie Grove on 7 Dec 1962 (1862).
Children of Mary Jane Norman Butler:

1: Martha "Mattie" Butler, born 29 May 1844 in Giles Co., Tenn.,
    died Nov 1930 at Republic, Mo., married in Missouri to John
    Knox McConnell, born 12 Feb 1848 at Shelbyville, Tenn., died
    25 March 1917, Republic, Mo. The Family lived on a farm 12
    miles west of Springfield, Mo., then retired to Republic.
    They had ten children, not used in the listing, but submitted
    by Mrs. Thomas.

2: John Calvin Butler, born 13 Jan 1846 at Shelbyville, Tenn.,
    died 9 March 1895, buried Purcell, Oklahoma (Indian Territory),
    married (1) Michael Lucretia Greer, (2) Alice Elizabeth Ecken-
    berger. After his first marriage in 1872, he lived six months
    in Greersburg, Ark., then moved to Whitesboro, Texas. He was
    converted into Methodist Church 1867 near Greersburg, lived in
    Mason Texas from late 1873 to 1890, serving alternately as
    Sheriff and Deputy. During this period he drove cattle and
    traveled much to return prisoners and deliver prisoners. By
    his first marriage there were 4 children: by his second there
    were two children. Descendants were submitted but are not be-
    ing used in this sketch.

3: Mary Elizabeth Butler, born 25 Aug 1848 in Perry County, Tenn.,
    died 27 Oct 1926 in Madill, Okla.; married 22 March 1866 in
    Benton County, Mo., to William Stewart Derrick, born 1847,
    died 1925. They had five children.

4: David A. Butler, born 25 July 1850 in Tennessee, died 1867 in
    Prairie Grove, Washington County, Ark.

Eliza E. Norman, daughter of Robert Norman, born 29 Nov 1821, married 11
April 1839 to William Noblett. Children of Eliza E. Norman Noblett;

1: Tom Noblett (Dr.)
2: William Noblett
3: John Noblett
4: David Noblett married Annie _____.

William Allen Norman, son of Robert Norman, born 4 Aug 1823 in Maury Co.,
Tenn., died 24 Oct 1895; married (1) 30 Dec 1849 to Mary Ann Gib-
son, born 6 Oct 1829, died 20 March 1879, daughter of John and
Patsey (Harper) Gibson. He married (2) on 27 March 1886 to Cynthia
C. Barrett, born 14 Oct 1836; married (3) 5 Nov 1889 to Rachel F.
Roundtree, born 27 Oct 1844.
Children by first wife:

1: Martha Jane Norman, born 4 Oct 1850 in Tennessee, died 7 Dec

1888, married Elias Orr in Brookline, Mo.
2: John Ransom Norman, born 20 Nov 1851 in Tennessee, died 6 June 1863.
3: William Franklin Norman, born 29 Sept 1855 in Tenn., died 8 Feb 1935, married in Springfield, Mo., to Mary "Mame" White.
4: Permelia Alice Norman, born 20 Aug 1858 in Greene Co., Mo., died 24 March 1895; married Frank White in Missouri.
5: George Marshall Norman, born 16 Sept 1861 in Greene Co., Mo., died July 1927 in Shawnee, Okla.; married third to Ella ___.
6: Annie Emmerilah Norman (twin), born 5 Sept 1866, died 28 Feb 1910; buried at Mt. Comfort; married 30 June 1897 to David Dillard Appleby. Had two children.
7: No Information
8: No Information

Robert Porter Norman, son of Robert Norman, born 16 March 1836, died 20 Nov 1900 at Brookline Cemetery, Mo., married on 4 Nov 1858 in Greene Co., Mo., to Mary Lucretia Phillips, born 3 July 1840, died 1 Nov 1925. Children of Robert P. Norman:
1: Ida Norman, born ca 1863 in Missouri, married Ira Joel Treesh. They had three children.
2: Ellen Elizabeth "Bet" Norman, born ca 1865 in Missouri, married _____Sumler.
3: William Willie Norman, born 21 July 1876 in Brookline, Mo., Greene County, died 31 Dec 1939, married 24 Sept ___, to Della Estella Lindsey, born 3 Sept 1880 in Urbana, Hickory County, Mo., died 28 Dec 1919 at Springfield, Mo., after her death he married again and by second marriage had two daughters. He had one child by his first marriage.

U. G. PASCHAL BIBLE

In possession of Mrs. J. H. Neeley, Shelbyville, Tennessee
Publisher: Cranston and Curts, Cincinnati, O. Chicago, Ill. St. Louis, Mo. 1881

U. G. Paschal Bible, Oct 10th 1894

The Rite of Holy Matrimony was celebrated between Ulysses Grant Paschal of Shelbyville, Tennessee, and Mattie Ellen Stephenson of Shelbyville, Tennessee on June 11th 1893 at Shelbyville, Tennessee.
                        by Rev. George Cook
Witness: Spencer Neeley and H. H. Rittenberry

MARRIAGES:
James Daniel Paschal, son of U. G. and Mattie Paschal was born on the Fourteenth day of May in the year of our Lord One Thousand Nine

and three. (May 14, 1903)

Edith Maye Paschal, daughter of U. G. and Mattie Paschal was born on
the Twenty-sixth day of July in the year of our Lord One Thous-
and nine Hundred and Five (July 26, 1905).

Harriet Morey Paschal, daughter of U. G. and Mattie Paschal was born
on the twenty-second day of April in the year of our Lord One
Thousand Nine Hundred and Eight (April 22, 1908).

Pauline Paschal, daughter of U. G. and Mattie Paschal was born on the
thirteenth day of August in the year of our Lord One Thousand
Nine Hundred and Thirteenth (Aug 13, 1913).

James Paschal, Sr. was born June 2, 1795, Died June 22, 1855

Elizabeth (Parker) Paschal was born Feb 5, 1801. Died Aug 6, 1873.

Wilburn Parker died at New Orleans during the War with England 1812-15.
Soldier.

William Ernest Paschal, son of U. G. and Mattie E. Paschal was born on
the twenty-fourth day of May in the year of our Lord, One Thous-
and eight hundred and ninety four (May 24, 1894).

Paul Paschal, son of U. G. and Mattie E. Paschal was born on the twenty-
fourth day of October, in the year of our Lord, One Thousand
Eight Hundred and Ninety Six. (Oct 24, 1896)

Charles McCabe Paschal, son of U. G. and Mattie E. Paschal was born on
the twenty fifth day of January, in the year of our Lord One
Thousand Nine Hundred. (Jan 25, 1900)

Ruth Ellen Paschal, daughter of U. G. and Mattie E. Paschal was born on
the 26th day of May, in the year of our Lord, One Thousand Nine
Hundred and one. (May 26, 1901)

J. C. J. Paschal was born Sept 28, 1841

Rachel (Muse) Paschal was born May 17, 1844, died March 8, 1910.

Thrusa A. F.(Ann Francés)(Brame) Muse was born Oct 18, 1818, died Oct 6,
1902.   Jacob Muse (Jacob Colson Muse, husband
of Thrusa)

DEATHS:

J. C. J. Paschal Died March 28, 1920. Age 78 years, 6 months.

Paul Paschal departed this life on the morning of June 15th 1898,
Age 1 yr, 7 mo. & 21 da.

Charles McCabe Paschal departed this life May 16, 1900, aged 3 months &
22 days.

Pauline Paschal departed this life on Oct 11, 1915, aged 2 years, 1 mos.
& 28 days.

Ulyssess Grant Paschal departed this life Dec 12th 1915. Age 45 years,
10 mo. & 20 days.

Mattie Ellen Paschal departed this life March 3rd, 1955, age 84 years,
8 months.

J. D. Paschal, departed this life Nov 21st 1918. age 15 years, 6 months
and 7 days.

Edith Maye Paschal Departed this life Sept 22, 1921. age 16 years, 1
month, 27 days.

William Ernest Paschal departed this life Oct 10, 1968, age 74 years,
4 months, 16 days. Burial Holy Cross Cemetery, Akron, Ohio.

REV. G. W. BLANTON BIBLE

In possession of Mrs. J. H. Neeley, Shelbyville, Tennessee
Publisher: A. H. Redford, agent for the M. E. Church, South
        Nashville, Tenn.   1873

Presented by my Father, W. C. Blanton.

This Certifies that the Rite of Holy Matrimony was celebrated between:
William C. Blanton of Unionville, and Elizabeth Tilford of Shelbyville,
daughter of Namie (Brown) and David Tilford, on 21st Jan. A.D. 1838 at
R. W. Lock's by Jas. Anderson, Esq.

H. H. Blanton says E. T. had brothers, Sam, James, John Tilford, sisters,
Lucy Ann and Mary, born near Shelbyville.

BIRTHS:
William C.(Crisp) Blanton born December 27th 1817
Elizabeth Blanton born August 6th 1820

E. A. Blanton Born January 4th 1839.
Green L. Blanton Born October 8th 1840.
Lucy J. Blanton Born July 10th 1842.
John C. Blanton Born July 12th 1844.
Sophia P. Blanton Born August 21st 1846.
James L. Blanton Born August 30th 1848.
William L. Blanton Born December 28th 1850.
Hiram H. Blanton Born August 7th 1853.
David T. Blanton Born November 14th 1855.
George W. Blanton Born September 24th 1857.
Laura Blanton Born May 25th 1863.
Mirion Blanton Born Jan 22, 1889,
        Baptised by Rev. T. J. Duncan March 1, 1889.
William C. Blanton Born Mar 11, 1892, Baptised by Rev. T. B. Fisher,
        June 5, '92 (1892).

MARRIAGES:
John C. Carney maried to Lucy J. Blanton, June 12, 1862.
E. A. Blanton maried to Minnie Thompson, A.D., July 10, 1862.
Sophy P. Blanton maried to J. A. Knott, A.D., Sept 10, 1863.
J. C. Blanton maried to Jane B. Maupin, A.D.,
Nannie L. Blanton maried to E. W. Ellis, A.D., Dec 4th 1873.
H. H. Blanton maried to Sallie Brunson, by Rev. T. A. Hoyte, Nashville,
        Tenn., Feb 13, 1879.
G. W. Blanton to Laura Sutton Dec 21, 1885.
W. L. Blanton to Sarah E. Allen Oct 7, 1884.
E. A. Blanton to Mattie Bounds Apr 1879.
H. H. Blanton to Alene Pennington Oct 14, 1887.
W. L. Blanton to Gertrude Burns dale?
H. H. Blanton to Blanche Ray
Lucy J. Blanton to Dr. A. W. Manier, Tullahoma, Tenn.

Smiley Blanton to Margaret Leslie Gray Oct 18, 1910.

DEATHS:
Green L. Blanton Departed this life August 22nd 1842.
David T. Blanton Departed this life Oct 22nd 1856.
Nannie L. Blanton Departed this life March 16th 1883.
Sophy P. Knott Departed this life July 9th 1884.
W. C. Blanton Departed this life Oct 24th 1887.
Elizabeth Blanton departed this life on May 21, 1898.
Sarah E. Blanton, wife of W. L. B. Aug 2nd 1905.
Minnie Blanton, wife of E. A.B. March 7, 1877.
Sallie B. Blanton, wife of H. H. B. June 1, 1886.
Jennie M. Blanton, wife of J. C. B.
E. A. Blanton d. Gainesville, Texas Feb 18, 1919.
Lucy J. Blanton Carney Manier d Aug 13, 1926.
Hiram Harris Blanton d   Nov 3, 1944.

William Crisp Blanton was the son of Meridith Blanton (and Nancy Crisp).
His stone in Unionville, Tennessee Reads: "A Soldier of the War of 1812
Merideth Blanton, Born in Cumberland Co., Va. June 9, 1792, Departed
this life July 5, 1879, aged 87 years 16 days," "In God we trust".

Nancy- Wife of Merideth Blanton, Born March 7, 1791, Died November 14,
1885, aged 94 years 3 mo 7 days.

A Newspaper report says married over 65 years, i.e. 1814. He served as a
Private in Captain Allen Wilson's Company of Infantry from Aug 28, to
Dec 3, 1814 (Truehart's Regiment of Virginia Militia).
Nancy Crisp b- Lynchburg, Va., probably, Mar 7th 1791, m. April 7th 1814
to Merideth Blanton, at Lynchburg (Probably).

KNOTT BIBLE

In possession of Mrs. J. H. Neeley, Shelbyville, Tennessee
Publisher: Dallas Publishing Co., Dallas, Texas   1881

Presented to Willie L. Knott by Thomas E. Knott. December 25, 1894.

MARRIAGES:
Mr. T. E. Knott to Mrs Willie L. (Trolinger) Williams in Dallas, Texas,
    Nov 2nd, 1890.
Mr. T. E. Knott to Mrs Elizabeth McElhaney in Dallas, Texas, Sept 1900.
Mr John Neeley to Tennessee Malinda Knott, Nov 29, 1894.
Mr Joseph Hiram Neeley to Ruth Ellen Paschal, January 1, 1922.
Mr Joseph Paschal Neeley to Jean Claire Robertson, September 27, 1947.
Mr Robert Albern Williamson to Margaret Mae Neeley, September 14, 1947.

142

BIRTHS:
Willie L. Knott Born Sept 23rd 1862.
Thomas E. Knott Born Nov 5th 1866.
Jessie Frank Knott Born Oct 22nd 1885 (hers before married Mr. Knott)
Henry Cornelious Knott Born Aug 18th 1887 ("   "   "   )
Thomas Ewing Knott Born June 16th 1894.
Joseph Hiram Neeley Born February 15, 1896.
Newt Neeley Born Oct 15, 1898.
Ruth Ellen Paschal Neeley born May 26, 1901.
Joseph Paschal Neeley   September 7, 1923.
Margaret Mae Neeley   ˙ February 3, 1926
Martha Ruth Neeley   August 28, 1928
Robert Albern Williamson January 24, _____
Jean Claire Robertson   April 24, 1926
Joseph Paschal Neeley, Jr. Nov 4, 1948
Robert Daniel Neeley   June 21, 1950
Margaret Ellen Williamson March 25, 1952

DEATHS:
Thomas Ewing Knott Died Aug 6th 1896 at 4:20
Willie L. Knott Died June 11th 1899 at 9:30
Thomas Elisha Knott Died October 15, 1951
Elizabeth McElhaney Knott Died Aug 25, 1938
Newt Neeley died April 1918
Malinda Tennessee Knott Neeley Oct 19, 1899.
John Shaw Neeley   May 11, 1931

STEPHENS BIBLE

Photocopy by Mrs. Robert Elam, Shelbyville, Tennessee
Publisher: Collins's Sterotype   New York   1818
          "Martha A. Stephens Book"
          April 10th Day A.D. 1855

NOTE: Inserted on same page: "The date April 10th Day A.D. 1855, probably
      is the date of her (Martha) death."

MARRIAGES & BIRTHS:
Ely Jr, Stephens was born July 23 day 1829
Lafayette Stephens was born the 28th of February 1831
Tranquilla A. Stephens, wife of Thomas Thompson was maried the 1st Day
      of February 1844.
Eli Stephens was married to Sarah E. Fisher the 21st of November 1850.
Martha R. Stephens was born the 13th day of March A.D. 1852.
Allen Stephens was born May 17th 1797
Josiah Stephens was born November 1801
Willey Stephens was born February 1804
John Stephens was born March 3, 1806.

James Stephens was born June 28, 1808
Salley A. Stephens was born May 11, 1810
Ransom Stephens was born Dec 22, 1816
Martha Gulley, wife of John Stephens was born February 21, 1796

Negro Amy, Sept 21, 1821
Tranquilla Stephens was born May 31 day A.D. 1827.
Thomas Thompson was born August the 2, 1824
Joseph H. Stephens was born August 18, 1868 on Tuesday.
John Stephens was born October 10th, 1819
Louizy D. Stephens was born November 30, 1827
Mikel was born November the 27, 1834, negro
Larha J. Stephens was born 10th of February 1845
Squire (Bob) E. Stephens was born the 17th of April 1839
James Preston was born Aprile the 5th 1844
Selah was born Dec the 6th 1842
George was born Feb 1st 1847
Joseph, negro, was born the 12th day of March 1849
Jno. B(lagg) was married to Sarah Stephens, Aug 11/12, 18__.
Gilbert was born September 13 day 1820
Phillip was born July 11 day 1821
Moses was born July   1819
Lindy was born May 10th, 1822
Willis was born February the 15th day 1851
                              by E. H. Stephens
Negro- Lewis was born March the 9th 1855
Margaret F. Robinson was born October the 12th 1840
William Fates Stephens was born Saturday April 16, 1855
Tranquilla A. Thompson departed this life April the 1st, 1860
Ransom Stephens, Jr., was born Thursday May the 22nd day A.D. 1862
Kate Stephens was born Wednesday July the 26th A.D. 1865.
J. M. L. Stephens married to Margaret F. Robinson the 24th day of Nov-
      ember A.D. 1858.
NOTE: J. M. L. Stephens was called "Fate".

BENNETT BIBLE

In possession of Mr Milton R. Bennett, Shelbyville, Tennessee
Publisher: Phinney & Co., Buffalo   New York
            Ivison & Phinney   1854

MARRIAGES:
Nehemiah Bennett and Sarah Slusses was married May A.D. 1817
Charles Bennett, son of Nehemiah B., married Nancy Dickensheets, Feb
      17, 1848
Milton Bennett and Ella Emley was married Jan 30th A.D. 1873
Harry Bennett and Mary R. Joslin married Dec 13, 1894
Charles Bennett & Grace Stevenson Nov 8, 1908

BIRTHS:
Nehemiah was born April the 3, 1793
Saly was born March the 26, 1799
Births of there children
Stephen   September 12, 1818
Tobias   December 11, 1820
Nathan   June 5, 1823
Charles   October 22, 1825
Jacob   February 22, 1825
Eliza   November 25, 1830
Clarisa   January 19, 1834
Saraha   June 15, 1837
Henry   July 31, 1839
Rebecca Ales   May 24, 1854

Milton Bennett, grandson of Nehemiah Bennett and son of Charles and
Nancy Bennett was born Dec 19th A.D. 1851.
Ella Bennett, daughter of A. H. and Rebecca Emley was born April 25
A.D. 1852.
Harry E. Bennett, son of Milton and Ella Bennett was born Nov 5th A.D.
1873.
Charles O. Bennett, son of Milton and Ella Bennett was born Oct 9th
A. D. 1887.
Charles Robert Bennett, son of Charles O. & Grace Bennett, born July
22, 1916

DEATHS:
Nehemiah Bennett departed this life 25th of Jan A.D. 1883
Sarah Bennett, wife of Nehemiah Bennett departed this life Sept 5,
        A. D. 1879
Charles Bennett, son of Nehemiah died June 26, 1895
Nancy D. Bennett died Feb 26, 1883
Milton Bennett died Nov 7, 1921
Ella Bennett died Mar 22, 1927
Charles Bennett their son died August 13, 1916
Harry Ensley Bennett died April 1, 1941 10 o'clock at St. Rita hospital
        of complications

Seperate paper:
This Certifies that Charles Bennett and Nancy M. Dickensheets were solemnly united by me in the Holy Bonds of Matrimony at David Dickensheets
on the 17th day of February in the year of our Lord One Thousand Eight
Hundred and 1848. In presence of H. S. Conklin.
                        Signed: John F. Frazier

Seperate paper: Sidney, Ohio
Charles Bennett, was born in Franklin Township, Shelby County, Oct 25,
1825, lived in Franklin Township all his life with the Exception of one
year which he lived in Sidney married to Nancy Dickensheets, Feb 17th,
1848 by this union there was born to them 8 children, 5 of whom are
living, 3 sons and 2 daughters. His wife died Feb 26, 1883. In the year,

145

He married Miss Lizzie Yinger who survives him.

Newspaper Clipping:
"Aged Franklin Township (Ohio) Resident Dead"
Mrs. Susan Elizabeth Bennett Died Saturday afternoon of General De-
bility (Sept 5, 1914). Mrs Elizabeth Bennett died at her home in Franklin
Township Saturday afternoon after an extended illness, aged 81 years, 4
months and 1 day. She was born in Miami County May 4, 1833 and with her
mother and brother Dennis Yinger and sister Mrs Sarah Critton, moved to
Shelby County in April 1841 and entered the home where she lived the
rest of her life. In 1885; she was married to Charles Bennett, of Franklin Township, who died in 1895. She was consistent member of the M. E.
Church for fifty years. On account of her hearing she was deprived of
the priveleges of attending services for the past several years. She was
of a jovial disposition and was always doing something for those around
her. She is survived by eleven nieces and nephews who will all feel the
loss of Aunt Lizzie. She was ready and anxious to pass away and often
expressed the desire to die. The funeral services were held Monday afternoon at   o'clock and interment was in Pearl Cemetery at Swanders.

Newspaper Clipping: Sidney, Ohio
"Milton Bennett Died Monday Night at his Home in Bennett Heights
of Heart Trouble." (Nov 7, 1921)
One of Sidney's well known and highly respected Citizens. Public Spirited. Always found ready to assist in Betterment of Community.
Early Tuesday Morning the news of the death of Milton Bennett
spread rapidly over our City and came as a shock, for none even knew that
he was ill. Mr Bennett was at his place of business on West Poplar Street
Monday morning, but before noon he was taken ill and went to his home in
Bennett Heights and summoned a Physician, he was found to be suffering
from neuralgia of the heart and gradually grew worse until death came at
11:30 o'clock Monday night. Mr Bennett's death removes one of our public
spirited Citizens who was always willing to aid in the betterment of
the community in which he lived. Mr Bennett was born in Franklin Township this County on December 19, 1852, the son of Charles and Nancy
(Dickensheets) Bennett. Mr Bennett spent his entire life in Shelby County. In 1872, he was united in marriage to Miss Ella Emley of Franklin
Twp. To this union two children were born Harry E. Bennett and Charles
Bennett (deceased). He is survived by his widow, one son Harry E. Bennett,
one sister, Mrs Rebecca Fosnight who made her home with Mr Bennett and
wife, and one brother, J. E. Bennett of Anna. Also two grandsons, Milton
and Charles, Jr., and one granddaughter, Miss Ruth Bennett.
Thirty five years ago, Mr Bennett, located at his present residence in Bennett Heights and for many years manufactured drainage tile. Since then he has been interested in many industries, the H. E. Bennett
Realty Co., The Citizens' Ice Coal and Supply Co., and was Contractor
on many public works having built many of Shelby County's Pikes. It was
through the activities of Mr Bennett and his son Harry that the Sidney
Chautauqua was first started. For about 50 years, Mr Bennett has been a
member of the K. of P. and Odd Fellow Lodges in Shelby. Mr Bennett always had a smile and a pleasant word, which won him a host of friends

who will miss him. In politics, he was a staunch Republican and always active in his party cause. Persons wishing to view the remains may call at the residence in Bennett Heights between the hours of 2 to 5 p.m. and 7 to 9:30 p.m. Wednesday. Funeral Services will be held at the home in Bennett Heights Thursday afternoon at 2 o'clock. Interment will be made at Graceland.

Newspaper Clipping: 1927
     "Well Known Lady has passed Away."
     Mrs Ella Bennett died at her home early Tuesday Morning after a Few Weeks Illness." Mrs Ella Bennett, daughter of A. H. Emley and Reb-ecca Toy Emley, was born near Mount Holly, New Jersey, April 25th, 1852. She was married to Milton Bennett, January 30th 1873, and to this union was born two sons, Harry E. and Charles C. Bennett, the latter being deceased. She is survived by one son, Harry E. Bennett, three grand-children, Ruth B. Emmons and Milton Bennett, Jr., of Sidney, Ohio and Charles Robert Bennett of Everett, Washington. She is survived by three half brothers: William, David and Thomas Emley of Spokane, Washington and Love Landreth of Readan, Washington; the latter being with her at the time of her decease. She and Milton, established their home immedia-tely North of Sidney, over 40 years ago where, after the death of her husband in November 1923 (1921) she continued to live until her death. Mother Bennett was always glad to extend shelter, hospitality and ser-vice, and her home was always freely opened to her relatives and driends. She died at 8:10 Tuesday morning after an illness of about ten weeks. A host of friends will miss her association and companionship-
                            Mar 22, 1927

SMITH BIBLE

In possession of Mr & Mrs James Madison Smith, Fayetteville, Tennessee
Publisher: John A. Hertel Co.   1955
Taken from: Lincoln County Tennessee Bible Records by Tucker & Waller.
          Vol. 5

PARENTS:
Married 28 Sept. 1950 Shelbyville, Tenn
Husband: James Madison Smith (born) 9 March 1915 Charity, Moore County,
          Tenn.
Wife: Ella Mae Head (born) 8 July 1917 Bedford County, Tenn.
          Were married by County Judge

Children's Register:
1: Naomie Charlotte (Smith) Born 15 August 1951 Shelbyville, Tenn.
          married- Aug 19, 1970 James E. Palmer- Fort Payne, Ala.
2: Cynthia Madge Smith born 30 June 1953 Shelbyville, Tenn.
3: David James Smith born 30 Oct 1954 Shelbyville, Tenn.
          married Debby Jean Bunn June 28, 1974 Fayetteville, Tenn.

4: Emma Mae Smith born 22 Oct 1956 Lewisburg, Tenn. Married 8 June
     1973 Chestnut Ridge to Stephen Nichols Raby.

Grandparents:
William (Bill) Washington Smith Born 23 April 1878. Death 13 Jan 1951
Emma Bell Laws Smith Born 21 July 1879 died 6 July 1944.
     Married 28 July 1901

Great Grandparents:
James Madison Smith Birth 1856   Death 1890
Josie Young   Birth 1858   Death 1913
Rufus Laws
Judy Ann Smith

Great Great Grandparents:
(Andrew) Jackson Smith (great, great grandfather father's side)
Mark Young (great, great, grandfather- mother's side)

Inportant Events:
Husbands side:
(Children of William Washington Smith & Emma Bell Laws)
Annie Ozella Smith born July 8, 1902 at Belleville Lincoln Co., Tn.
Lee Roy Smith Born 6 Jan 1904 at   "   " "   ".
Nora Mable Smith Born 29 Dec 1905 Chestnut Ridge, Tenn. LCT
William Alford Smith born 26 Oct 1907 Howell, Tenn. LCT
Birdie June Smith born 16 July 1909 Belleville   "
Maudie "L" Smith born 11 Oct 1913 Belleville   "
James M. Smith born 9 Mar 1915 Charity   "
Robert D. Smith born 14 May 1918 Belleville   "

(Children of Newsom Henry Head & Ida May Reynolds Head)
James W. Head Born 4 Jan 1916 Pleasant Grove Bedford Co., Tenn.
Ella Mae Head Born 8 July 1917 near Bedford, Bedford Co., Tenn.
Janie Ruth Head Born 18 July 1919 Pleasant Grove Bedford Co., Tenn.
Harold Head Born 3 May 1922 Pleasant Grove   "   "   "
Alice Francis Head 30 April 1927 "   "   "   "   "
Newsom Henry Head Jr. 7 Sept 1925 "   "
Hazel Ann Head 29 June 1929   "   "

Grandparents (Mothers Side)
(Parents of Ella Mae Head Smith)
Newsom Henry Head (father) Born Sept 2, 1886 Richmond Ridge, Bedford Co.
     Tenn. Death Oct 8, 1959 Shelbyville, Tenn. Married Nov 2, 1914
     Shelbyville, Tenn., Bedford County.
Ida May Reynolds Head (mother) Born Mar 26, 1889 Lincoln Co. near Peter-
     sburg Death Sept 1, 1973 Shelbyville, Tenn.

Great Grandparents
Amzie Reynolds May 22, 1853 (born) Death Dec 27, 1918
Clarass Reavis Reynolds Birth Feb 11, 1854 Death April 12, 1917

James W. Head Birth 1848   death 1926
Carolina Gambille Head   Birth 1856 death 1889

David Reavis 33 years old died in Civil War (brother of Clarassa
        Reavis Reynolds)
Claressa Brown Reavis Birth 1833 Death 1873 (mother of David Reavis
        & Claressa Reavis Reynolds)

Great Great Grandparents (Mothers side)
Cravin Head Birth 1821 Aug 1899 Death
Jane Mise Head   .   .

Bradly Gambille Birth 1829 Death 1909
        Anderson

Great Great Grandfather Mothers side
Green Reynolds

(Grandchildren of Mr. & Mrs James Madison Smith)
Sheila Diane Palmer Birth 13 Mar 1971 Fort Payne, Ala.
Christopher Scott Palmer Birth 19 Nov 1973   "   "
(Children of Mr & Mrs James E. Palmer)

ALLISON BIBLE

The Original Bible from which this copy was made belongs to Mr & Mrs
R. T. Jarrell, Shelbyville, Tennessee. Copied by Mrs. Sarah Jones,
Wartrace, Tenn. May 14, 1939.

MARRIAGES:
Kimbrough Alison and Sally Ogilvie were married on the 28th of Decem-
        ber 1819.
T. L. Whitaker and Sarah A. Allison was married Sept 17th 1851.
B. F. Jarrell and Nancy B. Allison were married April 27th 1859.
John W. Chambers and Nannie Allison were married Sept 22nd 1870.

BIRTHS:
Kimbrough Allison was born January 1st 1794.
Sally Ogilvie was born January 3rd, 1804.
Newton P. Allison was born 26th of Sept 1822.
Richard S. Allison was born the 10th of August 1825.
James H. Allison was born November 14, 1827.
Robert Franklin Allison was born May 22, 1829.
John Newman Allison was born July __ 1831.
Sarah Ann Allison was born April 29th 1834.
Nancy B. Allison was born June the 22nd 1840.

DEATHS:
Kimbrough Allison departed this life 18th June 1868.
Newton P. Allison departed this life May 16th 1823.
Richard S. Allison departed this life April 24, 1869.
James H. Allison died August 26th 1833.
Robt. F. Allison died August 9th 1830.
John N. Allison died December ___ 1832.
Sarah Allison departed this life November 19th 1879.

BLACKMAN BIBLE

This Bible was found at the home of Mr & Mrs C. M. Dean, Wartrace,
Tenn.,copied by Mrs. Sarah Jones, Wartrace, Tennessee July 23, 1937.
Publisher: Henry Alteman Philadelphia, Pennsylvania   1889

BIRTHS:
Burrell Blackman was born March 25, 1811.
Frances Blackman was born March 15, 1824.
(First wife of Burrell Blackman was Sarah Heard, but no data given)

MARRIAGES:
Burrell Blackman and Frances Holt were married January 1, 1857.

DEATHS:
Burrell Blackman died April 12, 1897
Frances Blackman died about 5 years later.

Elias C. Holt died February 21, 1897.
Joseph M. Holt died June 22, 1896.

THE CLEVELAND FAMILY RECORD

This Record is found at Mr R. P. Websters home one and one-half miles
from Wartrace on the Old Dirt Road between Wartrace and Haley Tenn.,
West of N.C.&St. L. Railroad. Copied by Mrs. Sarah Jones, Wartrace,
Tenn.

BIRTHS:
Sarah Philadelphia Cleveland was born April 4th 1835
Elizabeth Dawkins Cleveland was born September 23rd 1839
Thomas Stone Cleveland was born April 25th 1840
        (Children of Jeremiah & Sallie)
Mary Harriett Cleveland was born August 9th 1842
Jeremiah Cleveland was born August 20th 1844
Mary Cleveland was born April 7th 1847

(Children of Jeremiah and I think it must mean Mary, but this
    is the way it looks "Massy")
Annie W. Cleveland was born March 2nd 1848. Thomas' wife.
Jeremiah Cleveland was born February 4, 1806
Sarah Elizabeth Stone was born December 9, 1816
Mary A. Stone was born June 20th 1820

Cleveland Webster was born June 27th 1856
Robert P. Webster was born January 24, 1858
    (Children of John G. & Eliza D. Webster)

Sallie Stone Cleveland was born September 10, 1868
Lizzie Harper Cleveland was born March 28, 1870
Hattie D. Cleveland was born November 29, 1872
Annie Laurie Cleveland was born June 23, 1875
Carrie Choice Cleveland was born July 6, 1882
    (Children of T. S. & A. W. Cleveland)

Paul Dargan Willingham was born October 7, 1889
Infant daughter born to Jessie and Lizzie H. Cleveland Dec 23, 1894.

MARRIAGES:
Jeremiah Cleveland was married to Sarah E. Stone, 17th Sept 1833.
Jeremiah Cleveland was married to Mary S. Stone, 27th Oct 1841
Sarah P. Cleveland was married to Walter H. Sims, 22nd Sept 1853.
Thos. S. Cleveland was married to Annie E. Wright, Sept 4th 1867.
Paul D. Willingham was married to Sallie S. Cleveland, Nov 14th 1888.
Jesse Cleveland was married to Lizzie H. Cleveland, Dec 20, 1819
John G. Webster was married to Eliza Cleveland, October 3rd 1855.
Marion H. Massee was married to Annie Laurie Cleveland, Nov 13, 1895
Augustus Cicero Felton, Jr. was married to Hattie Cleveland, June 30,
    1896

DEATHS:
Sarah E. Cleveland, consort of Jeremiah Cleveland died May 23, 1840
Eliza D. Webster, daughter of Jeremiah & Sarah Cleveland and consort of
    J. G. Webster, departed this life April 16, 1860
Sallie P. Sims departed this life May 19, 1862
Jeremiah Cleveland, Sr., died May 19th at Greenville, C. H., South
    Carolina 1877.
Cleveland Webster died March 27, 1884
Lizzie H. Cleveland, wife of Jessie Cleveland, died December 24, 1894
Infant daughter of Jesse & Lizzie Cleveland died December 23, 1894
Mary Cleveland, consort of Jeremiah Cleveland died July 23, 1847
Mary Cleveland, daughter of Jeremiah & Mary Cleveland departed this life
    on Wednesday May 29, 1861
Jeremiah Cleveland, Jr., was killed at Durry's Bluff on May 16, 1864
John G. Webster departed this life September 17, 1870
Annie W. Cleveland, wife of Thos. S. Cleveland, died June 31st 1902 at
    5 p.m.
Thomas Stone Cleveland departed this life Sept 11, 1907 Wed. 12:05 a.m.

151

REMARKS:

Mary Ann Pepper, born March 2nd 1848
Henry Pepper, born July 28, 1849
Elizabeth Hightower Pepper, born February 14, 1851
Jane B. Pepper, born May 28, 1826, departed this life July 13, 1852.
(The above Record was placed here at the request of Wm. Pepper, father
   of the above children and the husband of the deceased wife, this the
   9th day of April, 1859)

Wm. Pepper departed this life the 13th of March, 1862.
J. G. Webster and Mary A. Pepper were married the 3rd of December 1867.

COBLE BIBLE RECORD

The following Record was copied from a Bible owned by C. R. Coble,
Wartrace, Tennessee. Copied by Mrs. Sarah Jones, Wartrace, Tennessee,
on Dec 9, 1939.

Neely Coble, born January 17, 1802. Died September 30, 1866.
Martha Robertson, born January 10, 1802. Died December 26, 1836,
         married Dec 21, 1820.
Mary Ann Coble, born November 11, 1823. Died May 22, 1857, married to
         B. F. Pannell, January 9, 1845.
John Daniel Coble, born June 25, 1828. Died March 7, 1912, married to
         Mary R. Miller, February 11, 1868.
Martha Catherine Coble, born August 26, 1836, died August 12, 1882.
James Jackson Miller, born March 7, 1810, died September 26, 1870.
Margaret Daniel, born April 27, 1810, died January 20, 1884, married
         Feb 10, 1831.
William Jasper Miller, born Mar 11, 1832, died November 29, 1849.
Wiley Martin Miller, born August 14, 1834, died _____, married to
         Harriet Jenkins.
Mary Rebecca Miller, born November 1, 1836, died _____, married to
         John D. Coble Feb 11, 1868.
Newton Emaly Miller, born January 21, 1839, died Feb 28, 1853.
Margaret Elizabeth Miller, born May 9, 1841, died _____, married to
         E. B. Phillips.
Lettitia Eliza Miller, born August 25, 1843, died _____.
Andrew Jackson Miller, born Aug 25, 1845, died _____, married to
         Louisa Berry.
James Washington Miller, born Feb 10, 1848, died Oct 1884, married Ada
         Belle Gardner.
Henry Jefferson Miller, born July 1, 1850, died July 20, 1930, married
         Fannie Bomar.
Charles Robert Miller, born May 2, 1853.
John Burton Miller, born Sept 16, 1856, died _____.

PARENTS:
John Daniel Coble, born June 25, 1828, died Mar 7, 1912.
Mary Rebecca Miller, born Nov 1, 1836, died July 10, 1921, married
      Feb 11, 1868.
Children:
Infant Daughter, Born & Died Apr 9, 1869
Maggie, born June 30, 1870, died July 2, 1933
Neely, born July 26, 1872.
Mattie, born Nov 19, 1875, died June 9, 1918
Charles Robertson, born Dec 4, 1880.
Mattie Coble, married to T. E. Fisher, Oct 9, 1904.
Daughter, Margaret Fisher, born June 30, 1909

SEHORN-STRAYHORN-ALEXANDER BIBLE

Typed Copy. From Bible Records of Murfreesboro, Tennessee, Library.
Publisher: J. B. Lippincott & Co., Philadelphia   1859

MARRIAGES:
John Martin Sehorn and Mary Biddle Caldwell were married December the
      11th A.D. 1855.
Sally Erwin Sehorn and Robt. L. Singleton were married Dec 18, 1877 in
      the Church of the Redeemer, Shelbyville, by Bishop Quintara.
Dan W. Shofner and Florence Sehorn were married Jan 6th 1892 in the Church
      of the Redeemer, Shelbyville, Tennessee, by Rev. F. F. Martin,
      Rector of St. Anne's Church, Nashville, Tennessee.
Clarence Fussell Alexander and Sadie Shofner were married Nov 27th 1917
      in the Presbyterian Church of Mt. Pleasant, Tennessee by Dr.
      H. C. Tolman, D.D., Nashville, Tenn.
Nathaniel Sehorn Shofner and Ethel Yeatman Mallard married Sat. the
      4th April 1925 at Emmanuel Church, Cleveland, Ohio, by Rev.
      Kirk O'Ferrall.
C. F. Alexander, Jr. and Marian E. McEwen married Dec 2, 1943 in
      Columbia, Tennessee.

BIRTHS:
John M. Sehorn born 6th of March 1815- wife Mary S. Sehorn born Nov
      20th 1832.
Children of J. M. & M. B. Sehorn:
Sally Erwin Sehorn born in Shelbyville, Tennessee Oct 23rd 1856
George Sehorn born in Shelbyville, Tenn., April 16, 1859
John Sehorn born in Shelbyville, Tenn., April 24th 1861
Nathaniel Sehorn born in Shelbyville, Tenn., Dec 14, 1865
Mary Florence Sehorn born in Shelbyville, Tenn., July 26, 1868
Robert Lipscomb Singleton, Jr., born in Shelbyville, Tenn., June 20,
      1879
John Sehorn Singleton born in Shelbyville, Tenn., April 18, 1882
Clare Singleton born in Shelbyville, Tenn., April 8, 1883.

Sadie Shofner born in Erin, Tenn., Sept 19th 1893 6 p.m.
Nathaniel Sehorn Shofner born in Erin, Tenn., June 2, 1895, 7 a.m.
Clarence Fussell Alexander, Jr., son of Clarence & Sadie Shofner Alex-
        ander born in Mt. Pleasant, Tennessee Feb 2nd 1921 3 p.m.
Mary Florence Shofner, daughter of N. S. Shofner and Ethel Shofner born
        in Columbia, Tennessee, Maury Co., at King's Daughters Hospital
        Dec 24th 1925 7:30 a.m.
Barbara McEwen Alexander, daughter of C. F. Alexander, Jr. and Marian
        McEwen Alexander born Nov 24, 1944 at King's Daughters Hospital
        George Williamson, doctor.
Angela Shofner Alexander, daughter of C. F. Alexander and Marian McEwen
        Alexander, born at K. D. Hospital, Columbia, Dec 30, 1950, Watt
        Yeiser, Doctor.
Clarence Fussell Alexander, III, son of Marian & Clarence Alexander,Jr.,
        born Nov 1, 1951 at King's Daughters Hospital in Columbia, Tenn.,
        Robin Lyles, Doctor.
William Daniel Alexander born Jan 12, 1959 in Columbia, Tenn., at Maury
        Co. Hospital, son of C. F. Alexander & Marian M. Alexander of Mt.
        Pleasant, Tenn. Robin Lyles, Doctor.

DEATHS:
John Martin Sehorn died Tuesday August 11th 1885 at 6:05 o'clock A.M. and
        was buried Wednesday August 12, 1885 at 10 o'clock A.M. Funeral
        Services by the Rev. H. R. Howard.
Nathaniel Caldwell Sehorn died Oct 14th 1888 and was buried Oct 15th at
        2 P.M. Funeral Services by the Rev. H. R. Howard.
Mary Biddle Sehorn died at Mt. Pleasant, Tenn., March 14th 1903, and was
        buried March 16th 1903 at Shelbyville, Tenn. Funeral Services by
        the Rev. Arthur Howard Noll.
John Sehorn died July 17th 1928 at noon in San Antonio, Texas also
        buried there.
Florence Sehorn Shofner died Nov 22, 1936 at home of her son, Nat, in
        Nashville. Buried in Mt. Pleasant Nov 23, at Arlington Cemetery.
Daniel Wilson Shofner died in Mt Pleasant, Tenn., Nov 10, 1936 at his
        home. Buried Nov 11 at Arlington Cemetery, Mt. Pleasant, Tenn.
Clarence Fussell Alexander, Sr. died Feb 1, 1946 at his home in Mt.
        Pleasant, Tenn. Buried at Arlington Cemetery.
Sadie Shofner Alexander died Sept 28, 1961, Mt. Pleasant, buried in
        Arlington Sept 29. William Boyd, Minister. Services from her home
        at 10 A.M. Friday. Widow of C. F. Alexander, Sr.

OBIT:
John Martin Sehorn, born March 6th 1815, died Aug 11, 1885, age 70
        years, 5 months, and 5 days. Funeral services tomorrow at 10
        o'clock at his late residence, by the Rev. Dr. Howard. Burial at
        Willow Mount Cemetery, Shelbyville, Tenn., August 11, 1885.

OBIT INVITATION:
        The friends and acquaintances of Mrs. Sophia W. Davidson are re-
        quested to attend her funeral, from the residence of Mr. John M.
        Sehorn, tomorrow morning at 10 o'clock. Services at the Presby-

terian Church, by Rev. J. H. Bryson, July 13th, 1870.

FUNERAL NOTICE:
      Mrs. Mary B. Sehorn, wife of late John M. Sehorn, died at Mt.
      Pleasant, Tenn., March 14th, 1903. Her friends and acquaintances
      are respectfully invited to attend her funeral services at the
      residence of Robt. L. Singleton, Shelbyville, Tenn., Monday
      March 16th, 1903, at 1:30 P.M., by the Rev. Arthur Howard Noll.
      Buried at Willow Mount Cemetery. Honary Pall Bearers:
      Dr. G. C. Sandusky, Edmund Cooper, George Calhoun, Jno. W. Ruth.
      Active Pall Bearers: James A. Woods, C. A. Warren, Dr. S. J.
      McGrew, H. L. Dayton, H. C. Ryall & E. Shapard, Shelbyville, Tenn.,
      March 16th, 1903.

CARD IN BIBLE:
      This is to Certify that Sadie Shofner received Holy Baptism in
      Saint Ann's Church, Nashville, Diocese of Tennessee on Friday
      the 20th day of July in the year of our Lord, 1894. Parents
      Daniel W. Shofner, Florence Shofner. Sponsors: Mrs. S. C. Erwin,
      Mrs. J. W. Rudolph. Born Sept. 19th 1893. F. F. Martin, Rector.

THOMPSON BIBLE

Photocopy by Paul K. Delk
Publisher: B. Warner, Philadelphia, Pa.   1819

RECORD:
Joseph Thompson was born 30th March 1782 and was married 20 Dec 1804
      to Elizabeth Thompson, born 15 Aug 1780.
Children:
1: Anna Thompson born 26 January 1799
2: Eliza Thompson born 29 November 1805
3: James Thompson born 6 January 1807
4: Harriet Thompson born 4 April 1809
5: Calvin Thompson born 22 March 1811
6: John A. Thompson born 27 March 1813
7: Patsey J. Thompson born 17 April 1815
8: William F. Thompson born 9 Dec 1817
9: Newton Cannon Thompson born 25 December 1819
10: Isabella Thompson born 30 August 1821

Martha Thompson Born 3 Oct 1760 Died Jan 6, 1841
Zilpha Windrow born 18 Feb 1786 Died 18 June 1851

Calving Thompson died 24 March 1852
Eliza Thompson died 27 Sept 1811
Joseph Thompson died 30 March 1824
William Thompson died 16 Oct 1826

Harret (Thompson) Richardson died 5 May 1830
John A. Thompson died 20 June 1840
James Thompson died 26 Dec 1841 at 5 p.m. Age 32 years, 11 months, and
    26 days.

Children of Newton Cannon Thompson:
1: Hattie Floyd Thompson born 28 Aug 1867, died 3 a.m. Wed. 15 Nov 1933
2: Emma Jane Thompson born 27 Feb 1869, died 7a.m. Monday 16 Jan 1939
    Emma Jane Thompson married 28 Dec 1892 to Joshua Vernon Delk who
    was born 8 Jan 1863. Children:
    1: Howard Porter Delk born 19 Sept 1893
    2: Horace Cannon Delk born 26 Aug 1896
    3: Harry Hunter Delk born 16 June 1900
    4: Floyd McLean Delk born 25 Nov 1901
    5: Paul Kennedy Delk born 17 Feb 1904
    6: Allen Freed Delk born 10 Mar 1906

DEATHS:
J. V. Delk died 30 Oct 1944
Emma Jane Thompson Delk died 16 Jan 1939
Harry Hunter Delk died 20 June 1901
Horace Cannon Delk died 6 Oct 1947
Floyd M. Delk died 8 Feb 1960
Howard P. Delk died 19 Sept 1964

Children of Geney Chelders, who was the colored Cook for Newton Cannon
Thompson and his wife Elizabeth Green Thompson:
Mary, born 1 June 1851
Daniel, born 26 Dec 1853
Nancy, born 10 Feb 1856
Nathan, born 15 Nov 1859
Malinda, born 28 Feb 1862

Thompson History in Old Joseph Thompson Bible:
    Joseph Thompson (30 Mar 1782-30 Mar 1824) was a son of John
Theophilus Thompson(7 Dec 1759-10 April 1826), accepted by the DAR as
a Soldier of the Revolution, was born in Frederick County, Maryland, he
went from there to North Carolina and then came to Bedford County, Tennessee, in the early 1800's, he was a son of Richard Thompson born in Dec.
1735 a resident or possibly a native of Frederick County, Maryland and
of his wife Mary. His grandparents are believed to have been Sarah and
John Thompson. Theophilus Thompson died in Bedford County.
    On 1780, Theophilus fought under DeKalb at the Battle of Camden,
S. C. and again in that year commanded a Company at King's Mountain
and subsequently at the Battle of Cowpens in 1781, he was in the Battle
of Guilford Court House.
    Theophilus Thompson married Mary Newcom in North Carolina and
they had three sons: Joseph, Samuel and Newcom. They may have had other
children but these three are known. The Family crossed the Mountains in
Ox Carts traveling in Creeks to keep from being tracked by the Indians.
    The information about Theophilus Thompson's Military history was

obtained from DAR application in Mollie Thompson Davidson, National No. 18195, other information as well as his Military history is contained in the Solomon Family History, compiled by Marion Solomon.

In Sampson County, North Carolina, on 20 Jan 1787, Martha Thompson, for love and affection Deeds to her "beloved daughters" Elizabeth and Zilphia, two Negro Slaves. This Deed is recorded in Sampson County, North Carolina, 1787 after being proven in open Court by a witness, Roger Snell, registered in Book B, page 320-321. This same Deed is registered in Bedford County, Tennessee, 12 July 1814, Book D, page 442.

The above information shows or indicates that the Martha Thompson (3 Oct 1760- 6 Jan 1841) who is recorded in Joseph Thompson's Bible is the Mother of his wife Elizabeth Thompson born 15 Aug 1780, and Zilphia Windrow born 18 Feb 1786 died 18 June 1851, Zilphia probably married and outlived a Windrow.

This all being true would show that Joseph Thompson's wife Elizabeth was a Thompson before she married Joseph Thompson. This Elizabeth Thompson born 15 Aug 1780 lived to be over 80 years old as she is listed in the 1860 Census but don't appear in the 1870 Census.

In the Old Joseph Thompson Bible, page 780, John: 20:17, where the page is torn there is two little stitches X X where Elizabeth Thompson repaired the tear.

Newton Cannon Thompson and Elizabeth Green were married by W. C. B. Thompson a Minister of the Gospel, 17 Mar 1866.

LAWRENCE BIBLE

Typed Copy
Publisher: Missing

Thomas W. Davis born Feb 22, 1810
Martha Hogin born July 8, 1809

James Lawrence & Marry Harris was married April 18, 1834
Mary Harris Lawrence born Oct 9, 1814
Child:
Elizabeth born Sept 5, 1835, died April 6, 1928
Nancy born Nov 2, 1837
Emmeline born Jan 7, 1839
Milly Ann born Mar 20, 1842
Mary born Aug 20, 1844
Margaret born July 18, 1847
Sarah Menerva born Oct 6, 1849
William born Dec 6, 1829
Samuel T. born Oct 2, 1831
George W. born Dec 5, 1835, died Jan 27, 1914
Elisha H. born Nov 8, 1843
Charles T. born Dec 6, 1847

Richard N. born Nov 8, 1851
Lemuel R. born Sept 10, 1854
Will--- Susan J. born Sept 16, 1846
Richard---William G. Davis born Dec 13, 1869
Catherine L. Allen born Sept 23, 1824
Will... Thomas A. Davis born Aug 23, 1871
Richard... Martha R. Davis born April 18, 1873
Richard... Neal R. Davis born Sept 13, 1874
Elisha..: Phebe E. J. Davis born June 25, 1878
N. R. Davis & M. S. Davis were married Oct 12, 1894

This Bible was in the possession of James Davis, Shelbyville, Tennessee
    in the 1960's.

ALLEN BIBLE

In possession of Rosalinda Brown Allen Eads, a Zerox copy of the Bible
which is owned by Mrs. J. E. Jones, Denton, Texas.
Taken from "Footprints" Vol. 15, No. 3, Aug 1972, Ft. Worth, Texas.

Parents names	Where	& by whom	born		Died
Richard F. Allen,			Sept 22, 1810		Nov 26,1851
Rosalinda Brown,	Tennessee	Thos. Coffee	Mar 20, 1812	Tenn	
Children:					
Elizabeth A.Allen	Texas	Thos. Calloway	Sept 23, 1833	Tenn	Mar 9, 1855
Martha A. Allen	"	H. Bennet	Nov 10, 1835	Mo.	
Hugh B. Allen	Idaho	Moses Fowler	Jun 11, 1839	Mo.	
Sabrina Allen	Texas	Scarberry	Mar 19, 1841	Mo.	
Cyrena Allen	"	"	Feb 24, 1843	Mo.	
Mayrilda Allen			Feb 15, 1845	Mo.	Nov 20,1845
Thos. R. Allen	Texas		Oct 23, 1846	Mo.	
Linda C. Allen			Jul 29, 1849	Texas	Apr 11, 1864
Sarah M. Allen			May 15, 1851	"	Dec 23, 1854
Jesse Eads	Texas	Thos Calloway	Jun 17, 1795		May 30,1875

Notes: Richard F. Allen, son of Thomas J. and Permelia (Lindsay) Allen,
was born Bedford County, Tennessee. He came to Texas from Moniteau Co.,
Mo., with wife and children, and is buried in an unmarked grave in Med-
lin Cemetery, Denton County, Texas. The Family is on the 1850 Census of
Tarrant County, Texas. His widow, Rosalinda, married Jesse Eads, a
widower, and they and connections are on the 1860 Census of Wise County,
Texas. Of the Allen Children: Elizabeth A. is said to have married a
McDonald and died in Tarrant County. Mary Ann married Thomas Henry Calloway. Hugh Brown married Hannah Elizabeth Schooler. Sabrina married Jordan
J. Eads, son of Jesse Eads, and they were enumerated in 1860 in Wise Co.,
living next to Jesse and Rosalinda Eads, having "Married within the year".
Cyrena married (1) William Caldwell (od a family that had come to the
area from Navarro Co.) and lived near the Eads in 1860; she married (2)

William Shoemake, probably the one who was a neighbor in 1860. Permelia Allen, of the 1850 Census, and Serena Caddell, of the 1860 Census, are obviously one and the same person. Dr. Thomas Richard Allen married Rhoda Catherine Gage, daughter of Jeremiah Gage who lived near the Eads in Wise County in 1860, Catlett Creek Post Office.

BIBLE OF DR. JOSEPH H. ALLEN

In possession of Mrs. J. E. Jones, Denton Texas.
Fly-leaf: "The Student's Bible", by Orville J. Nave, D.D., L.L.D. and Anna Semans Nave, M.L.A., Sixty-Third Thousand nd.
The Abington Press, New York, Cincinnatti, Chicago.

FAMILY RECORD:
Husband's Father: T. R. Allen (Thomas Richard)
Husband's Mother: R. C. Allen (nee Rhoda Catherine Gage)
Wife's Father: J. C. McDaniel
Wife's Mother: H. E. McDaniel
Husband: J. H. Allen
Birthplace: Greenwood, Texas   Date: Oct 17, 1877.
Wife: E. B. Allen (Effie B. McDaniel)
Birthplace: Decatur, Texas   Date: Dec 26, 1879.
Place of marriage: J. C. McDaniel's, Greenwood, Texas
Date of marriage: June 5, 1907
Officiating Clergyman: J. W. Sweeton, Decatur, Texas
Witnesses: J. E. Allen, Minnie McDaniel, Hattie McDaniel Cora McDaniel
        and Rachel Gage and Luty Gage.
Names of Children:
Clarence Edward Allen, June 5, 1908
Joseph Ellwood Allen, July 24, 1910
Lorena Catherine Allen, July 7, 1913

MARRIAGES:
Clarence Edward Allen to Louella Fry, Denton, Texas, Feb 8, 1927
Joseph Ellwood Allen to Margarett Brown, Denton, Texas, Oct 10, 1936
Lorena Catherine Allen to James Evans Jones, June 6, 1939

JONES BIBLE

In possession of Mrs. Josie Jones Briley, Stephenville, Texas.
Copied by Mrs. T. B. Cawyer, Stephenville, Texas for Footprints,
        Vol. 16, No. 2, May 1973.

This is to Certify that the Rite of Holy Matrimony was Celebrated be-
tween Mr. J. W. Jones of Corinth, Ark., and Miss Susan Murray of Corinth,
Arkansas on the 16th day of June 1870 at the home of the Bride, by
N. McClure, J.P.

BIRTHS:
J. W. Jones was born Nov 4, 1848
Susan D. Jones was born April 3rd, 1850
Leona Jane Jones was born Feb 17, 1871
Reese Basket Jones was born (no date)
Isaac Newton Jones was born August 2, 1874
Mary Rebecca Jones was born August 16, 1876
Minerva Malinda Jones was born December 22, 1880
David D. Jones was born (no date)
Josie Annie Jones was born December 29, 1884

DEATHS:
Mary Rebecca Metsgar died July 2, 1908
Susan D. Jones died December 13, 1926
John Wiley Jones died August 31, 1936
Isaac Newton Jones died May 24th, 1949

FAMILY RECORD OF D. D. JONES FAMILY:
        D. D. Jones and Minerva Reese was married Oct 17th, 1833
William Campbell and Rebecca Catherine Jones was married Feb 1854
Larkin Acree and Mariah Frances Jones was married April 10th, 1856
Charles Watson and Sarah Elizabeth Reese was married Feb 10th, 1845
J. G. Reese and Catherine Womack was married Feb 28, 1844

BIRTHS:
D. D. Jones was born Feb 13, 1814*(see Note)
Minerva M. Jones was born March 18, 1817
Rebecca Catherine Jones was born August 15, 1835
Walter W. Jones was born Feb 26, 1837
Mariah Frances Jones was born November 28, 1838
Charley W. Jones was born October 2, 1843
Sloman Woodford Jones was born April 3, 1846
John Wiley Jones was born November 4th, 1848
Nancy Elizabeth Jones was born Jan 28, 1851
Tacy Jane Jones was born June 9, 1853
Sally Eliza Jones was born March 24, 1856
David Jordan Jones was born April 28, 1859

*Note: David Dickens Jones was a son of Charles Jones and Rebecca Norman,
       both born at Jones Ferry, S. C. Several related families moved
       about 1805 to Bedford County Tennessee and between 1845-1850 to
       Corinth, Arkansas. Many of their descendants later moved to Erath
       County, Texas and settled in the Huckabay Community. Charles Jones,
       born 1777, died in Bedford County, Tennessee in 1833. His widow,
       born 2 February 1781, died in Corinth, Arkansas. Their children
       were:(1) Sarah, married Mike Womack; (2) Catherine, married Elli-
       son Cox; (3) Wiley B.; (4) Fannie, married Charles Crawford; (5)
       Jack, married a Lucas; (6) Tacie, married Wiley Watson; (7) David
       Dickens; (8) Rebecca, married Riley Yates; (9) Margaret; married
       Walter Watson; (10) Charles Brooks, married Jane Chesshir; (11)
       Samuel, married Pauline Chesshir; and (12) Eliza Jane, married

Sloman W. Reese. (Reese, S.B., <u>Corinth, Arkansas and Its Kinfolks</u>, 1931)

FAMILY RECORD:
Father:W. C. Mauldin, born April 12th, 1849 in Mississippi, died August 29, 1917, married 10th Sept 1874 at Corrinth, Arkansas to
Mother:T. J. Mauldin, born June 9th, 1853 in Arkansas, died 21 Dec 193_.
Children:

 1: S. E. Mauldin born 18 July 1875, died 4 June 1886(?)
 2: D. M. Mauldin born 31 Jan 1877 in Ark., died 10 Sept 1879
 3: J. G. Mauldin born 15 August 1879 in Ark., died 1937
 4: J. W. Mauldin born 12 August 1881
 5: M. G.(?) Mauldin born 6th Nov 1883, died 5-'59
 6: Whit Mauldin born 8 Sept 1886, died Jan 11, 1919
 7: El. Mauldin born 8 Sept 1886
 8: B. B. Mauldin born 14th April 1888, died 3rd July 1945
 9: C. D. Mauldin born 30 Jan 1890
 10: O. L. Mauldin born 6th Feb 1895, died 7th Oct 189_.
 11; D. M. Mauldin born 2nd April 1896
 12: Teddy Mauldin born 7th July 1898

Loose page:
Manervia M. Reese was born 18th March 1817
Sally Eliza Jones was born 24th March 1856
Rebecca Catherine Jones was born August 15th A.D. 1835
David Jordan Jones was born 28th April 1859
Walter M. Jones was born Feb 26th 1837
Mariah Frances Jones was born November 28th 1839
Charles W. Jones was born 20th October 1843
Slayman (Sloman)? Woodford Jones was born 3rd April 1846
John Wilie Jones was born 4th November 1848
Nancy Elizabeth Jones was born Jan 28th 1851
Tacy Jane Jones was born 9th June 1853
C.(G?) D. Jones and Manervia M. Reese was married 17th Oct 1833
William Campbell and Rebekah Marine Jones was married Feb 1854
Larkin H. Acree and Mariah Frances Jones was married 10th April A.D. 1856
J. G. Rees and Catherine Ann Womack was married 22rd Feb 1844
Charley(torn) and Sarah Eli(torn) married 10th Feb 1845

Note: These are the names of persons entered in the D. D. Jones Family Bible, with a few discrepancies in dates. See Bible Record of John Wiley Jones in this issue.

DAVIDSON BIBLE

In possession of Mrs. J. D. Elkins, McMinnville, Tennessee
Publisher: Missing.
Copied from Bible Records in North Carolina Archives and History,
Raleigh, North Carolina.

Name of Family: Major William Davidson and wife Margaret McConnell
Location: Duck and Obrion River, Tenn.
      The branches of the Davidson family who went to Tenn. from
Buncombe County, N.C. Major Wm. Davidson was a Major in the Revolution.
He went to Swannanoa, Buncombe County and made the first white settle-
ment west of the Blue Ridge in N.C. He was granted a large tract of
land in Tennessee. So many of his sons and daughters went to the Duck
River and Obrion River section of Tennessee to settle. This Major William Davidson was a first cousin of General William Lee Davidson who fell
at Cowans Ford, North Carolina.

BIBLE

      This is the Duck River branch of the Davidson family who emi-
grated from N.C. to eastern Tennessee. Davidson family from Iredell
County went to Buncombe County, North Carolina then to Tennessee.
      William Davidson, first cousin of General W. L. Davidson was 1st
Lt. 3rd Penn Batallion in 1776, afterwards commissioned Major in 4th
N. C. Regiment. Children of this Major William Davidson and Wife, Mar-
garet McConnell according to list in an Old Bible in possession of Mrs.
J. D. Elkins of McMinnville, Tennessee.
Children born to this marriage:
Mary Davidson, born October 4 ____
John Davidson, born Oct 4, 1764 married Martha Davidson, the daughter
      of James Davidson.
George Davidson, born January 1, 1768
Hugh Davidson, born January 5, 1768, married 1796 Jean Vance, daughter
      of David Vance.
Jane Davidson, born June 1, 1772
Sarah Davidson, born July 29, 1774, married William Lusk, son of Wm.
      Lusk killed at Battle of Kings Mountain.
Ruth Davidson, born November 2, 1777
William M. Davidson, born Jan. 1780, married Elizabeth Vance, daughter
      of Col. David Vance.
Samuel W. Davidson, born April 2, 1782, married 1st a McRee, 2nd Eliza-
      beth Vance Davidson, widow of his brother William M.
Elizabeth Vance Davidson was born July 1, 1775.

The Children of John and Martha Davidson are:
Hugh Davidson, born January 29, 1795
James Davidson, born September 12, 1796, died 1824
Mary Katherine, daughter of Jas. Davidson Married Louis Tillman
William Davidson, born July 8, 1798, died November 3, 1816
George Davidson, born March 10, 1800

Lorenzo Davidson, born June 29, 1804

Margaret M. Davidson born December 26, 1807, married Frances Smart of
    Warren County
Andrew M. Davidson born October 22, 1811 (all of these children were
    born in Buncombe County, North Carolina).

This Bible Record was copied and sent to William Bethell Williamson
of Asheville, North Carolina in 1930.

BIBLE RECORDS OF DAVIDSON FAMILY OF BUNCOMBE CO., N.C. AND DUCK RIVER,
    TENNESSEE.
Brief History of the Davidson Family compiled from published and un-
published Records owned by John Mitchell Davidson(1829-1917) Kingston,
Georgia. Now in possession of his son John Lee Davidson, Quitman, Ga.

Emigration of William Mitchell Davidson and Family
from Buncombe County, North Carolina to Texas in 1844
                A Reminiscence by John Mitchell Davidson (1829-1917)
Original manuscript in possession of John L. Davidson, Jr., Tarrytown,
New York and copied by his. (1955)

                    BRIEF HISTORY OF THE DAVIDSON FAMILY
                    AND SOME OF THEIR BIBLE RECORDS

John Davidson with his brother George came from Ireland and settled in
Pa.   They moved from there to Iredell Co., N. C., about 1748. They
were of Scotch-Irish descent.
John Davidson married Mrs. Morrison. Their children were:
Major William, married Margaret McConnell.
Samuel (twin of Major Wm.), married Miss Smith. He was killed by
Indians at Swannanoa Gap, N.C. about 1784. His only child Ruth married
James Wilson and left descendants.
Rachel married John Alexander, later moved to Crowder's Creek in that
part of Lincoln Which is now Gaston Co., N.C.
Betty married Ephraim McLean, settled near Nashville, Tenn., on the
Cumberland River, still known as "McLean's Bend".
Margaret or Peggy married James Smith, emigrated to middle Tenn., soon
after the Revolution, left descendants.
George emigrated to Tenn., settled near Shelbyville, left (NB-error-
Geo., son of John, was Col. George of Centre Church, Iredell County,
N.C./G.F.B.JR.)
Thomas settled in S. C., many of his descendants still live in that State
many others in Fla., Ala., Texas, and other S.W.States.
There is some confusion as to--
John who married Nancy Brevard. Some say he was the John Davidson kill-
ed 1776 by Indians on Mill Creek, near Old Fort, N.C. Some say he emigrated to Tenn., and settled near Columbia. It is more probable he was
the one killed by Indians. (NB- The John who married Nancy Brevard was
probably the son of Col. George. G.F.B.Jr.)

William Davidson was appointed Major of the 4th North Carolina Regiment, Apr 1775. He took a prominent part in the preparation made by the North Carolinians for the Battle of Kings Mountain. In 1791, Major William Davidson was Representative from Rutherford County. David Vance was Representative from Burke County. David Vance introduced the bill creating the County of Buncombe. Maj. William Davidson seconded the motion, the bill was passed and the new County was organized in William Davidson's house in 1792 on the banks of the Swannanoa River, where Biltmore now stands. Major William Davidson was the first state Senator from Buncombe County. (NB- Here the writer has Maj. William confused in part with Col. William, a different person, but living in the same area. G.F.B. Jr.)

The DAR have erected a monument to Major William Davidson on the Old Davidson Homestead where the Bee Tree Creek empties into the Swannanoa River, the inscription as follow:
" Major William Davidson 1744-1810. Soldier of the Revolution. House of Commons 1790. Senate 1792. One of the earliest settlers of the French Broad Valley. He was prominent in the organization of Buncombe County." On the reverse side: " Erected by the DAR."

These dates must be incorrect as an Old Family Record shows that William Davidson died May 16, 1814, age 78 years. His wife Margaret (McConnell) Davidson, died Nov. 13, 1806, age 58 years.

DAVIDSON FAMILY BIBLE RECORD

NAME OF FAMILY	Hugh Davidson
Location:	Duck River Section of Tennessee
Bible:	Date of Publication Unknown
Owner:	Hugh Davidson descendants in Normandy and Obrion River section of Tennessee

BIRTHS AND DEATHS	BORN	DIED
Hugh Davidson	Jan 5, 1768	Sept 19, 1841
Jane Vance	Nov 30, 1777	Jan 12, 1858
Children:		
Wm. Mitchell Davidson	Aug 21, 1797	March 7, 1874
Priscilla Davidson	July 6, 1799	Aug 29, 1840
Margaret M. Davidson	Aug 18, 1801	April 21, 1868
David Vance Davidson	Nov 29, 1803	Nov 3, 1869
Angeline Davidson	July 26, 1806	Apr 16, 1849
John Q. Davidson	Jan 26, 1808	Oct 12, 1879
Sarah E. Davidson	Apr 28, 1810	Dec 27, 1810
Samuel L. Davidson	Apr 19, 1812	Dec 31, 1870
Hugh L. Davidson	Apr 17, 1814	Apr 30, 1889
Robert Brank Davidson	Mar 12, 1817	
Eliza Jane Davidson	June 3, 1819	Sept 18, 1822
Martha Ann Davidson	Dec 16, 1821	May 5, 1851

MARRIAGES:

Wm. Mitchell Davidson	Mary Caruthers	July 4, 1837
Priscilla Davidson	Wm. A. Brittian	Jan 2, 1821
Margaret M. Davidson	Ransom Gwynn	Nov 1, 1832
David Vance Davidson	Sarah C. Hall	Jan 29, 1829
Angeline Davidson	(1) Thos. J. Bryan	Dec 28, 18--
	(2) Harwood Morgan	May 8, 1837
John Q. Davidson	Susan S. Hord	Dec 3, 1833
Hugh L. Davidson	(1) Edie Harrison	Apr 24, 1838
	(2) Mrs. Eliz. R. Nice	Oct 28, 1861
Martha Ann Davidson	Wm. B. Watterson	Dec 24, 1840
Robert Brank Davidson	(1) Narcissa Harrison	Aug 21, 1843
	(2) Mrs. Virginia S.	
	Buchanan	Mar 16, 1871

Copied by Mrs. J. L. Davidson for DAR, Gastonia, North Carolina.

DAVIDSON BIBLE RECORDS:

In possession of Mrs. Elizabeth Williamson Dixon, Gastonia, North Carolina
Publisher: J. B. Bunn and Hyde, Hartford, Conn.

Allen Turner Davidson, born May 9, 1817
Elizabeth Adeline Howell Davidson born April 8, 1824
Theodore S. F. Davidson, born Sunday, March 30, 1845
Wilbur S. Davidson born Sunday, April 9, 1847
William Edwin Davidson born Tuesday, March 27, 1849
Ella H. Davidson, born Sunday March 30, 1851
Robert V. Davidson, born Saturday, July 23, 1853
Cora I. Davidson born Saturday, February 23, 1856
Mary Elizabeth Davidson, born Friday May 20, 1859
Allen Turner Davidson Jr., born Friday June 7, 1861
Addie Lee Davidson born June 5, 1864

Grandchildren of Allen T. Davidson and Elizabeth A. Howell Davidson:
Mariella Davidson, born Wednesday July 8, 1874
Wilbur E. Davidson born Friday February 25, 1877.
James Harold Morrison, born July 23, 1878
Nannie Knox Davidson born July 14, 1880
Thomas Jack Davidson born January 18, 1882
Thedore D. Morrison born Feb 9, 1883
William Spencer Child born July 27, 1883
Allen Turner Morrison born March 23, 1886
Wilbur S. Davidson born October 10, 1886
Ella Varick Morrison born October 8, 1887 (Eleanor Morrison) or (Nell)

Allen Turner Davidson and Elizabeth Adeline Howell married October 12;
    1842
Theodore Fulton Davidson and Sallie Kate Davidson married November 6,
    1866
William Edwin Davidson and Hannah Mira Smith married Oct 14, 1873

Ella Henrietta Davidson and Theodore S. Morrison married June 12, 1877
Mary Elizabeth Davidson and William Spencer Child married October 12, 1882
Robert Vance Davidson and Laura Jack were married July 14, 1879, Galveston, Texas
Theodore Fulton Davidson married 2nd to Sarah Lindsey Carter October 12, 1893 in Raleigh, North Carolina

DEATHS: ·
Cora L. Davidson died Saturday September 20, 1862
William Edwin Davidson died December 21, 1877
James Harold Morrison died August 29, 1833
William Spencer Child, Jr. died July 22, 1884
Allen Turner Davidson, Jr. died June 11, 1888
Elizabeth Adeline Davidson died Thursday, 3 o'clock A.M., May 4, 1917
Allen Turner Davidson died Tuesday, January 24, 1905
Wilbur Sevier Davidson died Saturday January 7, 1928 at Houston, Texas
Theodore F. Davidson died Thursday June 11, 1931, in Asheville, North Carolina
Robert Vance Davidson died July 2, 1925 in Dallas, Texas
Allen Davidson Williamson died April 14, 1939
William Bethell Williamson died December 4, 1939
Addie Davidson Williamson died June 16, 1940
Mary Elizabeth Davidson Child died...

Copied by Mrs. Kay Dixon, Gastonia, North Carolina.

WILLIAM MITCHELL DAVIDSON BIBLE RECORD

NAME OF FAMILY: William Mitchell Davidson Son of
                                   Major William Davidson of the
                                   Revolution, Haywood County, N.C.
This Record is taken from two different Bibles in the possession of
Davidson Family. Owned by Elizabeth Dixon, Gastonia, N.C., and Edmund
B. Norvell, Murphy, North Carolina.

BIRTH AND DEATHS

	Born	Died
William Mitchell Davidson	July 2, 1780	May 31, 1846
Elizabeth Vance	Mar 23, 1787	Apr 14, 1861
Children:		
David Vance Davidson	Feb 23, 1807	Sep --, 1807
Margaret Elvira Davidson	Feb 13, 1805	Apr 10, 1891
William Edwin Davidson	Jul 9, 1809	Jul 7, 1847
Priscilla Eliza Davidson	Sept 20, 1811	Mar 21, 1901
Hugh Harvey Davidson	Mar 27, 1814	Jul 1, 1889
Celia Emeline Davidson	Oct 11, 1816	May 29, 1896
Allen Turner Davidson	May 9, 1819	Jan 24, 1905
Samuel Winslow Davidson	Mar 3, 1823	Oct 13, 1895
Robt. Brank Vance Davidson	Nov 21, 1826	Jan 7, 1871

John Mitchell Davidson   Oct 21, 1829   Jan 17, 1917

MARRIAGES:
Margaret E. Davidson   (1) Joseph H. Walker, July 5, 1821
                              (2) Thos. L. Gaston, July 12, 1842
Priscilla E. Davidson   (1) Rev. Paxton : ...
                                  Cumming,   Sept 21, 1842
Hugh H. Davidson   Lucinda Emaline
                                  Moody   Oct 27, 1840
Celia E. Davidson   (1) Ezekiel Enloe   Jan 21, 1834
                              (2) Henry Moss   Nov 17, 1861
Allen T. Davidson   Eliza. A. Howell   Oct 12, 1842
Samuel W. Davidson   Margaret J.
                                      Alexander   Dec 27, 1853
Robt. Brank Vance Davidson   Ann E. Harris   Sept 1, 1852
John W. Davidson   (1) Julia A. Dunn   Nov 1, 1855
                              (2) Jennie D. Parrott Oct 21, 1890

Copied by Mrs. Kay Dixon, Gastonia, North Carolina.

DAVIDSON BIBLE RECORDS

NAME OF FAMILY: Major John Davidson's Family
Location: Mecklenburg County, Hopewell
                              Section, North Carolina.

        Mary Davidson was the daughter of Major John Davidson
(Signer of Mecklenburg Declaration of Independence) and wife
Violet Wilson. Mary Davidson married Dr. William McLean, Surgeon's
mate, Revolution, of Lincoln (now Gaston County) North Carolina.
They lived in the South Point Section of Gaston County.
        Major John Davidson was born on the 15th of December 1735;
married to Violet Wilson on the 2nd of June 1761- Alias Violet Wilson
Davidson was born August 13, 1742 and died on the 3rd of December 1818.

Children:
Rebecca Davidson, their first child, was born on the 20th of March, 1762.
Isabella Davidson was born on the 21st of September 1764 Died on the
        13th of January 1808.
Mary Davidson was born on the 13th of December 1766.
Robert Davidson was born on the 7th of April 1769.
Violet Davidson was born on the 28th of August 1771. Died on the 20th
        of October 1826.
Sarah Davidson was born on the 13th of June 1774.
Margaret Davidson was born on the 8th of February 1777.
John Davidson was born on the 12th of November 1779.
Elizabeth Davidson was born on the 15th of September 1782.
Benjamin W. Davidson was born on the 23rd of May 1787, died on the 25th
        of September 1829 at eleven o'clock at night.

DEATHS:
Violet Wilson, wife of John Davidson, died December 3, 1818
Isabella D. Graham died January 3, 1808.
Violet D. Alexander died October 26, 1821.
Margaret D. Harris died July 30, 1830. Age: 53 years, 6 months.
Rebecca Davidson Brevard died November 23, 1824.
Major John Davidson died Tuesday the 10th of January 1832.
Elizabeth Lee Davidson died April the 27th 1845.
Sarah D. Calwell died February 3, 1842.

Copied by John McLean, Belmont, North Carolina.

McARTHUR BIBLE

Submitted by Georgia Elise McArthur Troupe, Normandy, Tennessee

Daniel McArthur was born in Scotland in the year 1741. He with his wife
Jeanette were married in 1774, and that year, came to America, settling
in North Carolina, Robeson County.

Their first child, Mary, was born April 14th, 1775. Following are the
other ten:
Sara, born February 12, 1777
Duncan, born March 4th, 1779
Charles, born May 25th, 1780
John, born April 7th, 1782
Peter, born March 2, 1784
Archibald, born September 28, 1786
Neil, born November 2, 1788
Alexander, born February 6, 1791
Allen, born July 6, 1793
Isabella, born November 10, 1796

Daniel arrived in this Country just about the time the Revolution was
getting under way. The long and turbulent times in Scotland left little
love for the established government in England, and so Daniel threw in
his lot with the Colonies. He served in the North Carolina Regiments.
He was paid for his services by Voucher #1595, recorded on page 4, Long
book, State of North Carolina.
It is on this record that many applicants for the DAR base their claims.

Daniel set a pattern that was followed for generations by his descendants.
He was 33 years old when he married. His wife was 22. In most of his
descendants, this same tendency was followed. Most of his sons and the
daughters followed the same pattern.

Daniel and Jeanette spent all their years in this Country in North
Carolina, while their sons, many of them, came into Georgia to settle

and rear their families.

Note: Georgia Elise Troupe said her father was also 33 years old when he married.

SNELL BIBLE RECORDS

Submitted by Mrs. Virginia McBride, Shelbyville, Tennessee
Publisher: Missing.

James Thomas Snell, born Oct 4, A.D. 1846, died 11-20-1918
Nancy Jane Hasting born April 26, 1849, died Dec 22, 1919, married
     Aug 20, 1865.

Albert Robert Snell born July 13, 1867, died July 3, 1946
Georgie Ann Snell born ___ 8, 1869, died Nov 21, 1917
Mary Belle Snell born Dec 29, 1871

Wiley B. Snell, born April 17, 1798, died Jan 1, 1888

Albert G. Snell, born July 20, 1820, died Nov 15, 1855
Cassande M. Snell Born May 4, 1820

Robert Hastings Born Nov 11, 1820
Thomas S. Word was born June 29, 1820, died Aug 28, 1890

Martin S, Shoffner born May 27, 1840, died Feb 14, 1906
Mary Ann Shoffner, born Aug 29, 1847, died Sept 16, 1920

HIGGINS BIBLE

In possession of Mrs. Margaret Stokes, Shelbyville, Tennessee
Publisher: Bowen, Stewart & Co., No. 18 West Washington St.,
     Indianapolis, Ind.   1881

Presented to Eugene J. Higgins, by _____ 1884.

This Certifies that the Rite of Holy Matrimony was celebrated between:
     Eugene J. Higgins of Fayetteville, Tenn. and
     Addie Woodard of Fayetteville, Tenn., on
     Jan. 24th 1884 at Mrs. Mary Woodard's by Rev. J. H. Graves.
     Witness: R. N. Hutton & H. K. Bryson

MARRIAGES:
Walter Higgins & Vic Whitaker, Apr 9th 1907
Edith G. Higgins & J. J. Moyers, July 26th, 1910
Robert S. Higgins & Mayme Shelly, Jan 31st 1912
Rosa Annah Higgins & Elmer Ross Caughran, Oct 20, 1925
Eugene B. Higgins & Mary Frances Bagley, Feb 23, 1944
Dan Higgins Caughran & Maria Peck Lane Barkdull, Aug 2, 1952
Charlotte Moyers & Jerry Clendenin, Dec 12, 1935
Margaret Lynn Higgins & Wm. Pruitt Stokes, Dec 20, 1927

BIRTHS:
Eugene J. Higgins born May 7th 1853
Addie Woodard born Oct 27th 1865
Walter Woodard Higgins born May 23rd 1885
Robert Stone Higgins born Sept 23 1886
Roseanna Higgins born Dec 6th 1887
Edith Gentry Higgins born Mar 10th 1890
Mary Eugenia Higgins born Mar 11th 1901
Frances Owen Higgins born Feb 5th 1906
Dan Higgins Caughran born Oct 2, 1932
Charlotte Higgins Moyers born Sept 12, 1911
Margaret Lynn Higgins born Jan 17, 1908
Eugene B. Higgins born Aug 12, 1918

DEATHS:
Eugene J. Higgins died' Feb 16th 1909
Frances Owen Higgins died Jan 24th 1910
Gena Higgins died Nov 9, 1915
Addie W. Higgins died July 12, 1917
Jas. Jackson Moyers died Jan 12, 1937
Vic Whitaker Higgins died June 17, 1940
Robert Stone Higgins died May 25, 1941
Walter Woodard Higgins died June 11, 1942
Rose Higgins Caughran died Jan 17, 1961
Elmer R. Caughran
Edith Higgins Moyers

STOKES BIBLE

In possession of Mrs. Margaret Stokes, Shelbyville, Tennessee
Publisher: Name missing.   1886

This Certifies that James A. Stokes of Shelbyville and Cleaver C.
Christian of Shelbyville, were joined by me in the Bonds of Holy Matri-
mony at Home of Bride on the fourth day of November in the year of our
Lord, 1875. In the presence of Redden G. Purdy, & Abraham Sewell.

MARRIAGES:
Edward C. Stokes to Myrtle Pruitt on February 17, 1902
William Pruitt Stokes to Margaret Higgins on December 20, 1927

BIRTHS:
James A. Stokes, Born Sept 14, 1854
Cleaver C. Stokes, Born Dec 1, 1855
Edward C. Stokes, Born Sept 13, 1876
Albert M. Stokes, Born April 30, 1878
John W. Stokes, Born Oct 2, 1881
Wm. Pruitt Stokes, Born Oct 8, 1904

DEATHS:
John W. Stokes, died July 30, 1908
Albert M. Stokes, died July 26, 1915

WHITAKER BIBLE

In possession of Mrs. Margaret Stokes, Shelbyville, Tennessee
Publisher: Missing

I. B. Whitaker of Mulberry, Tenn., and Mary Lou McDaniel of Fayetteville,
Tenn., on the 7th of May 1878 at Col. C. A. McDaniel's by A. J. Orman of
Culeoka, Tenn.

BIRTHS:
Isaac Benj. Whitaker was born May 10th 1855
Mary Lou Whitaker was born April 25th 1859
Ambie Lee Whitaker was born February 7th 1879
McDaniel Whitaker was born Nov 5th 1880
Margaret Lynne Whitaker was born May 1st 1883
John Mark Whitaker, Sept 19th 1885
Victoria Terry Whitaker, March 17, 1887
Holland Benjamine Whitaker, Feb 9, 1890
James Fielden Whitaker, Jan 31, 1892
Coleman Rutledge Whitaker, Aug 6, 1894
Mary Whitaker, born March 8, 1897

MARRIAGES:
Mr. Walter W. Higgins to Miss Victoria T. Whitaker on April 9, 1907
Robert Lee Motlow to Margaret Lynne Whitaker on Aug 24, 1910
McDaniel Whitaker to Emma Banough of Kentucky, June 20, 1911
Coleman Rutledge Whitaker to Mable Scott, Petersburg, on Oct 10, 1917
Mary Whitaker to Jas. Lawton Shannon of Dresden, Tenn., on Jan 3, 1918
Holland Benjamine Whitaker to Mary Martha Gillespie of Petersburg, Tenn.,
     on Dec 4, 1919
John Mark Whitaker to Ida Harris of Chattanooga, May 25, 1923.

DEATHS:
Ambie Lee Whitaker died May 7th 1880
James Fielden Whitaker died Sept 25, 1896
Isaac Benjamin Whitaker, Feb 1st 1931
Victoria Whitaker Higgins died June 17, 1940
Mary Lou McDaniel Whitaker died March 14, 1943
John Mark Whitaker died Nov 13, 1949
Coleman R. Whitaker died May 1961
Lynn Whitaker Motlow died Nov 8, 1968
MacDaniel Whitaker died Sept 17, 1971

WOODARD BIBLE

A Photocopy in the possession of Mrs. Margaret Stokes, Shelbyville, Tenn.
Publisher: William Flint, 807 Market Street, Philadelphia

MARRIAGES:
Robert S. Woodard to Mary McKinney, 29 December 1842

BIRTHS:
Robert S. Woodard, born 16th January 1821
Mary McKinney, born 14th August 1824
James L. Woodard, born 16th November 1843
Galen D. Woodard, born 25th February 1845
Buena A. Woodard, born 1st January 1848
Milton W. Woodard, born 8th August 1846
Mary E. Woodard, born 7th September 1849
Andrew B. Woodard, born 8th September 1851
Robert P. Woodard, born 8th March 1853
John R. Woodard, born 5th August 1855
Sallie Woodard, born 29th November 1856
Willie K. Woodard, born 12th August 1859
Adda Woodard, born 27th October 1865

DEATHS:
Robt. S. Woodard died May 14th 1877
Sallie Woodard Francis died Sept 16th 1883
Mary Woodard died Nov 10th 1897
Galen Woodard died Feb 2nd 1904
Andrew Woodard, May 24th 1907
Jas. L. Woodard, Dec 5th 1910
Jno. R. Woodard, Jany 11th 1914
M. W. Woodard Feby 24th 1916
Robt. P. Woodard, Mar 13th 1917
Addie Woodard Higgins, July 12th 1917
W. K. Woodard died Dec 12, 1924
Mary E. Hatcher died Nov 4, 1925
Ann Woodard Dryden died Dec 10, 1929

HIGGINS BIBLE

In possession of Mrs. Margaret Stokes, Shelbyville, Tennessee
Publisher: Missing

This Certifies that Victoria Terry Whitaker of Fayetteville, Tennessee
and Walter Woodard Higgins of Fayetteville, Tennessee were united in
Matrimony according to the ordinance of God and the laws of Tennessee
at Fayetteville on the nineth day of April in the year of our Lord 1907.

MARRIAGES:
Margaret Higgins to Pruitt Stokes, December 20, 1927, Bedford Co., Tenn.
Eugene B. Higgins to Mary F. Bagley, Feb 23, 1944, Lincoln Co., Tenn.
Doris Stokes to John K. McCord, June 24, 1947, Bedford Co., Tenn.
Victoria Lynn McCord to James Vannatta Ransom
Mary Battle Higgins to Bob Ford Thompson

CHILDRENS NAMES:
Margaret Lynn Higgins, 1-17-08 (to Vic & Walter), Lincoln Co., Tenn.
Eugene Benjamin Higgins, 8-12-18 (to Vic & Walter), Bedford Co., Tenn.
Doris Marie Stokes, 9-28-28 (to Margaret & Pruitt), Bedford Co., Tenn.
Walter Lawrence Higgins, 2-21-46 (to Gene & Mary), Bedford Co., Tenn.
Mary Battle Higgins, 7-20-47 (to Gene & Mary), Lincoln Co., Tenn.
Robert Eugene Higgins, 6-11-50 (to Gene & Mary), Bedford Co., Tenn.
Victoria Lynn McCord, 8-30-48 (to Doris & John), Bedford C., Tenn.
Michael David McCord, 8-6-52 (to Doris & John), Bedford Co., Tenn.
Eugene Benjamin Higgins, Jr.,(to Gene & Mary), Bedford Co., Tenn.
Jennifer McCord Ransom, June 8, 1969 (to Vic & Van), Knox Co., Tenn.
Edward Ward Carmack Ransom, April 6, 1971 (to Vic & Van), Ft. Knox, Ky.

DEATHS:
Victoria Whitaker Higgins, June 17, 1940
Walter Woodard Higgins, June 11, 1942
William Pruitt Stokes, Feb 11, 1975

STOKES BIBLE

In possession of Mrs. Margaret Stokes, Shelbyville, Tennessee
Publisher: Missing.

Front: Edd Cooper Stokes, Sept 13th 1876
              and
       William Pruitt Stokes, Oct 8, 1914
                        Oct 3rd 1924
Family Register
Family Names:
Husband: Edd Cooper Stokes. Born Sept 13, 1876
Wife: Fannie Myrtle Pruitt. Born June 2, 1883, Married Feb 17, 1901

To this union was born two sons. One died in infancy and the other son, William Pruitt Stokes, reached maturity, and married.

Children Names:
William Pruitt Stokes was born Oct 8, 1904
Doris Marie Stokes was born Oct 28, 1928
Victoria Lynn McCord was born August 30, 1948
Michael David McCord born August 6, 1952
Jennifer McCord Ransom born June 8, 1969
Edward Ward Carmack Ransom born April 6, 1971

MARRIAGES:
William Pruitt Stokes to Margaret Lynn Higgins, December 20, 1927
Doris Marie Stokes to John King McCord, August 24, 1947
Vicki Lynn McCord to James Vannatta Ransom, November 7, 1968

DEATHS:
William J. Pruitt died Feb 9th 1915
Fannie Myrtle Stokes died Dec 26th 1918
Cleaver C. Stokes died Dec 24th 1922
James Alex. Stokes died Feb 3rd 1924
Edd Cooper Stokes died Dec 18, 1929
William Pruitt Stokes died Feb 11, 1975

NEWSPAPER OBIT: Wartrace, Tenn., Dec 28 (Special)
        Mrs. Myrtle Pruitt Stokes, wife of Ed C. Stokes, who died at
        their Country home, near Shelbyville, Thursday, after a linger-
        ing illness of tuberculosis, was buried Friday at Horse Mount-
        ain Cemetery. The Rev. E. W. Brown of Nashville, who was former-
        ly Pastor of the Methodist Church here, conducted the funeral
        services from the residence. The deceased was a member of the
        Methodist Church, was 35 years old, and is survived by her Hus-
        band and one son, Pruitt Stokes, beside a large number of other
        relatives. She had lived in Wartrace for ten or twelve years.

DAVID ASHLEY VAUGHAN BIBLE

In possession of Miss Wilma Chunn, Shelbyville, Tennessee
Publisher: H. & E. Phinney, Buffalo, F. W. Breed   1848

BIRTHS:
David Ashley Vaughan was born March 16, 1824
America Clementine Smith was born August 19, 1840
Harriet Irene Vaughan was born October 18, 1861
Emmett Oliver Vaughan was born May 30, 1864
Charles Ashley Vaughan was born December 31, 1866
Ervin Parks Vaughan was born March 3, 1869
Mattie Dare Vaughan was born November 15, 1871

Kate Anna Vaughan was born September 15, 1874
Florence Virginia Vaughan was born August 13, 1877
James David Vaughan was born April 7, 1880
Benjamin Oscar Vaughan was born July 18, 1882
Elizabeth John Vaughan was born February 18, 1885

MARRIAGES:
David Ashley Vaughan and America Clementine Smith were married December
    18, 1860.
Hattie Vaughan and William B. Lawler were married December 28, 1886
Emmett Vaughan and Janie Scruggs were married December 8, 1892
E. Parks Vaughan and Katherine Edwards were married Nov 8, 1894
Mattie Vaughan and Wm. E. Chunn were married Dec 17, 1896
Charlie Vaughan and Mollie Harris were married _____
Florence Vaughan and Robt. A. Smith were married October 17, 1900
Oscar Vaughan and Maude Flippen were married August 24, 1904
Elizabeth Vaughan and Dr. Ernest Holmes were married Oct 18, 1905

DEATHS:
David Ashley Vaughan departed this life November 25, 1888
America C. Smith Vaughan departed this life December 26, 1916
Emmett Vaughan died July 1, 1934
Kate Vaughan died July 27, 1945
Elizabeth V. Holmes died Aug 10, 1947
Oscar Vaughan died May 21, 1949
Parks Vaughan died Sept 5, 1949
Charlie Vaughan died Nov 2, 1951
Jimmy Vaughan died March 30, 1955
Mattie V. Chunn died June 18, 1955
Hattie V. Lawler died Sept 28, 1955
Florence V. Smith died Aug 22, 1956

WILLIAM ELDRIDGE CHUNN BIBLE

In possession of Wilma Chunn, Shelbyville, Tennessee
Publisher: London and New York, Collins' Clear-Type Press,
          Glasgow. Toronto. Sydney. Auckland.
          Printed in Great Britain (no date)

PARENT'S NAMES
Husband: William Eldridge Chunn, born Feb 24, 1875, died April 8, 1952
Wife: Mattie Vaughan, born Nov 15, 1871, died June 18, 1955
Married, Dec 17, 1896 Bondsman A. L. Chunn; Minister: Rev. Green P.
Jackson.

Children:
1: Infant Daughter, stillborn Sept 18, 1897
2: William Guy, born April 13, 1899

3: Wilma Chunn, born Aug 24, 1908
4: David Lancelot, born June 29, 1918

MARRIAGES:
Wm. Guy Chunn and Mary Holmes Landers were married Sept 27, 1922
David L. Chunn and Rebecca Lee Keele were married July 27, 1942
Wm. Guy Chunn and Mrs. Iola (McCall) Slean were married July 13, 1957

GRANDCHILDREN:
1: Stephen Lawrence, son of David and Rebecca, was born Nov 19, 1945,
        married Julie Ann Groover, Jan 4, 1973
2: Wilma Jeanne, dau of David and Rebecca, was born March 7, 1948,
        married David Keathley Wright, March 16, 1968

ANDREW LANCELOT CHUNN BIBLE

In possession of Wilma Chunn, Shelbyville, Tennessee
Publisher: Jno. A. Dickson Publishing Company, Chicago, Illinois
        Copyright   1905

Grand Parents:
Father's   William Jordon Chunn, born Aug 31, 1821, died July 30, 1897
Father:
Father's
Mother: Martha Susan Vannoy, born Aug 30, 1823, died July 21, 1905

Mother's
Father: Alfred Mallard, born Oct 4, 1813, died July 17, 1854
Mother's
Mother: Sarah Comer, born _____, died _____

Parents:
Father: Andrew L. Chunn, born May 26, 1847, died Jany 6, 1921
Mother: Eliza Mallard, born June 23, 1846, died Jany 1, 1929

MARRIAGE:
A. L. Chunn to Eliza Mallard. I Certify that I solemmized the rites
of Matrimony between the within named people, Sept 24, 1868
Security: W. J. Chunn   T. B. Marks, M.G.

Children:
1: Horace L., born July 24, 1870, died Lindsay, Cal., married Tennie
        Barber.
2: Minnie Tennessee, born July 24, 1872, died Sept 26, 1878
3: William Eldridge, born Feby 24, 1875, died 4/8/1952, married Mattie
        Vaughan, 12/17/1896
4: A. Edgar, born Sept 29, 1877, died 9/_/1958, mar'd Jennie Sanders
        11/29/1911

5: Annie Eureta, born July 25, 1887, died 5/23/1955, married
      James Davis Temple, 8/31/1912

THORNTON MALLARD BIBLE

In possession of Wilma Chunn, Shelbyville, Tennessee
Publisher: Charles Ewer, Boston   1816

Thornton Mallard, born October 13, 1769, died July 13, 1842
Elizabeth Mallard, born December 22, 1769, died November 20, 1845

Children:
1: John Mallard, born September 4, 1789, died December 28, 1814
      (War 1812)
2: George Mallard, born March 6, 1791
3: Sarah Mallard, born October 29, 1794
4: Eldridge Mallard, born September 26, 1797
5: Richard Mallard, born September 4, 1800
6: Deborah Mallard, born Feb 8, 1802, died Oct 8, 1844
7: William Mallard, born May 2, 1804, died August 11, 1806
8: James Mallard, born April 29, 1806, died March 11, 1829
9: Joseph Mallard, born March 21, 1809
10: Rebecca Mallard, born February 22, 1811
11: Alfred Mallard, born October 4, 1813, died July 17, 1854

Eldridge married Katherine Byler in 1819 and migrated to Alabama then
      to Texas.

ANDREW VANNOY, SR. BIBLE

In possession of Wilma Chunn, Shelbyville, Tennessee
Publisher: American Bible Society, New York, Instituted in the year
        MDCCCXVI   1850

MARRIAGES:
Andrew Vannoy & Betsey A. Dogan was married November 30, 1809
Andrew Vannoy and Jane McMichael was married Jany 11, 1821

BIRTHS:
Andrew Vannoy was born Nov 30, 1783
Jane McMichael was born July 24, 1796
Joseph H. Vannoy, son of Andrew and Elizabeth his wife was born October
      18, 1810
James Hervey Vannoy their son was born May 26, 1812
Anderson Vannoy their son was born April 17, 1814

Sarah Vannoy their daughter was born 13 March 1816
Nathaniel Vannoy their son was born July 30, 1818

Elizabeth Vannoy daughter of Andrew Vannoy and Jane his wife was born .
    Nov 9, 1821
Martha Susan Vannoy their daughter was born August 30, 1823
Jesse Franklin their son was born 2nd day of April 1825
John Vannoy their son was born the 20th September 1826
Mary Ann Vannoy was born May the 14th 1829
Andrew Vannoy was born the 7th day of June 1832
Margaret Jane Vannoy was born October 22nd 1836
William S. Watkins son of W. S. and E. Watkins was born June 17, 1848

DEATHS:
Elizabeth Vannoy wife of Andrew Vannoy died 31st day of August 1819.
    In the 29th year of her age.
Sarah Vannoy daughter of Andrew and Elizabeth Vannoy died February 2,
    1820. Age 4 years.
Nathaniel Vannoy their son died October 8, 1826. Age 9 years.
Anderson Vannoy died June 30, 1833. Age 20 years.
James H. Vannoy died Sept 11, 1833. Age 22 years.
Margaret Jane Vannoy daughter of Andrew & Jane Vannoy died July 26,
    1840. Age 4 years.
Joseph H. Vannoy died June 17, 1854. Age 44 years.
Andrew Vannoy, Senior died Jan 25, 1869. Age 85 years
Jane Vannoy wife of Andrew Vannoy died Feb 5, 1872. 76 years.
Martha S. Chunn died July 21, 1905. Age 82 years.
Elizabeth Vannoy Booth died Sept 8, 1897. Age 75 years.
Jeremiah B. Booth died Nov 24, 1871. Age 59 years.

WILLIAM JORDAN CHUNN BIBLE

In possession of Wilma Chunn, Shelbyville, Tennessee
Publisher: Stereotyped by A. Chandler and Printed by D. Fanshaw for the
        American Bible Society,   1844   New York

Statement on front page of William Jordan Chunn's Bible in his handwriting
"My father Lancelott Chunn was born August 16th 1799 in Fredrick County,
Maryland and was married to Susan Gates Jordan of Bedford County, Tennessee on the 17th of Oct 1820 and died in Lamar County, Texas August 18,
1848. My Mother Susan Gates Chunn was born Nov 19th 1803 and died January
19, 1822."

MARRIAGES:
William J. Chunn and Martha S. Vannoy was married the 14th day of Novem-
        ber A.D. 1844.
Eldridge T. Mallard and Martha E. Chunn was married December 19, 1867.
James S. McCland (McClelland) and Emma V. Chunn was married June 25, 1885.

William A. Jordan and Susan J. Chunn was married 12th day of December
      1866.

BIRTHS:
William J. Chunn was born August 31, 1821
Martha S. Vannoy was born August 30, 1823
Children:
1: Susan Jane
2: Andrew Lancelott
3: Martha Elizabeth
4: Mary Ann
5: Sarah Tennessee
6: Emma Virginia

Susan J. Chunn was born Oct 2, 1845
Andrew L. Chunn was born May 26, 1847
Martha E. Chunn was born Aug 2, 1849
Mary Ann Chunn was born April 1 A.D. 1851
Sarah Tennessee Chunn was born Feb 24, 1854
Emma Virginia Chunn was born Sept 28, 1856
James S. McClelland was born Oct 4, 1854
Jimmie McClelland infant son of James S. and Jennie E. McClelland was
      born July 16, 1886
William A. Mallard was born Dec 24, 1869

DEATHS:
Mary Ann Chunn departed this life July 13, 1869
Martha Elizabeth Mallard departed this life August 5, 1870
William J. Chunn departed this life July 30, 1897
Martha S. Chunn departed this life July 21, 1905
Jennie E. McClelland died June 6, 1938
Miss Tennie Chunn died January 23, 1939
James S. McClelland died July 31, 1886
Jimmie McClelland, infant, died August 24, 1886

                        MARK WHITAKER BIBLE

In possession of Mrs. Margaret Stokes, Shelbyville, Tennessee
Publisher: Missing.

Mark Whitaker, born June 9, 1806 in Ky., died Aug 28, 1887 Lincoln
County, Tennessee, married Rosanna Rutledge about 1833 in Lincoln
County, Tenn., born Feb 29, 1812 in Surry County, North Carolina,
died Sept 8, 1895. Both buried in Whitaker Cemetery, Lincoln County.
Tennessee.

Children:
1: Charles Lafayette Whitaker, born July 4, 1834, Lincoln County, Tenn.,

died 1834 in Lincoln County, Tennessee.

2: Mary Jane Whitaker, born May 12, 1836, in Lincoln County, Tennessee, died 1840 in Lincoln County, Tennessee.

3: John Franklin Whitaker, born Feb 24, 1838 in Lincoln County, Tennessee, died about 1865, C.S.A., buried near Atlanta, Ga., never married.

4: William Boone Whitaker, born Jan 10, 1840 in Lincoln County, Tennessee, died May 16, 1862, C.S.A., buried in Corinth, Mississippi, married Jan 24, 1860(1861) to Nannie Susan Kimbrough, born Oct 8, 1841 in Lincoln Co., Tenn., died Oct 13, 1867 in Lincoln C., Tenn.

5: Virginia Katherine Whitaker, born Nov 10, 1841, Lincoln Co., Tenn., died 1931, Lincoln Co., Tenn., never married, buried in Rose Hill Cemetery, Fayetteville, Tennessee.

6: America Fredonia Whitaker, born Nov 26, 1842, in Lincoln Co., Tenn., died 1877 in Lincoln Co., Tenn., buried in Whitaker Cemetery, married to William Polk Tolley, born 1839 in Illinois, died 1909 in Lincoln Co., Tennessee.

7: Rebecca Maneda Whitaker, born Mar 19, 1844, in Lincoln Co., Tenn., died 1914 in Memphis, Tenn., married April 28, 1880 to John Eaton, born 1832, died 1914 in Memphis, Tenn.

8: Victoria Josephine Whitaker, born Nov 10, 1845 in Lincoln Co., Tenn., died 1913 in Lincoln Co., Tenn., buried in Rose Hill Cemetery, Fayetteville, married Nov 2, 1867 to E. Simpson Terry, born 1844 in Bedford County, Tenn., died 1924, buried in Rose Hill Cemetery, Lincoln County, Tennessee.

9: Rosanna Whitaker, born Feb 24, 1847 in Lincoln County, died _____, buried in Rose Hill Cemetery, Fayetteville, married on Aug 7, 1872 to Rufus Medicus Holman born July 25, 1840 in Lincoln Co., Tenn., died Aug 9, 1883 in Lincoln County, Tennessee.

10: Ruth Ann Whitaker, born Aug 6, 1849 in Lincoln Co., Tenn., died Aug 22, 1877 in Lincoln Co., Tenn., buried in Whitaker Cemetery, married Sept 8, 1873 to Frank P. Taylor, born _____, died May 3, 1888 Lincoln Co., Tenn., Rose Hill Cem.

11: Mark Whitaker, III, born Feb 8, 1851 in Lincoln Co., Tenn.(Mulberry), died 1890 in Lincoln Co., Tenn.(Mulberry), married Dec 23, 1880 to Willie Caldwell, born & died in Lincoln Co., Tenn.

12: Laura Fannie Whitaker, born Aug 21, 1852, in Lincoln Co., Tenn., died Sept 6, 1933 in Oklahoma, married Aug 12, 1886 in Lincoln Co., Tenn., to John Mark Hall, born Nov 12, 1842 in Davidson Co., Tenn., died Sept 4, 1911 in Oklahoma.

13: Isaac Benjamin Whitaker, born May 10, 1855 in Lincoln Co., Tenn., died Jan 31, 1931 in Lincoln Co., Tenn., married May 7, 1878 in Lincoln Co., Tenn., to Mary Lou McDaniel born April 25, 1859 in Lincoln Co., Tenn., died Mar 13, 1944 in Lincoln Co., Tenn.

14: James Chamberlain Whitaker, born May 27, 1858 in Lincoln Co., Tenn., died 1932 in Lincoln Co., Tenn., buried in Rose Hill Cemetery, married Feb 10, 1886 to Mary Addie Sugg born July 25, 1867 in Lincoln Co., Tenn., died Feb 7, 1957 in Lincoln Co., Tenn., Rose Hill Cem.

15: Delia Whitaker, born Jan 8, 1861 in Lincoln County, Tenn., died July 24, 1893 in Lincoln Co., Tenn., married May 7, 1883 in Lincoln Co.,

Tenn., to William Jones Osborne, born June 3, 1860 in Bedford
Co., Tenn., died Feb 7, 1936 in Lincoln Co., Tenn.

OSTEEN BIBLE

This Record was copied in 1939 by Mrs. Sarah Jones, Wartrace, Tenn.,
The Bible was in the possession of the R. L. Jarrell Family, 1939,
        in Shelbyville, Tennessee
Publisher: Not listed.

MARRIAGES:
W. J. Osteen and M. P. Wadley was married Jany the 17th 1839
W. H. H. Osteen & L. Allison was married March the 18th 1869
J. D. Wall & M. J. Osteen was married the 5th of Nov 1866

BIRTHS:
W. J. Osteen was born March the 11th 1819
M. P. Osteen was born Nov 9th 1821
John E. Osteen, son of W. J. Osteen, was born June the 29th 1840
Elie Jenning Osteen was born Jany the 31st 1842
T. J. Osteen was born Nov 21st 1844
W. H. H. Osteen was born Oct the 24th 1847
Mary J. Osteen was born Oct the 7th 1850
J. R. Osteen was born Feb the 6th 1853
An E. Osteen was born April the 12th 1855
G. E. L. Osteen was born April the 2nd 1859
J. F. W. Osteen was born July the 10th 1863

DEATHS:
John E. Osteen died May the 26th 1856
Elizabeth J. Osteen died June the 20th 1856
Thomas J. Osteen died July the 28th 1848
Rev. Edward Osteen died Jany the 3rd 1869
Elizabeth, wife of Rev. Ed. Osteen, died May the 16th 1863
John Wadley died March the 17th 1861
Mary Wadley, wife of John Wadley, died Oct 15th 1862

W. H. H. O'STEEN BIBLE

This Bible Record was copied in 1939, the record was copied from a
Bible belonging to Mr & Mrs R. L. Jarrell, Shelbyville, Tennessee.
Copied in 1939 by Mrs. Sarah Jones, Wartrace, Tennessee.

W. H. H. O'Steen and Sarah E. Allison was married by the Rev. A. S.
        Riggs, March 18, 1869.

Della A. O'Steen was married to Robert L. Jarrell by the Rev. Sam
    Thompson, December 18th 1895
T. Myrtle O'Steen was married to William E. Stephens by Dr. G. C.
    Sandusky, October 21, 1901
Charlie D. O'Steen was married to Mrs. Bessie Thompson by the Rev.
    C. S. Gabard, October 9th 1908
Robert F. O'Steen was married to Miss Irene Daly by the Rev. J. T.
    Baird, June 10th 1908

STEVENS BIBLE

This Bible Record was copied in 1936 by Mrs. Sarah Jones, Wartrace,
Tennessee, from the Bible owned by Mr. T. L. Davis, Wartrace, Tenn.
Publisher: Not known.

BIRTHS:

John Stevens	February 10, 1765
Elizabeth Stevens	February 22, 1788
Sally Stevens	August 22, 1788
William Stevens	November 1st 1792
James Stevens	January 22nd 1795
Middleton Stevens	June 10th 1798
Boyer Stevens	May 18th 1801
Eliza Stevens	July 18th 1800
John Stevens	March 10th 1803?
Thomas Stevens	June 22nd 1803? (5)
Daniel Stevens	February 9th 1808
Micah Stevens	February 10th 1809
W. G. Keller	August 4th 1837
Nancy C. Keller	July 29th 1838

MARRIAGES:
Boyer Stevens was married November 1819
Thomas Stevens and Rebecca W. Puryear, April 26th 1832

ACREE
Larkin, 160
Larkin H., 161
ADAMS
A. P., 80
Fannie, 77
John, 116
AGNEW
J. W. C., 12
William N., 12
William Walter, 12
W. W., 12
AIKEN
Dr., 46
AILES
Amrette Webb, 6
John W., 6, 7
AKIN
Louis G., 109
ALDEN
Elizabeth F., 9
ALEXANDER
Angela S., 154
Barbara McE., 154
C. F., Jr., 153, 154
Charles F., III, 154
Charles Fussell, Jr.,
154
Clarence F., 153,
154
John, 163
Margaret J., 167
Marian McE., 154
Sadie S., 154
Violet D., 168
William D., 154
ALLEN
Catherine L., 158
Clarence E., 159
Cyrena, 158
Dr. Joseph H., 159
Dr. Thomas R., 159
E. B., 159
Elizabeth A., 158
Hugh B., 158
J. E., 159
J. H., 159
Joseph E., 159
Linda C., 158
Lorena C., 159

ALLEN
Martha A., 158
Mary Ann, 158
Mayrilda, 158
Permelia, 158, 159
R. C., 159
Richard F., 158
Sabrina, 158
Sarah E., 141
Sarah M., 158
Thomas J., 158
Thomas R., 158
T. R., 159
ALLISON
Bettie, 75
Cleopatra, 76
Elvira V., 75
Harris, 75
James, 75
James H., 149, 150
James K., 75
Jennie B., 76
John, 75
John N., 149
Kimbrough, 75, 149,
150
Kimbrow, 75
L., 181
Margaret E., 75
Minnie L., 75
Miss, 82
M. L., 119
Nancy, 75
Nancy B., 149
Nannie, 149
Newton P., 149, 150
Richard D., 76
Richard S., 75, 149,
150
Robert, 75
Robert F., 149, 150
Ruth F., 76
Sallie, 75
Sally, 75, 149
Sally Jane, 75
Sarah, 75, 150
Sarah A., 149
Sarah E., 181
Sarah V., 76
William R., 75

AMECK
Sue, 77
ANDERSON
_, 149
Adlaid, 24
Amanda H., 24
Bettie, 80
Bryant, 34
Charles M., 34
Chester C., 88, 89
Claiborne W., 88, 89
Cora, 81
Edmund, 88, 89
Jacob, 126
James, 94, 95, 141
James A., 88, 89
John H., 33, 34
John T., 88, 89
Louisa, 88, 89
Margaret, 34
Mary E., 88, 89
Mollie E., 88, 89
Nancy, 88, 89
Nora, 88
Permelia, 88
Rachele, 88
Rev. R. C., 119
Robert S., 88, 89
Sallie V., 24
Warner P., 88, 89
ANSHUTZ
J. J., 86
ANTHONY
Adam, 44
Barbara, 44
Betsy, 44
Carl, 43
Cornelia L., 43, 45,
77
Dorothy, 44
Eliza Jane, 77
Eve, 44
Henry, 44
Jacob, 44
Katie, 44
Margaret, 44
Mary, 44
Nicholas, 44
Nick, 43
Robert H., 43, 54, 76

ANTHONY
    Sallie, 44
    W. D., 43
    Will D., 44
    William, 45, 76
    William H., 43
APPLEBY
    David D., 139
    Hazel, 55
ARENDALE
    Nancy T. P., 19
ARMSTRONG
    Atlanta J., 61
    Cenia T., 69
    Dr. James L., 62
    Mrs. John, 69
    Rev., 84
    Sophia, 62, 124
ARNETT
    Agnes, 9
    Joseph B., 9
ARNOLD
    Arabella, 93, 94
    Arch T., 80
    Argie M., 50, 51
    Aubry D., 50
    Benjamin K., 80
    Bertha L., 50, 51
    Capt. Thomas, 90
    Clara U., 50
    Clay, 48
    Daniel, 93
    Dayton R., 50
    Della T., 81
    Elijah, 80, 93
    Elijah W., 80
    Elisha, 93
    Eliza, 93
    Elizabeth, 80, 93,
        94
    Fannie, 81
    Frank C., 81
    Gladis L., 50
    Gracie L., 49, 51
    Grady, 51
    Hannah, 93
    Horal M., 50
    Hugh, 97, 100
    Hugh T., 90, 91,
        92, 94

ARNOLD
    James, 90, 91, 92,
        93, 94, 96, 98,
        99, 100
    James H., 46
    Jarusha, 80
    Jarusha G., 80
    John, 93
    John W., 80
    Joseph, 93, 94
    Katherine L., 91, 92,
        95
    Katheryn, 96
    Katie, 94, 97
    Lamyra, 93, 94
    Laura B., 50
    Lois V., 49, 50
    Louisa, 93, 94
    Louisa H., 46
    Louise, 47
    Lucinda, 93, 94
    Lucy H., 46
    Mabel, 97
    Mabel C., 90, 91,
        94, 98, 99
    Margaret E., 93, 94
    Martha Ann, 93, 94
    Martha J., 80
    Marvin C., 50
    Mary, 80
    Mary D., 80
    Matchie, 91
    Mrs. James, 93, 96,
        98, 99
    Mrs. Marie, 127, 128
    Mrs. R. G., 51
    Nannie, 90, 93, 99
    Nannie F., 91, 92,
        100
    Odis G., 50
    Oliver, 93, 94
    Oliver P., 94
    O. P., Sr., 100
    Rachel T. V., 100
    R. G., 51
    Robert A., 81
    Rufus C., 50
    Rufus D., 50
    Rufus G., Jr., 49,
        50, 51
    Sam, 80

ARNOLD
    Samuel, 90, 93
    Samuel S., 81
    Sarah E., 80
    Sophia M., 93, 94
    Thomas, 93, 97
    Thomas F., 91, 92,
        93, 94, 98, 99,
        100
    Thomas M., 90
    T. M., 94
    Tommie, 99
    William, 80, 93
    William M., 50
    Willie C., 50, 51
    Winnifred W., 91, 100
ASHLEY
    Lillian Bell, 6
AWALT
    Polly, 111
AYERS
    Ellen, 70
    Lucinda, 69
    Mrs. Sallie, 69
    R. E., 119
AZAR
    Joanne, 58

BAGLEY (see page 187)
BAILEY
    Mary, 66, 67
    Rev. C. H., 92, 98,
        100
    Sarah, 66, 67
BAIRD
    Ann P., 31
    Ella May, 31
    Horace Ney, 31
    Jane E., 31
    Rev. J. T., 182
    Robert G., 31
    Sarah Jones, 31
    William E., 31
    Wm. E., 31
    Zenas, 31
BALL
    James Turner, 3
BANET
    Elizabeth A. C., 18
BANOUGH
    Emma, 171

BARBER
   Tennie, 176
BARBOUR
   Hattie Lee, 108
   Saphronia D., 106
BARKDULL
   Maria P. L., 170
BARNES
   Mrs. Ben, 75
BARRETT
   Capt., 136
   Cynthia C., 138
BARRINGER
   Daniel L., 116
   Gaither A., 117
BARTLETT
   J. E., 133
BASHAM
   Fenitte, 2
   Peter, 2
BASKETT
   John, 21
BASS
   Mary, 21
   Mary V., 90, 127,
      130
BATES
   Dr. Thomas, 117
   Mrs. Thomas F., 21
   Rev., 84
   Rev. T. F., 119
   Thomas Fletcher, 119
BATTE
   J. R., 33
BEAMS
   Miss, 124
BEARDEN
   John, 1
   W. S., 119
BEASLEY
   A. Lelia, 71
   Anna Lelia, 72
   Archibald, 71
   David H., 71
   D. H., 71
   F. R., 71
   Lelia, 71, 72
   Liberty, 71
   Mary A., 71
   W. T., 71

BECHMAN
   Col. Bernard, 60
BEDWELL
   Yullar, 133
BELL
   Hon. John, 40
   Rachel S. C., 18
BENNET, BENNETT
   Charles, 144, 145,
      146
   Charles C., 147
   Charles J., 146
   Charles O., 145
   Charles R., 145, 147
   Clarisa, 145
   Eliza, 145
   Ella, 145, 147
   Grace, 145
   H., 158
   Harry, 144
   Harry E., 145, 146,
      147
   Henry, 145
   Jacob, 145
   James S. J. A., 13
   J. E., 146
   J. M., 13
   Letitia, 13
   Margaret E., 14
   Margaret L., 15
   M. E., 13
   Milton, 144, 145,
      146, 147
   Milton, Jr., 147
   Milton R., 144
   Mrs. Elizabeth, 146
   Mrs. Susan E., 146
   Nancy, 145
   Nancy D., 145, 146
   Nathan, 145
   Nehemiah, 144, 145
   Nehemiah B., 144
   Rebecca Ales, 145
   Ruth, 146
   Saley, 145
   Sarah, 145
   Stephen, 145
   Tobias, 145
   Virginia, 13
BERRY
   Louisa, 152

BEVEL
   Mary, 101
BLACK
   Edward M., 67
   Elizabeth, 66
   Florena M., 67
   Florence M., 67
   Francis M., 67
   Frances Marion, 67
   James, 66, 67
   James L., 66
   James M., 66
   James N., 67
   Jane E., 31
   Jany June, 67
   J. M., 69
   John, 66
   John A. L., 66
   John C., 67
   John W., 66, 67
   Joseph C., 66
   Joseph R., 67
   J. W., 67
   Magdaline, 69
   Margaret, 66
   Margaret F., 66
   Margret C., 67
   Martha A., 66
   Martha L. R., 66
   Mary, 67
   Mary A., 67
   Mary Ann, 67
   Mary B., 66
   Mary Bailey, 66
   Mary E., 66, 67
   Mary N., 66
   Quincy B., 66
   Robert, 66, 67
   Robert Lee, 67
   Robert Scott, 66
   Sallie L., 67
   Sarah, 66
   Susan C., 67
   Susan G., 67
   Susannah H., 66
   William H., 66
   William W., 67
   W. W., 67
BLACKMAN
   A. B., 98
   Burrell, 150

185

BLACKMAN
  Frances, 150
BLACKWELL
  Margaret, 95
BLAKE
  Bennett, 42
  Rev. Bennett T., 42
BLAKEMORE
  Anne E. W., 177,
    118
  Dr. A., 118
  J. A., 120
  J. U., 117
  Mrs. Gartha, 188
  Row, 117
BLANTON
  David T., 141, 142
  E. A., 141, 142
  Elizabeth, 141, 142
  George W., 141
  Green L., 141
  H. H., 141
  Hiram H., 141, 142
  James, 141
  J. C., 141
  Jennie M., 142
  John C., 141
  John T., 141
  Laura, 141
  Lucy A., 141
  Lucy J., 141
  Lula, 98
  Mary, 141
  Merideth, 142
  Minnie, 142
  Mirion, 141
  Mrs. B. W., 98
  Nancy, 142
  Nannie L., 141, 142
  Sallie B., 142
  Sam, 141
  Sarah E., 142
  Smiley, 142
  Sophia P., 141
  W. C., 141, 142
  William C., 141,
    142
  William R., 141
BOLES
  Rev. G. L., 91, 98

BOMAR
  Fannie, 152
  Virginia, 65
  W. S., 120
BOONE
  Elizabeth, 1
  Howard, 1
  H. L., 54
  Ida, 30
  Rhoda, 125
BOOTH
  Elizabeth V., 178
  Jeremiah B., 178
BOSTWICK
  Harry, 97
BOUNDS
  Mattie, 141
BOWEN
  Ann, 21
  Arthur, 18, 21
  Elizabeth, 21
  John, 18, 21
  Moses, 18, 19, 21
  Rebacha, 21
  William, 21
BOWLING
  Arthur, 92
  Irving, 92
BOYD
  Leona, 133
  William, 154
BRADEN
  Cassander A., 15
  Eliza J., 15, 16
  Francis O., 15
  Giles W., 16
  Harvy L., 16
  Irene A., 15
  James W., 15, 16
  Jennie E. Ray, 16,17
  John W., 15, 16
  Leroy Calvin, 15, 16
  Lucinda C., 15, 16
  Mary M., 15
  Nancy P., 15
  Narcissa E., 15
  Patrick Harvy, 15
    16
  Perry C., 15, 16
  Rachel, 15
  Sarah A. T., 16

BRADEN
  Sintha A., 16
  Sintha P., 15
  Sintha Porter, 15
  Susan J., 16
  Temple A., 16
  Thomas G., 15, 16
  Vera, 16, 17
  Vertna M., 16, 17, 18
  William H., 16
BRADSHAW
  Hattie May J., 131
  Zerelda, 87
BRANDON
  Percy, 48
BRANTLEY
  Ruth C., 64
BRAZELTON
  Wilson, 94
BREVARD
  Nancy, 163
  Rebecca D., 168
BRIDGES
  Anne E., 41
  C. Coldwell, 40
  Coldwell, 40
  Ethel M., 40, 41
  George W., 39, 41
  H. Erwin, 40
  James E., 40, 41
  Katherine, 40
  Mary, 52
  Sara R., 40
  Shirley Anne, 39, 40
  Warren, 52
  Warren P., 52
  W. P., 51
BRILEY
  Mrs. Josie J., 159
BRISTOL
  Dr. G., 61
BRITTAIN
  Jason T., 32
  Jesse Newton, 32, 33
  J. T., 32
  Maria, 32
  Mary Ann, 33
  William A., 165
BROCK
  George A., 115

BORDEN
  Mr., 138
BROOKS
  Virginia R., 10
BROWN
  America P., 134
  B. A., 133
  Elizabeth, 116
  Elizabeth D., 4
  F. A. B., 134
  Frances Ann B.,135
  Frederick, 134,
    135
  G. W., 116
  James H., 134
  Jennett, 134, 135
  J. H., 134
  John, 51, 52, 53
  John F., 135
  John T., 135
  Kittie P., 52
  Louisa J., 135
  Lucy F., 80
  Margaret H., 134,
    135
  Margaret J., 135
  Margaret M., 135
  Margarett, 159
  Martha J., 135
  Mary E., 53, 134
  M. E., 134
  Mrs. Jo I., 65
  Mrs. Thomas H., 73
  Nancy, 52
  Nancy I., 133
  Nancy M., 135
  Nona, 56
  Paschal, 52
  Pleasant L., 135
  Rev. E. W., 174
  Sarah, 103
  Sarah H., 51
  Sarah Hinton, 52,
    53
  Sarah M., 134
  Sarah Melissa, 135
  William D., 135
BRUNSON
  Sallie, 141
BRYAN
  G., 79

BRYAN
  James A., 79
  Nathaniel G., 79
  Thos. J., 165
  T. W., 79
  W. J., 79
BRYANT
  Nannie, 104
BRYSON
  H. K., 169
  Rev. J. H., 155
BUCHANAN
  Amanda, 94, 95
  Betsy, 95
  Catherine, 95, 97
  Catherine M., 94,
    96
  Elizabeth, 95
  George, 95, 97
  Hugh, 97
  James, 95, 97
  Jane, 94, 95
  Jimmie, 97
  Lola Clyde, 20
  Mary, 95
  Mary E., 94
  Mrs. Virginia S.,165
  Robert, 97
  Sarah, 95
  Sarah C., 94
  William, 94, 95, 97
BULLOCK
  _, 75
BUNN
  Debby Jean, 147
BURLIN
  Diania, 35
  Monroe, 35
BURBA
  Jean F., 17
BURNS
  Gertrude, 141
BURROW
  Emlie, 51, 52
  Philip, 124
BURTON
  Nat. L., 119
BUTLER
  David, 137
  David A., 138
  James S., 137, 138

BUTLER
  John C., 138
  Martha, 138
  Mary, 124
  Mary E., 5
  Mary Elizabeth, 138
  Mary Jane N., 138
  Rev., 84
  Samuel W., 4
BUXTON
  Virginia, 136
BYERS
  Alexander, 122
  Sallie B., 122
BYLER
  Katherine, 177

BAGLEY
  Edward, 93
  John, 93
  Margaret, 90, 93
  Martha, 93
  Mary Frances, 170,
    173
  Thomas, 93

CADDELL
  Serena, 159
CALDWELL
  Cassander, 51, 52
  Mary B., 153
  Rev., 84
  William, 158
  Willie, 180
CALHOUN
  George, 155
CALLOWAY
  Thomas H., 158
  Thos., 158
CALWELL
  Sarah D., 168
CAMERON
  Eugena, 128, 129
CAMP
  Mrs. Mary J., 39
CAMPBELL
  William, 160, 161
CANNON
  Almon, 82
  Andrew, 114

CANNON
 Archibald Y., 121,
 122
 Augustus D., 82
 Charles L., 25
 Clement, 25, 121,
 122
 Clement J., 26
 Clement, Jr., 121,
 122
 Clement, Sr., 25,
 26, 27
 Cora Y., 121, 122
 Dolly, 82
 Elizabeth, 82, 83
 Eliza M., 29
 George, 82
 George J., 82
 Henry, 25, 82, 83
 Hugh E., 82
 Jane, 82
 John, 82
 John J., 82
 John Julius, 82
 John S., 121, 122
 Lettie T., 26
 Lettitia T., 25
 Maria M., 83
 Marthey, 32
 Mary, 25, 82, 83
 Mary E., 78, 82
 Mary M., 25
 Mary Y., 122
 Melville, 83
 Newton, 83
 Rasha, 83
 Robert, 83
 Robert A., 82
 S. A., 82
 Sally B., 122
 Samuel C., 121,
 122
 Sarah, 82, 83
 Sarah Ann, 82
 Sarah B., 121, 122
 Sarah Blythe, 121
 Susan L., 26, 27
 Susan M., 82
 Susannah, 25
 Susanna W., 82
 Thomas, 83

CANNON
 Thos. B., 25
 William H., 81, 82
 William Henry, 82
 William H., Sr., 82
 William R., 83
CANTRELL
 Mary Lou, 72
CAPLES
 Pearl, 68
CAPSHAW
 Annie Lee, 61
CARNEY
 John C., 141
CARTER
 Joseph, 96
 Nancy, 13
 Sarah L., 166
CARUTHERS
 Mary, 165
CASHION
 Avus W., 126, 127
 Cora, 134
 James, 127
 Mary, 127
CASWELL
 Anne, 22, 23
 Benjamin, 23
 Charlotte, 23
 Christian, 22, 23
 Dallam, 22
 Eleanor, 23
 Elizabeth, 22, 23
 John, 22, 23
 Joseph, 23
 Joseph W., 22, 23
 Martin, 23
 Mary, 22, 23
 Richard, 21, 22, 23
 Sally, 23
 Samuel, 23
 Sarah, 22
 Shine, 23
 Susannah, 22
 William, 22, 23
 Winstone, 22
CATHEY
 Alexander, 78
 Andrew, 78
 Elizabeth, 77
 Frances, 78
 Frances H., 77

CATHEY
 George, 77
 George C., 77
 George, Sr., 77
 Henry, 77, 78
 Jean, 77
 John, 78
 Josias, 77
 Mary, 78
 Nancy A., 77
 Sarah, 77
CAUGHRAN
 Dan Higgins, 170
 Elmer Ross, 170
 Rose Higgins, 170
CAWYER
 Mrs. T. B., 159
CHAMBERS
 John W., 149
CHANDLER
 J. W., 75
CHARLES
 Mrs. Avva, 73, 74
 Ophni, 74
CHELDERS
 Daniel, 156
 Geney, 156
 Malinda, 156
 Mary, 156
 Nancy, 156
 Nathan, 156
CHERRY
 George, 82
 Susanna, 82
CHESSHIR
 Jane, 160
 Pauline, 160
CHILD
 Mary E. D., 166
 William S., 165, 166
 William S., Jr., 166
CHILTON
 Edith, 70
CHITTAM
 Mrs. Noel P., Jr., 133
CHITWOOD
 Stephen, 94
CHRISTIAN
 Cleaver C., 170
CHUNN
 A. Edgar, 176

CHUNN
A. L., 175, 176
Andrew L., 176, 179
Annie E., 177
David, 176
David L., 176
Emma V., 178, 179
Horace L., 176
Lancelott, 178
Martha E., 178, 179
Martha S., 178, 179
Mary Ann, 179
Mattie V., 175
Minnie T., 176
Rebecca, 176
Sarah T., 179
Stephen L., 176
Susan G., 178
Susan J., 179
Susan Jane, 179
Tennie, 179
William E., 175, 176
William G., 175, 176
William J., 178, 179
Wilma, 174, 175, 176, 177, 178
Wilma Jeanne, 176
W. J., 176
CLAPP
Barbara, 45, 76
Mr., 43
Mrs., 43
CLARDY
Mary An, 28
Mary F., 27
CLARK
G. W., 98
Rev. W. C., 119
R. W., 118, 119
CLAXTON
Buck, 50
Lois A., 49
Marvin, 49
Mrs. Marvin, 49, 50, 51, 54

CLAY
Sally, 62
CLEEK
Julia D., 135
Mrs. William T., 134, 135
CLENDENIN
Belle, 45, 76
Jerry, 170
CLEVELAND
Annie L., 151
Annie W., 151
A. W., 151
Benjamin, 128
Carrie C., 151
Eliza, 151
Elizabeth D., 150
Hattie, 151
Jeremiah, 150, 151
Jeremiah, Jr., 151
Jessie, 151
Lizzie H., 151
Mary, 150, 151
Mary H., 150
R. M., 98
Robert, 128
Sallie, 150
Sallie S., 151
Sarah, 127
Sarah E., 151
Sarah P., 150, 151
Thomas, 151
Thomas S., 150
Thos. S., 151
T. S., 151
CLIFFT
Asley, 35
David L., 35
Diania, 35, 36
D. L., 35
Jane D., 35
John W., 35
Mary E., 35
CLINE
Rev., 91
CLOWER
Katherine, 86
COATS
Emma, 78
COBLE
_, 124

COBLE
Charles R., 153
C. R., 152
John D., 152, 153
Maggie, 153
Margaret, 153
Martha C., 152
Mary Ann, 152
Neely, 152, 153
COFFEE
Martha, 136, 137
Thos., 158
COGGINS
Joel, 55
COLDWELL
Miss Sarah, 39
COLE
N. A., 16
COLEMAN
Alexander E., 9
Elizabeth F., 9
Esq. J. M. H., 73
Martha W., 9
W. E., 9
Wilford E., 9
COLLIS
G. B., 54
George, Jr., 54
Rebecca, 54
Rebecca K. K., 54
COMER
Sarah, 176
CONKLIN
H. S., 145
CONWELL
Ada R. S., 49
Mrs. Roxie S., 48
COOK
Catherine, 124
C. B., 105, 112
Rev. George, 139
Rose, 35
Sarah E., 104
COOP
Corrie M., 108
George W., 108
George W., Jr., 108
G. W., 108
Horatio, 108
Horatio, Jr., 108
L., 108

COOP
Laura K., 108
L. H., 108
Lillian, 108
Lillian F. K.,
108
Robert G., 108
COOPER
Carolzor, 12
Edmund, 155
Eliza A., 12
Eliza C., 12
Eliza Corine, 12
Henry Lee, 12
James W., 12
Mildred, 8, 12
Miller M., 12
Sara, 121
Thomas A., 12
William P., 8, 12
William P., Jr., 8,
12
W. P., 8, 118
CORBIN
Ada F. J., 131
CORDELL
Catharine, 6
Dawn, 6
Elizabeth, 6
John W., 6
CORLETT
Jemima M. A., 106
CORTNER
G. A., 98
Mary C., 64
COUCH
Abigail, 69
Almeda, 64
Arthur, 64
Ben, 64
Buckaniah T., 66
Calloway, 64
Catherine M., 66
Catherine P., 64
Charity A., 69
Christopher C., 69
Dr. Robert W., 64
Elijah, 64
Elijah P., 64
Elisabeth J., 69
George, 65

COUCH
Isaac, 64
Isaac A., 69
James, 69
James C., 69
James E., 64
J. E., 69
Jim, 64
Jimmie, 64
Joe, 64
John, 64
John A., 63, 64,
65, 132
John W., 69
Joseph, 64, 69,
126
Kenny E., 66
Lester, 64
Magdalena, 69
Martha D., 69
Mrs. Almeda H., 65
Mrs. J. A., 64, 65
Nancy, 69
Nancy C., 69
Reuben, 64
Reuben C., 64
Rhoda C., 69
R. L., Jr., 64
R. L., Sr., 64
Robert L., Sr., 64
Ruby, 64
R. W., 64
Sarah J., 132
Thomas, 126
Thomas F., 69
Tommie, 64
Will, 64
COUSER
Mevolene L., 111
Thelma C., 111
Thomas C., 111
COWLEY
Desso, 18
COWAN
O., 118, 119
COWDEN
Ada D., 132
Charlie N., 131
John, 131
Mary D., 131
Mildred, 131

COWDEN
Raith, 131
William E., 131
COWSER
Mary, 126
COX
Ellison, 160
Flora, 36
Grady, 36
Louis, 35
CRAIG
_, 137
CRAVY
Mrs. Betty J., 131
CRAWFORD
Alice E., 18
Blanche F., 17, 18
Carrie E., 20
Charles, 160
Charles S., 20
Ebinezer, 18, 19
Elizabeth Ann, 18
Emma L., 20
Evaline, 18
Exie Lee, 17, 18
Fannie E., 20
Frances E., 20
Fredna M. K., 21
George G., 19, 20
Georgia A., 20
Helen, 20
Helen Joe, 17, 72
Henry C., 16, 17, 18
Joe Kyle, 20
Joe W., 19, 20, 21
John J., 18
Joseph W., 17, 18, 21
Josie, 21
Lee Earl, 17
Lola C., 20
Maggie E., 20
Margaret A., 19
Mary E., 17, 18
Mary Etta, 19, 20
Meredith, 20
Merrill D., 21
Minnie G., 17, 18
Nancy E., 21
Nancy R., 19, 20
Nancy T. P., 18
Phebe T., 18

CRAWFORD
Rachel, 16, 19
Rachel S., 18
Rachel T., 18, 19
Rececahah, 18
Richard G., 18
Sally S.,18
Titus, 18
Vertna M. B., 16, 17
Virgil G., 20
William, 18, 19, 20
William A., 18
William D., 20
William R., 17
William Robert, 17, 18, 21
CRISP
Nancy, 142
CRITTON
Mrs. Sarah, 146
CROSS
Asel, 52
Elizabeth, 52, 51
CROW
John M., 114
Nancy M., 113
CROWELL
Lusinda, 28
CSUY
Debra Lynn, 47
James, 47
Steve James, 47
CUMMING
Rev. Paxton, 167
CUNNINGHAM
_, 94
Belle C., 64
Caye F., 135
Elizabeth, 124
G. W., 135
H. L. D., 135
Humphry, 134, 135
Inez, 68
J. A., 98, 135
James E., 135
J. W. C., 135
Margaret M., 134
Margaret P., 135
Mrs. Lucinda, 98

CUNNINGHAM
Oliver P., 92
Sarah, 125
Sarah C., 64
T. P., 135
W. N., 135
CURLEIN
Margaret, 61

DALEY
Miss Irene, 182
DALLAM
Christian, 22
DAMRON
S. A., 134
DANCE
J. T. S., 110 John, 44
J. W. M., 110
M. A. E., 110
Martha, 110
Mrs. Finetta, 110
Sarah, 110
S. E. H., 110
Stephen M., 110 Susan, 44
Susan F., 110
DANDRIDGE
_, 114
DANIEL
Galloway, 109, 111
Margaret, 152
Martha A. E., 109
Mrs. Vanzant, 109
Sena, 109, 111
DARNELL
Noah, 56
Sarah E., 56
DASHIELLE
Revd. Dr., 39
DAUGHTREY
Alsie, 35
Bonnie, 36
David, 35
Davy C., 36
Harvie, 36
John C., 35
John T., 36
Mrs. David C., 34, 35
Ray Clifford, 35
Susie B., 35
Tenny, 36

DAUGHTREY
Thomas, 35
Thos. F., 35
Tommie, 35
Winnie, 35, 36
DAVIDSON
_, 126
Addie Lee, 165
Allen T., 165, 166, 167
Allen T., Jr., 165, 166
Andrew M., 163
Angeline, 164, 165
Benjamin W., 167
Bettie, 94
Betty, 163
Celia E., 166, 167
Col. George, 63
Col. William, 164
Cora I., 165
Cora L., 166
David V., 164, 165, 166
Dryden, 35
Elizabeth, 167
Elizabeth A., 165
Elizabeth A. H., 165, 166
Elizabeth L., 168
Elizabeth V., 162
Eliza Jane, 164
Ella H., 165, 166
Gen. William L., 162
George, 39, 162, 163
Hugh, 2, 3, 162, 164
Hugh H., 166, 167
Hugh L., 164, 165
Isabella, 167
James, 162
Jane, 162
John, 162, 163, 167
John L., Jr., 163
John M., 163, 167
John Q., 164, 165
Lorenzo, 163
Major John, 167, 168
Major William, 162, 163, 164, 166
Mariella, 165
Margaret, 163, 164, 167
Margaret E., 166, 167

DAVIDSON
  Margaret M., 163,
    164, 165
  Martha, 162
  Martha A., 164,165
  Mary, 162, 167
  Mary E., 165, 166
  Mary K., 162
  Mollie T., 157
  Mrs. J. L., 165
  Mrs. Sophia W., 154
  Nannie K., 165
  Priscilla, 164, 165,
    166, 167
  Quincy A., 3
  Rachel, 163
  Rebecca, 167
  Robert, 167
  Robert B., 119,164,
    165
  Robert B. V., 166,
    167
  Robert V., 165,
    166
  Ruth, 162, 163
  Samuel, 163
  Samuel L., 164
  Samuel W., 162, 166
  Sarah, 35, 162, 167
  Sarah E., 164
  Susan H., 2, 3
  Theodore F., 165,
    166
  Theodore S. F., 165
  Thomas, 163
  Thomas J., 165
  Violet, 167
  Violet D., 168
  Violet W., 167,168
  Wilbur E., 165
  Wilbur S., 165,166
  William, 164
  William E., 166
  William Edwin, 165,
    166
  William M., 162,
    163, 164, 165,
    166
  William S., 165
DAVIS
  Catherine, 32

DAVIS
  Goodrum, 72, 73
  Henrietta, 72
  James, 158
  Martha R., 158
  M. R., 158
  Mrs. Scott, 93
  M. S., 158
  Neal R., 158
  Phebe E. J., 158
  Richard S., 93
  R. L., 98
  Sarah L., 72, 73
  Scott, 93
  Thomas A., 158
  Thomas W., 157
  T. L. 182
DAWSON
  John C., 3
  Mary E., 3
  Walter W., 3
DAYTON
  H. L., 118, 120,155
DEAN
  Adlaid A., 24
  C. M., 150
  Edward Elam, 24
  Edward Everett, 24
  John T., 24
  Louisa H., 46
  Margaret L., 24
  Minnie L., 24
  Mrs. C. M., 150
  Nancy G., 24
DEASON
  Dr. Timothy, 144
DELK
  Allen F., 156
  Emma J. T., 156
  Floyd McL., 156
  Harry H., 156
  Horace C., 156
  Howard P., 156
  James J., 134
  John, 135
  Joshua V., 156
  Julia, 135
  J. V., 156
  Paul K., 155, 156
DERRICK
  William S., 138

DICE
  Phoebe, 27
DICKENS
  Charles H., 57, 58
  Charles S., 58
  Jeanne S., 58
  Joanne A., 58
  John C., 58
  Joseph S., 58
  Leonard F., 58
  Loura E., 58
  M. Beatrice, 58
  Mrs. Beatrice, 57
  Paul S., 58
  Peggy Jean, 58
DICKENSHEETS
  David, 145
  Nancy, 144
  Nancy M., 145
DICKERSON
  Jennie, 4
DICKEY
  Emma L., 20
DITTO
  Fabra, 80
DIXON
  Frances, 32
  James, 32
  Mrs. Elizabeth W., 165,
    166
  Mrs. Kay, 166, 167
DOGAN
  Betsey A., 177
  Elizabeth, 127
DOWNING
  Isabel, 59, 61
DOZIER
  Ada M., 131
  Arabella, 131
  Cyntha Ann J., 132
  Infant Son, 131
  Joseph T., 131, 132
  Mary E., 131
  Narcissa C. T., 132
  Paul, 131
  Sarah Ann, 131
  William M., 131, 132
  William Z., 131
  W. M., 131, 132
  Zachariah, 131, 132
  _, 94

DRYDEN
   Ann W., 172
DRUMRIGHT
   Kizzie M., 108
DUGGER
   Rev., 84
DUGUAY
   Merideth C., 21
   Nestor, 21
   Richard C., 21
   Stephen B., 21
DUNCAN
   Annie, 81
   Edna, 81
   Rev. T. J., 141
DUNN
   Julia A., 169
   Mrs. Mary F., 113
DUTREAUX
   Marie A., 84
DYER
   Harrison, 94

EADS
   Jesse, 158
   Jordan J., 158
   Rosalinda B.A.,158
EAGAN
   Emily R., 6
EAKIN
   John R., 39
EARLE, EARL
   Mildred, 59
   Mrs. Martha R., 10
EARNHART
   Christiana, 27
   Margaret, 27
EAST
   Allie F., 73
EASTLAND
   Sally S., 19
EATON
   John, 180
ECKENBERGER
   Alice E., 138
EDGAR
   Revd. John T., 39
EDWARDS
   Arthur R., 17, 72
   Bettie, 83

EDWARDS
   Elizabeth H., 60
   Frances, 59
   George N., 59
   Hannibal, 59
   Hayden B., 59
   Henry B., 59
   Jacob, 59
   James, 59
   James B., 16
   Jane, 59
   John, 59, 60
   John W., 59
   Joshua, 59
   Katherine, 175
   Lenard, 59
   Lencil A., 59, 61
   Marsha M., 17
   Martha B., 59
   Martin, 59
   Melissa M., 17
   Minerva, 59
   Minus, 59
   Mr. James G., 59, 115
   Mrs. James G., 59,115
   Mrs. Melissa M., 60
   Narcissus, 59
   Peter, 59
   Peter B., 59
   Richard, 60
   Robert, 60, 61
   Robert B., 59
   Robert T., 59
   Sally R., 17
   Thomas, 59, 60, 61
   Thomas B., 59
   Timothy J., 17
   Van, 83
   Van E., 84
   Virginia G., 83
   William, 59, 60
ELAM
   Mrs. Robert, 143
ELEY
   Auguston B., 107
   Eliza J., Jr., 107
   Eliza J., Sr., 106,
      107
   Fannie, 107
   F. M., 106
   Francis M., 106,107

ELEY
   Frank S., 107
   Grover C., 107
   Harriet C. M., 106,
      107
   Irene, 107
   J. A., 106, 107, 108
   James W., 107, 108
   Jemima M. A., 106,
      107
   Jesse Lee, 106
   John F., 106, 107
   John W., 107
   Josiah, 106, 107
   Josiah A., 106, 107
   Mary, 106
   Mary A., 107
   Mary Ann C., 106, 107
   Mary M. A., 106, 107
   Mary W., 106
   Melvina L., 107, 108
   M. F., 107
   Mrs. Evie W., 106
   Sarah R. E., 107
   Sophronia B., 106, 107
   Thomas H., 107
   W. A., 105
   William A., 106, 107
ELKINS
   Mrs. J. D., 162
ELLIS
   Carrie E. C., 20
   Charles C., 20
   E. W., 141
   Fredna M., 20
   George B., 20
   James C., 20
   James O., 20
   Lewis, 74
   Vera, 74
EMERSON
   Esq. H. S., 3
EMLEY
   A. H., 145, 147
   David, 147
   Ella, 144, 146
   Rebecca, 145, 147
   Thomas, 147
   William, 147
ENOCHS
   David L., 109, 110

ENOCHS
Dora, 109
Dorah B., 109, 111
Dora L., 110
Dr. M. A. L., 111
Elsie S., 109
Fannie L., 111
F. P., 111
G. A. J., 110
George W., 109
G. W. F., 110, 111
Isaac, 110
James, 109
Jane T., 110
J. E., 109
J. E. M., 109, 110, 111
J. H., 109
J. M., 111
L. L., 110
M. A. L., 110
Margaret A. L., 109
Martha A. E., 109, 110
Mary E., 109, 110, 111
Mollie D., 110
Nannie M., 109, 110
Petway, 109
Polly M., 110
Rebecca, 110
Sally S., 110
Sarah, 110
Sarah M. L., 109, 111
Sena D., 110, 111
Sena E., 109, 110, 111
Stephen W. I., 111
Stephen W. J., 109
EMMONS
Ruth B., 147
ENLOE
Ezekiel, 167
ERWIN
Andrew, 41
Andrew, Jr., 39, 41
Andrew P., 40
Anne C., 39, 40
Elizabeth J., 39, 40, 41

ERWIN
Elvira J., 39, 40, 41
Frances A., 39, 40
Henry H., 39, 40, 41
H. H., 40
James P., 40, 41
John P., 39, 40
Joseph, 126
Mary, 82
Mrs. Sarah C., 41
Mrs. S. C., 155
Rev. J. B., 120
Robert S., 40
Sarah C., 40, 41
Thomas Y., 40
ESLICK
Frederick M., 24
Sallie V., 24
EULESS
Adam, 124
EVANS
N. P., 118, 119
EWER
Charles, 120, 177

FAIN, Mrs. Margie A., 106
FALLON
Hattie L., 35
FARRIS
Shirley F., 17
FAY
Irma, 84
FELTON
Augustus C., Jr., 151
FINLEY
Elizabeth, 62
FISHER
Amy, 27, 28
Anna, 27, 28
Charley, 28
Christiana, 27, 28
Elizabeth, 27
George, 27, 28
Jacob, 27
John, 27, 28
Margaret, 28, 153
Marthey, 32
Martin, 27, 28
Mary, 27, 28
Mary Ann, 27, 28
Michael, 27, 28

FISHER
Philip, 27
Rev. T. B., 141
Sarah, 27, 28
Sarah E., 143
T. E., 153
FITZGERALD
Lillian M., 89
FLANDERS
A. A., 72
Mary Lou, 73
FLINT
William, 172
FLIPPEN
Maude, 175
FLIPPO
Gracie L., 49
Gracy, 51
FLOYD
Ann I., 2
David, 125
Eld. John, 24
Elijah, 1
Elizabeth, 1
Emma, 2
Emma M., 2
E. T., 67, 68
Eugene T., 68
Fenitte J., 1, 2
George, 120
George W., 1, 68
Hester, 68
Ida, 68, 70
James S., 1
Jane, 1, 68
Jane Ann, 68
Jayne, 67, 68
J. D., 2
Jewell J., 68
Jno. E., 68
John D., 1
Kindred N., 1
Margarett L., 68
Mary A., 1, 2
Mary P., 67
Mildred T., 68
Nancy E., 1, 2
Orrie, 68
Orrie E., 68
Pauline I., 1, 2
Sallie, 1, 68

194

FLOYD
  Sydney, 1
  Synthia, 1
  Watson, 1, 2
  William, 1
  William I., 68
  William I.,Jr., 68
  William P., 1
  Walt, 1
FOGLEMAN
  Mrs. Mary V., 94
  Peter, 45, 76
FORD
  Leah, 59
FORT
  Bettie F., 83, 84
  Emily M., 83
  Faye, 83
  James H., 83, 84
  Mrs. R. B., Jr.,83,
    84
  Robert B., III, 83,
    84
  Robert B., Jr., 83,
    84
  Susan W., 83
FOSNIGHT
  Mrs. Rebecca, 146
FOSTER
  Betty Jane, 17, 72
  Jas., 94
  John B., 127
  Margie E., 18
FOWLER
  Moses, 158
FRANCIS
  Bettie, 96
  Col. Hugh, 99
  Dr. James, 96
  Dr. J. O., 99
  Elizabeth, 96
  George, 97
  Grant, 97
  Hannah, 97
  Hugh, 92, 94, 95,
    96, 97, 99, 100
  Joe, 97
  John, 96
  Joseph, 96, 97
  Joseph H., 96
  Judge Hugh, 92, 100

FRANCIS
  Katherine, 97
  Katie, 97
  Lonnie, 97
  Malinda W., 96
  Margaret, 96
  Mary, 96, 97
  Mary A., 92
  Mary E., 96
  Miller, 92, 97
  Mrs. Catherine M., 99
  Nannie, 90, 94, 96,
    97
  Sallie, 97, 99
  Sallie W., 172
  Susan M., 94, 96
  Teresa H., 95, 96
  Turner, 96
  William, 96
  Willie, 97, 99
  Woodson, 96
FRANKLE
  A., 30, 31
  Clarence W., 30, 31
  Elizabeth Y., 31
  George Y., 30, 31
  Lizzie Y., 31
FRAZIER
  Glenn E., 79
  John F., 145
FRAZOR
  Nancy B., 18
  Rebecca B., 21
FREEMAN
  Hartwell, 102
FRIERSON
  John W., 119
  Mrs. Felicia C., 119
  Mrs. Lucy S., 119
FROST
  Mr., 95
FRY
  Louella, 159

GABARD
  Rev. C. S., 182
GAGE
  Jeremiah, 159
  Luty, 159
  Rachel, 159

GAGE
  Rhoda C., 159
GAINES
  George R., 84
GALLANT
  Chas., 57
  Lee, 57
GAMBILL-GAMBILLE
  Addie V., 74
  Avva B., 74
  Bradly, 149
  Cleve, 74
  Elgin, 74
  Joshua C., 74
  Lucy T., 74
  Marvin E., 74
  Minnie E., 74
  Newton E., 74
  Nora Lee, 74
  Thomas J., 73, 74
  T. J., 74
GAMBLE
  Bonnie, 35
GARDNER
  Ada Belle, 152
GASTON
  Thos. L., 167
GAUT
  George M., 128, 129
  Mary Jane, 129
  Mrs. Jane, 129
GENTRY
  Lillian, 74
GARRETT
  Mary, 44
GERNERT
  Rev. J. W., 7
GIBBS
  Christine E., 86
GIBSON
  John, 19, 138
  John M., 137
  Lonnie Mai, 78
  Margaret, 19
  Martha H., 137
  Mary Ann, 137, 138
  Nancy R., 19
  Patsey, 138
  Sarah J., 137
GILES
  Rev., 84

GILL
  John, 133
  Sarah B., 16
  W. D., 15
GILLESPIE
  J. G., 24
  Margaret D., 24
  Mary M., 171
GILLIS
  J. S., 119
GILMORE
  Florence, 60
  John D., Jr., 61
GIVENS
  William, 96
GOODWIN
  Nancy, 4
GORDON
  Amzi J., 53
  Martha E., 31
  Mary Ellen, 47
  Robert, 31
GOWAN
  Eld., 24
  Sallie, 1
GOWEN
  Sydney, 2
GRAHAM
  Edward J., 102, 103
  Henry F., 102, 103
  Isabella D., 168
  James H., 103
  James, IV, 102, 103
  James, V, 102, 103
  Mary, 102, 103
  Nancy, 102, 103
  Nicholas, 33, 102,
    103
  William, 102, 103
GRAMMER
  Mary, 137
GRANT
  Mary E., 96
  Mattie E., 96
GRANTLAND
  Minnie, 18
GRAVES
  Rev. J. H., 169
GRAY
  _, 94
  Louise, 70

GRAY
  Margaret L., 142
GREEN-GREENE
  Dr. Sidney, 95
  Elizabeth, 157
  Helen N., 14
  Judge Nathan, 94
  Mary Ann, 67
  Nathan, 95
  Nathan, Sr., 94
  William S., 94
GREER
  Michael Lucretia, 138
GRIFFIS
  William, 32
GRIFFITH
  William, 96
GROOVER
  Julia Ann, 176
GULLEY
  Martha, 144
GUNN
  G. W., 80
GUTHERIE
  A. H., 136
  A. Hugh, 137
GWYNN
  Ransom, 165

HALL
  Anne, 60
  B. I., 98
  Elizabeth, 60
  John Mark, 180
  Sarah C., 165
  Thomas, 60
HALSELL
  Rev. William, 90
HAMBLE
  Elizabeth J., 58
HAMES
  Lillian, 35
HAMILTON
  Andrew J., 128, 129
  Mrs. Altha, 129
  Mylinda, 87
HAMPTON
  Rachel T., 19
HANCEFORD
  _, 126

HANNAH
  William, 126
HAND
  Jennie P., 3
  William C., 3
HANSON
  Mrs. Henry L., 33
HARDAWAY
  James D., 80
HARLEE
  William C., 81, 82
HARMON
  Frank C., 80
  Jarusha G. A., 80
  Thomas J., 80
HARNEY
  Rev. James, 93
HARPER
  Mrs. Gladys Eley, 104,
    105, 106, 111
HARRIS
  A., 86
  A. J., 3
  Alfred W., 37
  Almedia J., 102, 103
  Ann E., 167
  Ann W., 102
  Catherine B., 37
  Cyntha C., 37
  Elizabeth, 102, 103
  Elvira, 102, 103
  Emma N., 19
  Fannie B., 121
  Frances B., 42
  George N., 20
  Georgia A., 20
  Gillie P., 36, 37
  G. L., 36
  Hannah S., 102
  Harold C., 20
  Hiram, 102, 103
  Ida, 171
  James, 102
  James S., 102
  John, 102
  John B., 37
  John T., 36, 37, 102
  Julian N., 20
  Laura, 108
  Luiza M., 36, 37
  Margaret, 102

HARRIS
 Margaret A., 37
 Margaret D., 168
 Martha G. A., 36,
  103, 104
 Mary I., 37
 Mary N., 36, 37
 Melissa E., 36
 Mollie, 175
 Nancy T., 36
 Nicholas, 28, 102
 Polly, 102
 Safrona A., 36
 Sarah F., 37
 Sarah T., 102, 103
 Sarah W., 36, 37
 Watson R., 37
 William, 104
 William J., 37
HARRISON
 Edie, 165
 Joannah, 115
 Mary E., 115
 Narcissa, 165
HART
 Clytus R., 68
 Ed., 68
 E. E., 68
 Thomas E., 68
HARVEY
 Mary Ann, 86
HASKINS
 Dock, 35
 Malinda A., 34
 Redman, 34
 Susan, 34
HASTINGS
 Nancy J., 169
 Robert, 169
HATCHER
 Mary E., 172
HAYNES
 Enoch, 126
 Joseph, 126
 Kizia, 64
 Robert, 126
 Thomas H., 105
HEAD
 Alice F., 148
 Caroline G., 149
 Cravin, 149

HEAD
 Ella Mae, 147
 Harold, 148
 Hazel A., 148
 Ida May R., 148
 James W., 148, 149
 Jane M., 149
 Janie R., 148
 Newsom H., 148
 Newsom H., Jr., 148
HEARD
 Sarah, 150
HEATH
 Mrs., 95
HEMPHILL
 Nora A., 89
HENDERSON
 Howard D., 79
HENRY
 Frances, 77
 Hannah, 92
HENSON
 Rev. T. H., 117
HESTER
 Emily J., 9
 John W., 103
HICKERSON
 Charles, 94
 Mary C., 64
HIGGINS
 Addie W., 170, 172
 Edith G., 170
 Eugene B., 170, 173
 Eugene B., Jr., 173
 Eugene J., 169, 170
 Frances O., 170
 Gena, 170
 Lucie, 12
 Margaret, 173
 Margaret L., 170,
  173, 174
 Mary B., 173
 Mary E., 170
 Robert E., 173
 Robert S., 170
 Rosa Annah, 170
 Victoria, 172, 173
 Vic W., 170
 Walter, 170
 Walter L., 173
 Walter W., 170, 171,173

HIGHT
 W. G., 119
HILL
 E. R., 98
 James, 103
 John, 103
 Mrs., 98
HINES
 C. B., 3
 Maggie, 48
HODGE
 Mary, 74
 William, 81
HOGAN
 Rev. L. R., 99
HOGIN
 Martha, 157
HOLLAND
 _, 114
 Thomas B., 114
HOLLEN
 Marthey, 32
HOLMAN
 Rufus M., 180
HOLMES
 Dr. Ernest, 175
HOLT
 Betty, 47
 David, 44
 Elias C., 150
 Frances, 150
 Harriet V., 63, 132
 Joseph M., 150
 J. W., 98
 William, 124
HOOPES
 Harry, 6
 Laura Amrette, 6
HOOSER
 D., 63
 Daniel, 63, 64, 65,
  132
 Eliza A., 63, 64,132
 Frances, 63, 64, 65,
  132
 George M., 63, 65,132
 George M., Jr., 65
 Harriet L., 63, 64,
  132
 Margaret, 63
 Martha F., 63, 132

HOOSER
  Mary An, 25, 132
  Mary Ann, 63, 64,
    132
  Miss Edmund, 132,
    162
  Rachel L., 63, 132
  Sarah J., 63, 64,
    132
  Sara Jane, 63, 65,
    132
  Sefrona A., 63, 132
  Virginia A., 63,132
  William M., 63, 64,
    65, 132
HOOVER
  Christopher, 58
  Elizabeth L., 58
  James, 58
  Minerva Jane W., 58
HOPKINS
  Elizabeth D., 4, 5
  G. A., 4, 5
  Letticia V., 4
  Mira Louisa, 5
  William L., 5
HORD
  Susan S., 165
HOSKINS
  Malinda Ann, 33
HOUSTON
  Claude V., 119
HOWARD
  Pauline I., 1
  Rev. H. R., 154
  William H., 1, 2
HOWELL
  Elizabeth A., 165,
    167
HOYT-HOYTE
  Irene, 80
  Rev. T. A., 141
HUFF
  Mary, 62
  Rev. William, 99
HUFFMAN
  William, 15
HUGHSON
  E. M., 57
  G. C., 57
  H. E., 57

HUGHSON
  James S., 58
  J. C., 57
  J. S., 57
  M. S., 57
  Myrtle Effie S., 58
  T. M., 57
  W. F., 57
HUMMEL
  Helene, 108
HUNTER
  Florence, 117, 118
HURT
  Mrs. Mary, 47
HUTSON
  Jim L., 2
  Mary A., 2
HUTTON
  R. N., 119, 169

INGLE
  Alonza A., 45, 76
  Benny, 45, 76
  Ernest C., 45, 76
  Fred D., 77
  James W., 45, 76
  Koy C., 77
  Leta Marye, 77
  Lura Belle, 77
  Mable, 45
  Martha F., 45
  Prince Ernest, 76
  Ruphus C., 77
  Ruphus W., 45, 76
  Sara M., 45, 77
  Thadeus, 45, 77
  William T., 45, 76
INGOLD
  John, 44
INGRAM
  Rev. A. B., 3
IRONS
  Mary, 23
IVIE
  Chas. S., 120
  C. S., 119

JACK
  Laura, 166

JACKSON
  Andrew, 129
  Andy, 18
  Charlie, 18
  Gen., 62
  James L., 34
  Sarah J., 34
  Thomas J., 18, 34
JAMES
  Ben, 92
  Mrs. Ben, 92
  Robert, 92
JARMON
  Rev. L. B., 100, 101
JARRELL
  B. F., 75, 149
  Mrs. R. L., 181
  Mrs. R. T., 149
  R. L., 181
  Robert L., 182
  R. T., 149
JARRETT
  _, 94
JENKINS
  Edgar, 83
  Harriet, 152
  Margaret C., 84
  William, 84
JENNINGS
  Allen, 101
  Elizabeth, 101, 124
  James H., 114
  James W., 101
  Lucreecy, 101
  Martin, 101
  Nancy, 101
  Nancy A., 101
  Robert, 101
  Salley, 101
  Salley H., 101
  Sophy, 101
  Webb, 101
  William, 101
  William C., 101
  William K., 101
JOHNSON
  Ada F., 130, 131
  A. L., 80
  Alice E., 130, 131
  Cynthia, 94
  Cynthia A., 131

JOHNSON
    Earl C., 130, 131
    Grover C., 130,
      131
    Hattie M., 130,
      131
    James A., 130, 131
    Jane P., 103
    Joe, 94
    Major J. M., 130
    Malinda G., 130
    Margaret L. R., 130
    Millie, 94
    Mrs. Gust E., 116,
      117
    Nancy, 90, 94
    Nancy A., 94
    Rebecca, 94
    Rury, 94
    Sarah M., 130, 131
    Sophia, 94
    Wiley, 53
    W. M., 130, 131
JONES
    Benjamin F., 114
    Bryant C., 115
    Catherine, 160
    C. D., 161
    Charles, 136, 160
    Charles B., 160
    Charley W., 160,161
    David D., 160, 161
    David J., 160, 161
    E. D., 75
    Eliza J., 160
    Fannie, 160
    Francis, 56
    George W., 115
    Isaac N., 160
    Jack, 160
    James E., 159
    James M., 115
    John W., 160, 161
    Josie A., 160
    J. W., 159, 160
    Lawrence, 77
    Leona J., 160
    Louise A., 103
    Margaret, 160
    Mariah F., 160, 161
    Marthey J., 115

JONES
    Mary R., 160
    M. C., 115
    Milinday E., 115
    Minerva M., 160
    Mrs. J. E., 158, 159
    Mrs. Sarah, 149, 150,
      152, 181, 182
    Nancy E., 160, 161
    Peter R., 115
    Rebecca, 160
    Rebecca C., 160, 161
    Rebecca N., 136
    Rebecker E., 115
    Rebekah M., 161
    Reese B., 160
    Rev. J. E., 48
    Sally E., 160, 161
    Samuel, 160
    Sarah, 136, 160
    Sarah E., 160
    Sloman W., 160, 161
    Susan D., 160
    Tacie, 160
    Tacy J., 160, 161
    Thomas J., 115
    T. P., 115
    Walter W., 160, 161
    Wiley B., 160
    William R., 115
    W. R., 115
JORDAN
    Susan G., 178
    William A., 179
JORDON
    W. E., 4
JOSLIN
    Mary R., 144
JUSTICE
    A. S., 98
    J. E., 98

KEELE
    Rebecca L., 176
KEELING
    Bess, 4, 5
    Charlotte, 4, 5
    Charlotte E., 5
    Edmond, 5
    Eliz. F. C., 4

KEELING
    Eulalia A., 4, 5
    Gustavus C., 4, 5
    James H. H., 4, 5
    James L., 4, 5
    Letticia V., 4
    Lillian L., 4
    Mary E., 4
    Mary L., 4, 5
    Nancy C. A., 4, 5
    Reginald L., 4
    Thomas, 5
    Thomas A., 5
    Verbena O., 4
    Victor L., 4
    William J., 4, 5
    W. T., 4
KELLER
    Ann, 63, 81
    Charles, 81
    Charley P., 70
    Charlie, 63
    Faye, 70
    F. M., 69, 70
    Frances, 81
    Frances A., 81
    Frances H., 63
    Ida F., 70
    Jacob, 63, 81
    Jane, 70
    J. Lane, 70
    John, 63, 81
    Joseph, 63, 81
    Joseph L., 70
    Kittie, 70
    K. John, 81
    Klyne Jack, 63, 64,
      65, 67, 68, 69,
      70, 81
    Loucinda, 70
    Louise G., 70
    Mary Lou, 68, 70
    Nancy C., 182
    Rachel, 63, 81
    Rhoda C., 70
    Rob, 68
    Robert I., 68, 70
    W. G., 182
KEYSER
    Martha, 124

KIDD
  Poley, 101
  Polly, 101
KIMBRO
  Dewey Hix, 24
  Frances, 63, 132
KIMBROUGH
  Nannie S., 180
KIMES
  Fannie E., 19,
    20
KINCAID
  Edward A., 70
  Elisha R., 70
  James T., 71
  John F., 70, 71
  Margaret L., 70
  Samuel I., 70
KINDIECH
  Betsey, 59
KING
  Dale, 8
  Earl C., 55
  E. C., 54
  George M., 26
  Hoyt D., 8
  Mary D., 26
  Morton B., 8, 26
  Morton B., Jr., 26
  Mrs. Morton, 25
  Rebecca, 54
  Rebecca K., 54
  Rebecca K. C., 54
  Redden D., 8
  Redden Dale, 8
  R. D., 8
  Rev. A. J., 84
KINGREE
  Pearl, 35
KINGSTON
  Mary M. A., 106
KINNARD
  Mrs. Marvin, 75
KIRBY
  James M., 103
KIRKPATRICK
  Jane H., 137
KISSELL
  Harry, 54
  Rebecca C., 54

KITTRELL
  Lillian, 108
KLINE
  Rev., 90
KNIGHT
  Allen, 2, 3
  Baby, 3
  Charles E., 2, 3
  Elizabeth A., 2, 3
  Eva M., 3
  Gertrude, 3
  Grace, 3
  Jennie P., 3
  Jesse, 114
  John A., 2, 3
  Karl C., 40
  Lewis, 3
  Louis W., 2, 4
  Lucy Ann, 2, 3
  Margaret P., 2, 3
  Martha C., 2, 3
  Mary, 2, 3
  Mrs. Richard P., 39
  Quincy, 3
  Quincy A., 2, 3
  Richard C., 40
  Richard P., 39, 40
  Shirley Ann B., 40
  Susan M., 2, 3
  William G., 2, 3
KNOTT
  A. F., 34
  Albert F., 33, 34
  Alfred R., 34
  Alga M., 34
  Algie S., 33
  Charles R., 34
  Elizabeth, 34
  Elizabeth McE., 143
  Ella A., 33
  Henry C., 143
  J. A., 141
  James W., 33
  Jessie F., 143
  J. W., 33
  Laura F., 33, 34
  Lieullor A., 33
  Malinda, 34
  Malinda Ann, 34
  Mary Ann T., 33, 34
  Sallie J., 33

KNOTT
  Sarah J., 33
  Sophy, 142
  Susannah E., 33
  T. E., 142
  Tennessee M., 142
  Thomas E., 142, 143
  Thomas Elisha, 143
  Thomas Ewing, 143
  Virginia T., 34
  William, 34
  Willie L., 142, 143
KOONCE
  Jack, 55
  Jas. A., 13
  J. E., 54, 55
  Joel E., 54, 55
  John H., 54, 55
  John P., 13, 15
  Jno., 13
  Ladie B., 55
  L. B., 46, 54
  Lottie, 55
  Martha A., 54, 55
  Mollie F., 55
  Nancy C., 55
  Rebecca L., 55
  R. T., 54
  Sarah J., 55
  William W., 54
  W. W., 55

LaMAR
  Ruth Isabell, 77
LAMB
  Carolyn S., 86
LANDERS
  Ada, 33
  Anderson, 34
  Arthur L., 119
  Flavius S., 33, 34
  F. S., 33
  Mary H., 176
  Sarah, 34
LANDIS
  _, 75
  Abb S., 14
  Abel H., 13
  Abel J., 13, 14
  Absalom L., 13, 14

LANDIS
    Absalom M., 14, 15
    A. L., 13
    Douglas, 8
    Eran, 13, 15
    Helen N., 14
    James H. P., 13
    James K. P., 13, 14
    Jas. R. P., 13
    John, 13, 14
    John C., 13
    John T., 14
    Lavoy P., 14, 15
    Leelan, 14
    Lenora, 14
    Major A. L., 8, 14
    Margaret E., 13
    Mary, 14
    Mary A., 14
    M. E., 8
    Melissa E., 13, 14
    Melville A., 14,15
    Mildred, 8
    Nancy, 13
    Nancy C., 8
    Phebe A., 13, 14
    Phebe L., 14
    Robert W., 13, 14
    Sallie N., 14
    Sarah, 13
    Solon L., 14
LANDRETH
    Love, 147
LANE
    B. F., 108
    Carl T., 78
    Johnnie Jas., 78
    John T., 43, 44,
        76, 78, 81
    Mary E., 78
    Mary Emma, 78
    Mary Emma C., 78
    Mary H., 31
    Mrs. F. M., 78
    Robert Henry, 78
    Robert Henry, Jr.,
        78
LARGEN
    Eld., 24
LANGLEY
    Mrs. Carlysle, 115

LATTA
    Elizabeth, 90
LAWLER
    Hattie V., 175
    William B., 175
LAWRENCE
    Charles T., 157
    Elisha H., 157
    Elizabeth, 157
    Emmeline, 157
    George W., 157
    James, 157
    Lemuel R., 158
    Margaret, 157
    Mary, 157
    Mary H., 157
    Milly A., 157
    Nancy, 157
    Richard N., 158
    Samuel T., 157
    Sarah M., 157
    Susan J., 158
    William, 157
LAWS
    Emma Bell, 148
LEITER
    Amrette, 6
    Harry H., 6, 7
LENORD
    John W., 127
LENTZ
    Benjamin F., 104
    John J., 103
    Lora, 35
LEWELLYN
    John W., 53
LILE
    Benjamin, 122
    Clary, 122
    Elizabeth, 122
    Jackson, 122
    James H., 122
    Nancy, 122
    Rebecca, 122
    Sally, 122
    William, 122
LINDSEY
    Della E., 139
LIPSCOMB
    Rebecca, 117, 118
    T. C., 120

LITTLE
    Emily J., 25
    James, 114
    William D., 114
LOCK
    R. W., 141
LOCKE
    Minnie E., 24
    Susannah, 25
LONG
    Grace M., 120
LORANCE
    J. C., 70
    Mary L., 70
LOVVORN
    Jeffrey H., 47
    Thomas H., 47
LOWE
    Albert, 13, 15
    Mary, 13
    Nancy, 123
    William, 123
LUCAS
    _, 160
    Elizabeth, 110
LUCY
    Caroline E., 86
LUSK
    William, 162
LYLES
    Dr. Robin, 154
LYNCH
    Mrs. Sam K., 92
    Sam K., 92
    Sam K., Jr., 92

MABEE
    Charles A., 111
    Mrs. Mevolene, 109,
        111
MACKILWEAN
    Mary, 22
MAIN
    Charlotte E., 90
MALLARD
    Alfred, 120, 176, 177
    Alfred T., 121
    Clara B., 121
    Deborah, 120, 121,177
    Eldridge,120, 121,177

MALLARD
  Eldridge T., 178
  Eliza, 121, 176
  Elizabeth, 120,
    177
  Ethel Y., 153
  Fannie B., 121
  George, 120, 177
  George F., 120,
    121
  Grace M., 121
  Hattie T., 121
  Harriet T., 121
  James, 120, 177
  John, 120, 177
  Joseph, 120, 177
  Martha A., 121
  Martha E., 179
  Marvin M., 121
  Mary E., 121
  Mary J., 121
  Rebecca, 120, 177
  Richard, 120, 177
  Samuel B., 121
  Sarah, 120, 121,
    177
  Sarah C., 121
  S. B., 121
  Susan E., 121
  Thornton, 120, 177
  William, 120, 177
  William A., 179
MALONE
  Sam, 128
MANGIS
  Permelia, 89
MANGRUM
  Harriet C., 106
  H. C., 106
MANIER
  Dr. A. W., 141
  Mattie, 96, 97
MANSFIELD
  Elizabeth, 114
MARKIEWICZ
  Ray., 17
MARKS
  T. B., 176
MARSH
  Adelbert H., 71,72
  Annie A., 73
  Archabald P., 73

MARSH
  Clara J., 73
  Elizabeth, 72
  George W., 73
  Grady U., 71, 72, 73
  Helen C., 17, 90,101,
    122, 123, 125
  Henrietta E., 73
  James B., 73
  John B., 71, 72
  John L., 73
  John W., 72, 73
  Julia V., 73
  Laura S., 73
  Lelia, 71, 72
  Leslie D., 17, 72
  Marsha J., 17, 72
  Mary F., 72
  Mary T., 73
  M. G., 71, 73
  Michael, 72, 73
  Michael G., 71, 72,73
  Mrs. T. R., 70
  R. A., 71
  Richard A., 71, 72
  Robert A., 73
  Sarah F., 73
  Sarah G., 72
  Sara L., 72
  Timothy R., 17, 72
  William E., 73
MARSHALL
  Aldrige, 61
MARTIN
  Abigail, 42
  Anna F., 24
  Hannah, 43----Clarissa, 42
  Josiah, 42
  Marilla, 43
  Matilda, 43
  Matt, Sr., 62
  Mrs. S. M., 55
  Polly McD., 43
  Rachel P., 61
  Rev. F. F., 153
  Robert, 42
  Sally, 62
  William, 42, 43
MASSEE
  Marion H., 151

MATHEWS
  Blanche L., 72----Allie, 72
  John T., 72, 73
  Mary Lou, 72
  Nancy B., 21
  Thomas, 73
MATHIS
  Blanche L., 71
MAULDIN
  B. B., 161
  C. D., 161
  D. M., 161
  El., 161
  J. G., 161
  J. W., 161
  M. G., 161
  O. L., 161
  S. E., 161
  Teddy, 161
  T. J., 161
  W. C., 161
  Whit, 161
MAUPIN
  E. B., 8
  Edward B., 8
  Emily C., 64
  Jane B., 141
MEADOWS
  N. P., 71
MEDARIS
  E., 80
MELSON
  Frances, 115
MELVILLE
  Miss, 83
METFORD-MEDFORD
  Alene, 60
  Anne, 60
METSGAR
  Mary R., 160
MIAL
  Thomas, 42
MICHAEL
  Avus E., 127
  James A., 127
  John F., 127
  Josy Ann, 127
MILES
  Bertha A., 51
  Floyd, 51
  Louise, 51

202

MILES
    Margarett L., 50
MILLER
    Andrew J., 152
    Charles R., 152
    Henry J., 152
    James J., 152
    James W., 152
    John B., 152
    Lettitia E., 152
    Margaret E., 152
    Mary R., 152, 153
    Mrs. P. R., 60
    Newton E., 152
    Robert S., 119
    Wiley M., 152
    William, 103
    William J., 152
MILLIKEN
    Rebecca, 137
MILLS
    Charity, 69
MINATRA
    Brenda F., 84
MITCHELL
    Minnie, 86
    Thomas F., 15
MONTGOMERY
    Amy, 96
MOODY
    Dr. George W., 26
    George W., 25
    Georgie E. S., 25,
      26, 27
    G. W., 119
    Lettitia T., 26
    Lucinda E., 167
    Margaret, 25, 26
    Margaret L. W., 25
    Margaret W., 26
    Mary E., 26, 27
    Rev. Samuel S., 26,
      36
    Rev. S. S., 39
    Rev. T. L., 26, 27
    Sallie C., 26
    Samuel S., 25, 26,
      27
    Samuel S., Jr., 26
    Winston G., 25, 26

MOORE-MORE
    A. L., 68
    Allice M., 128
    Altha P., 129
    Asael, 88
    Augustus F., 30
    Charles M., 61
    Earl T., 68
    Eliza, 28
    Elizabeth R., 26, 27
    Ethel W., 84
    Fannie A., 80
    Floyd L., 67, 68
    Frederick A., 30
    Gen. William, 26, 27
    Hugh L., 84
    Jayne F., 68
    John, 7
    Lucinda, 30
    Margaret B., 26
    Missouri A., 128, 129
    Mrs. Viva, 90
    Nancy M., 30
    Rev. William T., 12
    Samuel B., 30
    Sarah H., 30
    Tabitha W., 6
    Troxel H., 81
MORFORD
    W. H., 119
MORGAN
    Alta E., 7
    General, 60
    George A., 99
    Harwood, 165
    Henry M., 7
    H. K., 6, 7
    James L., 7
    Lucile, 7
    Raymon, 7
    Rebecca, 7
    Tina S., 7
    Tina Webb, 7
MORRIS
    Sarah Ann, 124
MORRISON
    Allen T., 165
    Ella V., 165
    James H., 165, 166
    John F., 4, 5
    Rev. Silas, 126

MORRISON
    Theodore D., 165
    Theodore S., 166
MORTON
    Bessie Mai, 48, 54
    Betty Lou, 47
    Charles, 134
    Earl H., 46, 48, 55
    Eldridge L., 46, 48
    Fanny A., 46
    Frances L., 47
    George M., 46
    George W. C., 46
    Glenn, 45, 46, 47
    Glenn C., 46, 48, 51,
      54
    Gracie, 48
    G. W. C., 46
    Hazel, 48
    Hobert, 48
    Jack B., 48
    Jacob, 27
    James B., 45
    James C., 46
    James R., 46, 48
    Jesse, 135
    J. H., 46
    John H., 48, 54
    J. R., 46, 47, 48,54
    Julia A., 48
    Julia B., 46
    Julia E., 46
    Lady Belle, 48
    Larry D., 47
    L. B., 46, 48
    Lucy H. A., 45, 46
    Margaret A., 47
    Martha J., 46
    Mary M. L., 46
    Mrs. Glenn, 45, 46,
      47
    Nancy B., 47
    Patsy M., 47
    Ralph, 55
    Ralph B., 48
    Reizin, 134
    Robert C., 47
    Robert F., 46, 48
    Saphronia A., 46
    Wanda L., 47
    Wayne L., 47, 48

MORTON
    William H., 45,46
    Willie E., 46, 48,
      55
MOSS
    Henry, 167
MOSER
    Frederick, 44
    Henry, 44
    Sara, 44
MOTLOW
    Agness, 37, 38
    Elizabeth, 37
    Felix, 38
    James McE., 38
    John, 37, 38
    John M., 38
    Laraet, 38
    Lynn W., 172
    Mary, 37
    Negroes, 38
    Robert Lee, 171
    Susan B., 1
    William, 37
    Zadock, 38
MOYE
    Sarah, 82
    William, 82
MOYERS
    Charlotte H., 170
    Edith H., 170
    Jas. J., 170
    J. J., 170
MULLINS
    Andrew E., 80
    Joseph, 84
    Mary Wells, 83
MURPHY
    C. B., 98
    P. A., 98
MURRAY
    Susan, 159
MUSE
    Jacob, 140
    Mary Jane, 45
    Thrusa A. F., 140
MYERS
    Abram, 117
    Anne E. W., 118
    Ethel, 117. 118
    Henry, 118

MYERS
    Hu B., 117, 118
    Hugh B., 117
    Mrs. T. R., 118
    Paul B., 117, 118
    Thos. R., 117, 118,120
    Thos. R., Jr., 118

McARTHUR
    Alexander, 168
    Allen, 168
    Archibald, 168
    Charles, 168
    Daniel, 168
    Duncan, 168
    Isabella, 168
    Jeanette, 168
    John, 168
    Mary, 168
    Neil, 168
    Peter, 168
    Sara, 168
McBRIDE
    Mrs. Virginia, 169
McCALEB
    Catherine, 95
McCLANAHAN
    Mary Ann, 59, 61
McCLARY
    Robert, 43
McCLELLAND
    James S., 178, 179
    Jennie E., 179
    Jimmie, 179
McCLURE
    N., 159
McCONNELL
    John K., 138
    Margaret, 162, 163
McCORD
    John K., 173, 174
    Michael D., 173, 174
    Victoria L., 173, 174
McCRORY
    Minnie S., 16
McDANIEL
    Col. C. A., 171
    Cora, 159
    Hattie, 159
    H. E., 159

McDANIEL
    J. C., 159
    Mary Lou, 171, 180
    Minnie, 159
McDONALD
    _, 158
McDOWELL
    Mrs. Morgan, 110
McELHANEY
    Mrs. Elizabeth, 142
McEWEN
    Marian E., 153
McGAUGH
    Felix R., 71
    F. R., 71
    Mary A., 71
    Susana, 71
    W. M., 71
McGEE
    Rev. Jas., D.D., 43
McGREW
    Charlotte, 4
    Dr. S. J., 155
    James H., 31
    Mrs. Amie C., 34, 35,
      36, 120, 121
    Mrs. S. D., 29, 30, 31,
      32, 33
    Nancy, 4, 5
    Pattye E., 84
    William, 4, 5
McGUIRE
    Dr. John, 79
    Katie, 79
    Mary, 79
    Mary Ann, 79
    Neely, 79
    Polly, 79
    Sallie, 80
    Sarah, 79
    Sarah S., 80
    Synthia, 79
    Thomas, 79
    William, 79
McIVER
    Mary, 83
McKINNEY
    Mary, 172
McLEAN
    Dr. William, 167
    John, 168

McLEAN
  L. V., 112
  Miss, 94
McMICHAEL
  Jane, 127, 177
McMURRAY
  _, 94
McNATT
  A. E., 133
  Braxton, 134
  Boyd, 134
  Clarence, 133, 134
  Cora, 133
  D. C., 133
  E. B., 133
  Elizabeth R., 133
  Florence, 133
  Fred, 134
  G. A., 133
  Gilbert, 134
  Girtie A., 134
  Grady, 134
  Huston, 134
  J. B., 133, 134
  John, 133
  J. W., 134
  Leona, 133, 134
  Lisan, 133
  Loyd, 134
  L. T., 133
  Mable, 134
  Marvin, 134
  Mary, 133
  M. E., 133
  Nancy, 133
  Nancy I., 133
  Neely M., 133
  Ore Lee, 134
  Rev. B., 91, 96
  Rev. L. B., 96
  S. E., 133
  S. T., 133
  Willie, 133, 134
  W. O., 133
  Yullar, 133
McPHERSON
  Glenn P., 77
  Mrs. Glenn P., 44,
    76
McREE
  _, 162

McTAGGART
  Jennie W., 84
  Norris W., 83
  Ray S., 84
McTYNE
  Sarah Ann, 81, 82

NANCE
  Will, 116
NAVE
  Anna S., 159
  Orville J., 159
NEAL
  C. B., 33
  Charles B., 33
  S. M., 105, 112
NEELEY
  John, 142
  John S., 143
  Joseph H., 142, 143
  Joseph P., 142, 143
  Joseph P., Jr., 143
  Malinda T. K., 143
  Margaret M., 142,143
  Martha R., 143
  Mrs. J. H., 139, 141,
    142
  Newt, 143
  Robert D., 143
  Ruth E., 143
  Spencer, 139
NEESE
  Mary J., 76
NEIL
  Joseph P. L., 104
NEILL
  Donie L., 131
NELSON
  Amanda C., 114
  Andrew M., 114
  Charlie, 30
  C. L., 29
  Daughter, 114
  E. C., 29
  Elizabeth M., 114
  Elizabeth S., 29
  Elizabeth V., 114
  Frederick, 30
  Gladys L., 30
  H. L., 29

NELSON
  Ida Ann, 29
  James L., 29
  Jeff, 30
  Jeffey, 30
  J. F., 29
  John, 114
  John McC., 114
  Lawson B., 29, 30
  Lewis M., 30
  Lucy, 30
  Luther, 114
  Mary A., 113, 114
  Matthew, 29
  Matthew F., 30
  Maude, 114
  M. F., 29
  M. L., 29
  Nancy C., 29
  Nancy M., 114
  Napoleon B., 29
  N. B., 29
  Newton T., 30
  Rebecca B., 114
  Sally, 30
  Samuel B., 30
  Sarah H., 30
  S. B., 29
  S. B., Jr., 30
  Thomas R., 29
  William D., 29
NEWCOM
  Mary, 156
NEWELL
  Sallie, 96
NEWMAN
  Col. Tazwell, 95
  Tazewell W., 94
NEWTON
  Revd. George, 40
NICE
  Mrs. Eliz. R., 165
NICHOLAS
  Elizabeth, 59
NICHOLS
  Elizabeth, 61
  Gothie Y., 56
  J. R., 56
  L. O., 56
  Rev. Green, 133

NICOLAS
  Col. Lewis, 90
NOBLETT
  Annie, 138
  David, 138
  Dr. Tom, 138
  John, 138
  William, 137, 138
NOLL
  Rev. Arthur H.,154,
    155
NORMAN
  Agnes A., 9
  Amanda H., 137
  Annie E., 139
  Benjamin, 9, 10
  Betsey Ann T., 9
  Cornelius A., 10
  Dora, 137
  Elizabeth, 9, 10
  Elizabeth P., 137
  Eliza E., 137, 138
  Eliza H., 9, 10
  Ellen E., 139
  George F., 137
  George M., 139
  George T., 9, 10
  Hannah J., 138
  Ida, 139
  Infants, 137
  James C., 137
  James Mc., 137
  James S., 138
  Jane, 138
  John M., 137
  John R., 139
  Joseph C., 9, 10
  Judy, 9, 10
  Martha Ann, 137
  Martha J., 138
  Martha R., 10
  Mary Jane, 137,138
  Mary Jane F., 10
  Nancy A., 137
  Nancy H., 9, 10
  Nellie, 136
  Permelia A., 139
  Rebecca, 160
  Robert, 136, 137,
    138, 139
  Robert P., 137,139

NORMAN
  Thomas N., 137
  Wesley, 9, 10
  Wesley G., 10
  William A., 137, 138
  William F., 139
  William W., 139
NORVELL
  Edmund B., 166
  Edmund M. B., 80
  Nell, 79, 81
  Nell T., 80
NOWLIN
  Dr. J. S., 119
  James R., 47
  Jerry E., 47
  John D., 47
  J. S., 119
  Michael S., 47

O'FERRALL
  Rev. Kirk, 153
OGILVIE
  Annie, 75
  James, 75
  Margaret, 75
  Nancy, 75
  Richard, 75
  Sally, 149
  Sarah, 75
  Tabitha, 75
  William, 75
ORMAN
  A. J., 171
ORR
  David, 36, 103
  Elias, 139
  Gillie P., 36, 103
  Jane, 36, 103
OSBORNE
  Ann E., 85
  Clement N. B., 85
  Elizabeth V. M., 85
  Gabriel G., 84, 85
  G. G., 85
  G. G., 3rd, 85
  Henry P., 85
  James S., 85
  John F., 85
  Lucy N., 85

OSBORNE
  Margaret, 85
  Margaret H., 85
  Margaret M. T., 85
  Martha G., 85
  Mary, 85
  Mary Ann, 85
  Mary G., 85
  Nancy, 84, 85
  Nancy J., 85
  Nancy J., Jr., 85
  Nancy Jones, 85
  Rep. G., 85
  Sarah V., 85
  Sophia E., 85
  Susan P., 85
  William J., 85
  William J., 2nd, 85
  William Jones, 85
O'STEEN
  Charlie D., 182
  Della A., 182
  Robert F., 182
  T. Myrtle, 182
  W. H. H., 181
OSTEEN
  An E., 181
  Elie J., 181
  Elizabeth, 181
  G. E. L., 181
  J. F. W., 181
  John E., 181
  J. R., 181
  Mary, 181
  M. J., 181
  M. P., 181
  Rev. Edward, 181
  Thomas J., 181
  T. J., 181
  W. H. H., 181
  W. J., 181
OTT
  Amrette, 6
  Charles W., 6
  Mary E., 6
  Paul D., 6
  Wallace E., 6, 7

PALMER
    Christopher S., 149
    James E., 147, 149
    Mrs. James E., 149
    Sheila D., 149
PANNELL-PANNEL
    B. F., 152
    Frances H., 7
    Jane, 32
    L. C., 7
    Lee C., 6
    Nell, 7
PARK
    F. W., 87
PARKER
    Sarah C., 65
PARKS
    John, 93
PARROTT
    Jennie D., 167
PARSONS
    A. B., 28
    A. C., 28
    Amie, 28
    Benjamin S., 29
    Elizabeth J., 29
    George, 28
    George W., 28
    Jacob M., 28
    J. M., 28
    John W., 28
    Margaret C., 29
    Mary Ann, 28
    M. F., 28
    Michael F., 28
    Newton B., 29
    Permelia, 27
    Philip A., 29
    Thomas J., 29
    Thomas T., 27
PASCHAL
    Charles McC., 140
    Edith M., 140
    Elizabeth, 140
    Harriet M., 140
    James D., 139
    James, Jr., 140
    J. C. J., 140
    Mattie E., 140
    Paul, 140
    Pauline, 140

PASCHAL
    Rachel, 140
    Ruth E., 140, 142
    U. G., 139, 140
    Ulysses G., 139
    William E., 140
    William P., 140
PATTERSON
    Capt. Andrew, 136
    Louisy Jane, 134
    Myrtle, 76
PATTON
    Abigail, 126
    Elizabeth, 126
    Humphrey, 126
    James, 125
    Jane, 126   James E., 126
    Katherine, 126
    Keziah, 126
    Magdaline, 126
    Margaret, 126, 134, 135
    Mary, 126
    Nancy Ann, 126
    Rhoda, 126
    Sarah, 126
    Sarah C., 125
    Thomas, 126
PAYNE
    Margaret C., 64
PEACOCK
    Sarah L., 61
PEARSON
    Addie, 56
    Arminda, 3
    J. E., 68
    Mary L., 67, 68
    William E., 3
    William N., 3
PENN
    Angie, 80
PENNINGTON
    Alene, 141
PEPPER
    Agatha O., 84
    Elizabeth H., 152
    Henry, 152
    Jane B., 152
    Mary Ann, 152
    William, 152
PERRY
    Bernice, 6

PERRYMAN
    John Lee, 35
PETRIE
    J. C., 12
PETTY
    Robert, 94
PEYTON
    Rev. C. C., 98
    Rev. O. C., 91, 100
PHELPS
    Nancy, 75
PHILLIPS
    Adolphus J., 116
    Amanda, 116
    Bettie, 116
    Caldona M., 116
    Catherine E., 116
    E. B., 152
    Elizabeth, 115, 116
    Emily E. A., 116
    Emily W., 116
    George W., 116
    Jesse, 115, 116
    John, 116
    John G., 116
    Joseph G., 116
    Kate, 116
    Malinda J., 116
    Margaret J., 115, 116
    Margarett M., 116
    Maria, 137
    Martha Ann, 115, 116
    Mary L., 137, 139
    Mary M., 116
    Mathew J., 116
    Meck, 116
    Merica J., 116
    Sam, 116
    Samuel H., 116
    Tennessee, 116
    Tennie, 116
    Thomas G., 116
    William T., 116
PICKLE
    Betty, 35
    Charlie, 35
    Ella, 35
    John, 35
    Mag, 35
    Malissa, 34, 35
    Mollie, 35

PICKLE
  Thomas, 35
  Will, 35
PITTMAN
  Emma, 54
PLUMLEE
  M. G., 98
POLK
  Frances A., 41
  Genl. Lucius J., 39,
    41
  Mary E., 87
  Newton N., 86
POPE
  William H., 39
PORTER
  James D., 94, 96
  Sintha, 15
PORTERFIELD
  William T., 47
PRICE
  Ann G., 1
  Ann I., 2
  Caswell E., 41,42
  Fetney, 41, 42
  Needham, 41, 42
  Prentiss, 41, 42
  Rebekah, 41, 42
  Scheherazada, 41,
    42
  Thomas, 41, 42
  Washington, 41,42
PRIMROSE
  Parthena, 104
PRINCE
  Macon B., 54
PROSSER
  L. T., 133
PRUETT
  W. K., 98
PRUITT
  Archibald, 80
  Fannie M., 173
  Myrtle, 171
  William J., 174
PRYOR
  Henrietta, 72
PUCKETT
  James A., 104, 105
PURDY
  Redden G., 170

PURYEAR
  Rebecca W., 182
PYLANT
  Miss, 34
PYRDOM
  Charlie, 56

QUICK
  William, 60
QUINTARA
  Bishop, 153

RABY
  A. E., 133
  E. B., 133
  J. R., 133
RANDALL
  Rodolphus O., 86
RANSOM
  Edward Ward C., 173,174
  James V., 173, 174
  Jennifer McC., 173, 174
RAY
  Blanche, 141
  Charles H., 16, 17
  Jennie E., 16
  John, 68
  Lizzie C. W., 16
  Nancy J., 104
  Orrie, 68
  Robert Lee, 17
REAGOR
  Anthony, 125
  Anthony W., 125
  Jacob, 125
  John, 125
  Margaret S., 125
  Mary M., 125
  Rhoda B., 125
  William, 125
REAVES
  Chaney G., 50
  Elizabeth, 50
  Isham D., 50
  John, 50
  Mary B., 50
  M. J., 50
  Priscilla, 50
  Sarah A., 50

REAVES
  William, 50
  William H., 50
REAVIS
  Clarassa, 149
  Clarassa B., 149
  David, 149
REDNICK
  Pheby T., 18
REED
  Alice J., 39
  Andrew M., 38
  Benjamin F., 39, 51,
    53
  Charles N., 39
  Cordelia V., 39
  Elizabeth, 38
  Elizabeth L., 39
  Fred, 53
  Infant, 39
  James H., 38
  Jincy C., 38
  John, 38
  John L., 38
  Madison L., 38
  Mary I., 39
  Prentiss, 39
  Robert A., 38
  Samuel E., 39
  William, 38
  William W., 38
REESE
  J. G., 160, 161
  Mary, 127, 129
  Minerva, 160, 161
  Sarah E., 160
  Sloman W., 161
REEVES
  Margaret, 51, 53
REYNOLDS
  Amzie, 148
  Clarass R., 148, 149
  Green, 149
RICH
  Barbara H., 45, 76
  Cornelia L., 43, 45,
    76, 77
  Daniel, 43, 45, 76,
    77
  Elizabeth C., 45, 76
  Eliza J., 45, 76

RICH
Emily E., 45, 76
Henry M., 45, 76
James R., 45, 76, 77
Margaret T., 45, 77
Martha F., 45, 77
Mary A., 45, 76, 77
Sarah M., 45, 76
RICHARDSON
Harret, 156
RICHMAN
Jennie B., 76
RICHMOND
Bernice, 56
H. B., 57
Mrs. H. B., 57
RIDDLE
Lucinda, 58
RIGGINS
Barbara H., 45, 77
Jerome, 45, 76
RIGGS
Rev. A. S., 181
RIKE
Hardie S., 45, 76
Unie C., 45, 76
RIPPETOE
W. B., 48
RITHIE
Rev. Herman, 39
RITTENBERRY
H. H., 139
ROBB
Edith P., 3
ROBERTS
America P., 135
James R., 135
J. Gilbert, 81
Maggie, 75
R. R., 134, 135
ROBERTSON
A. B., 40
Jean C., 142, 143
Martha, 152
Rebekah, 41, 42
ROBINS
Rev., 84

ROBINSON
Margaret F., 144
Mary L., 49
ROGERS
George, 109, 111
Nannie M., 109
Nancy M., 111
Polly A., 109
ROHWER
Avalyn C., 81
ROPER
Margaret L., 130, 131
ROUNDTREE
Rachel F., 138
ROWLAND
Eliza J., 106
ROYSTER
Bebe, 11
Bro. Alexander, 10
Eliza, 10
Eliza A., 12
Eliza Ann, 11
Eliza H., 11
George M., 11
Ireneaus F., 11
James H., 11
J. C., 11
J. H., 11
John N., 11
Joseph C., 10, 11
Leander A., 11
Levin C., 11
Negroes, 11
Wesley W., 10, 11
William, 10, 11
William E., 11
William T., 10, 11
ROZEAR
Mrs. Marion, 106
RUDOLPH
Mrs. J. W., 155
RUDY
Bobby, 91
Robert, 91
RUSSELL
J. E., 98
RUSHING
_, 75
B. E., 98
RUTH
John W., 155

RUTLEDGE
Rosanna, 179
RYALL
H. C., 155

SANDERS
Jennie, 176
Nancy P., 42
SARLES
Elizabeth A., 3
John C., 3
Sarah, 3
SANDUSKY
Dr. G. C., 155, 182
Louisa, 88
SARRETT
Hiram, 125
James, 125
Joseph, 125
Nancy, 125
Samuel, 125
Samuel G., 125
Wilson, 125
SCALES
N. C., 54
SCARBERRY
_, 158
SCHOOLER
Hannah E., 158
SCOTT
Mable, 171
SCRUGGS
Henry P., 85
Janie, 175
John F., 85
Rachel Ann, 85
SCUDDAR
Abbie W., 90
SEABRIGHT
Virginia, 84
SEAGRAVES
J. M. E., 133
SEARCY
Ada R., 49
Alice E., 49
Elvira J., 39
Emmett, 49
Hattie E., 49
Hugh, 35
Laura B., 49

SEARCY
  Martha L., 49
  Mary L., 49
  Miss Lucile, 48, 49
  Rev. Daniel P., 48, 49
  Sarah C., 49
  Vincon E., 49
SEHORN
  Florence, 153
  George, 153
  J. M., 153
  John, 153, 154
  John M., 153, 154, 155
  Mary B., 154, 155
  Mary F., 153
  M. B., 153
  Nathaniel, 153
  Nathaniel C., 154
  Sadie, 153
  Sally E., 153
SEWELL
  Abraham, 170
SEYMOUR
  Mary Jane S., 90
SHANNON
  Jas. Lawton, 171
SHAPARD
  D. G., 118
  E., 119, 155
SHARP
  Daniel, 44
  Daniel E., 45, 76
  J. Emmie F., 7
  K. P., 80
  Mary Ann E., 7
  Morgan A., 7
  Tabbitha W., 7
  W. G. P., 6
SHAW
  C., 124
  Capt. Christopher, 124
  C. G. W. B., 124
  Cotesworth P., 124
  David A. J. B., 124
  Martha, 124
  Mary Butler, 124
  Robert C., 124

SHAW
  Thomas L., 124
  Washington B., 124
SHEARIN-SHEARON
  James F., 58
  Louvenia C., 58
  Mary Sue H., 58
  M. Beatrice, 58
  Rebecca, 28
  Ross, 6
  Sarah Mayfield, 58
  Thomas, 58
  William T., 58
SHELLY
  Mayme, 170
SHEPPARD
  Susanna, 127
SHINE
  Eleanor, 23
SHOEMAKE
  William, 159
SHOFFNER
  Amelia, 124
  Magdalena, 44
  Martin S., 169
  Mary Ann, 169
  Michael, 44
  Sarah E., 83, 84
SHOFNER
  A. J., 13, 14
  Alice, 8
  Anna B., 9
  Argentine, 8
  Argie, 8
  Austin, 124
  Christian, 124
  Dan W., 153, 154, 155
  Dr. Jenkins, 13
  Dorotha, 124
  Edna, 8
  Edora, 14
  Emma, 8
  Eran, 13
  Eran L., 15
  Ethel, 154
  Eva, 124
  Florence S., 154, 155
  Fred, 124
  Frederick L., 13
  Jacob M., 8, 13
  J. M., 8, 14

SHOFNER
  Joseph T., 13
  Katherine, 124
  Laura E., 6
  Margaret, 124
  Martin, 124
  Mary F., 154
  Melissa E., 8, 14
  Nathaniel S., 153, 154
  N. S., 154
  Robert N., 13
  Sadie, 154, 155
  Tessey, 124
  William, 15
  William C., 13
SHOOK
  Margaret, 125
SHRIVER
  Berry D., 79
  Thos. A., 79
SIKES
  Elizabeth An, 123
  Jese, 123
  John, 123
  Jones, 123
  Mary, 123
  Nancy, 123
  Rebecker, 123
  Robert, 123
  Sarah, 123
  Susanna, 123
  Thomas A., 123
SIMPSON
  Carrie, 74
  J. W., 70
  Kittie K., 70
SIMS
  Sallie P., 151
  Walter H., 151
SINGLETON
  Clare, 153
  John S., 153
  R. L., 119
  Robert L., 153, 155
  Robert L., Jr., 153
SLATER
  Mrs. Hattie E. S., 48
SLEAN
  Mrs. Iola, 176

SLOAN
  Amanda C., 77
  Calvin S., 77
  Samuel, 27
SLUSSES
  Sarah, 144
SMARTT-SMART
  Frances, 163
  Frederick, 91,
    93, 98
  Frederick W., 99
  Mabel A., 91, 93
  Mrs. F. W., 92,
    100
SMITH
  Addie P., 128
  Altha P., 128, 129
  Amanda V., 105, 11
  America C., 175
  Annie O., 148
  Bennett, 128, 129,
    130
  Birdie J., 148
  Camaro A., 128,129
  Cynthia M., 147
  David J., 147
  Egbert V., 128, 129
  Ella M. H., 148
  Emma B. L., 148
  Emma M., 148
  Ferdinand, 109
  Florence V., 175
  Frances E., 6
  George, 87
  Hannah M., 165
  Jackson, 148
  James, 163
  James M., 53, 148,
    149
  James Madison, 147,
    148
  John E., 87
  Joseph, 36
  Judge Bennett, 129,
    130
  Judy A., 148
  Kate, 128
  Lee Roy, 148
  Levi G. W., 105,
    112
  Levi T. M., 105

SMITH
  Levi T. M. A., 111
  Margaret, 96, 97
  Mary, 5
  Mary F., 105, 111,112
  Mary J., 128, 129
  Mary Jarret, 128
  Mary S., 129
  Maude L., 148
  Miss, 163
  Morgan, 6, 7
  Mrs. James M., 147, 149
  Mrs. Roberta F., 104
  Naomie C., 147
  Nora M., 148
  Phebe, 87
  Robert A., 175
  Robert B., 128, 129
  R. L., 128
  Samuel, 128
  Samuel J., 128
  Samuel T., 129
  Sarah, 80
  Sophia, 62
  Tabitha W., 5, 6, 7
  Vincent, 4
  William A., 148
SMOOT
  John B., 101
  Sarah W., 101
SNEAD
  Mrs. Mary, 126
SNEED
  Rev. Henry, 84
SNELL
  Acton Y., 51, 52, 53,
    54
  A. G., 51
  Albert, 52
  Albert G., 51, 52, 169
  Albert R., 169
  Asachel C., 52
  A. Y., 50, 51, 52
  Cassande M., 169
  Elisabeth, 51, 52
  Elizabeth Ann, 52
  Elizabeth C., 52, 53
  Frances, 51, 52
  Gartha A., 53
  Georgie A., 169
  H. B., 52

SNELL
  James C., 51, 52,
    53
  James T., 169
  J. C., 51
  Margaret J., 51
  Mary, 51
  Mary A., 53
  Mary B., 169
  Mary E., 50
  Mary S., 52
  M. E., 50
  Nancy, 51, 52, 53
  Roger, 157
  Sary Jane, 52, 53
  S. J., 51
  W. B., 52
  Wiley B., 169
  William R., 52, 53
  Willie C., 51, 52, 53
  Willie B., 51
  Willie Bell, 51, 53,
    54
  Willie T., 51, 52
  Willie U. B., 50, 51
SNELLINGS
  Dr. John B. R., 80
SOLMON
  Marion, 157
  Polly, 59
SORRELLS
  W. T., 56
SPARKS
  W. H., 109
STANCELL
  Dorothy, 91
  James A., 91, 96
  Katherine, 91
  Katherine A., 91
  Katherine L., 91
  Mrs. William M., 92,
    96, 100
  Prof., 96
  Prof. William M., 95
  William, 91
  William M., 91, 92,
    95, 96
STANFILL
  Mrs. R. C., 92
  R. C., Jr., 92
  R. C., Sr., 92

STEELE-STEEL
  Phebe, 87
  Thomas, 44
  T. J. G., 88
STEGALL
  Elvira A., 75
STEPHENS
  Allen, 143
  Carmie, 109, 111
  Daniel, 69
  E. H., 144
  Eli, 143
  Ely, Jr., 143
  James, 144
  J. M. L., 144
  John, 143, 144
  Joseph H., 144
  Josiah, 143
  Kate, 144
  Lafayette, 143
  Larah J., 144
  Louizy D., 144
  Martha A., 143
  Nancy C., 64
  Ransom, 144
  Ransom, Jr., 144
  Salley A., 144
  Sarah, 144
  Sena E., 109
  Squire E., 144
  Tranquilla A., 143, 144
  W. B., 109
  Willey, 143
  William, 111
  William E., 182
  William F., 144
STEPHENSON
  Mattie E., 139
STEVENS
  Boyer, 182
  Daniel, 182
  Eliza, 182
  Elizabeth, 182
  James. 182
  John, 182
  Micah, 182
  Middleton, 182
  Sally, 182
  Thomas, 182
  William, 182

STEVENSON
  Grace, 144
STEWART
  Garrett, 119
  Harrison, 24
  James, 88
STOKES
  Albert M., 171
  Cleaver C., 171, 174
  Doris M., 173, 174
  Edd Cooper, 173, 174
  Edward C., 171, 174
  Fannie M., 174
  James A., 170, 171, 174
  John W., 171
  William P., 170, 171, 173, 174
  Mrs. Margaret, 169, 170, 171, 172, 173, 174, 179
STONE
  Mary A., 151
  Mary S., 151
  Sarah E., 151
STORY
  M. M., 16
STREET
  Annie W., 84
  Donald M., 84
  Martha R., 84
STRINGFIELD
  Rev. Thomas, 40
STRONG
  Charles R., 26, 27
  Dr. George M., 26
  Georgie E., 26
  Hugh L., 26, 27
  Margaret B., 26, 27
STROTHER
  Ellen B., 19, 20
SUGG
  Mary Addie, 180
SULLIVAN
  Fannie, 110
SUMLER
  _, 139
SUTTON
  Atlanta J., 62
  Elizabeth, 62
  Elizabeth F., 61

SUTTON
  John, 62
  Laura, 141
  William B., 62
SWEETON
  J. W., 159
SWING
  Martha A., 54, 55
  S., 48
  Salie, 48
  Sallie, 55

TALBOT
  Martha L., 117
TALLEY
  Elizabeth A., 131
  Narcissa A., 131
  N. C., 131
  William, 131
TARPLEY
  Fletcher, 4
  Sarah J., 33
TARVER
  Rachel, 94
TAYLOR
  Frank P., 180
  Mrs. W. Nowlin, 27
  Rev., 84
  Rev. W. S., 120
  Sarah A., 16
  Shirlene, 47
TEAGUE
  Elizabeth, 123
  James, 123
  John, 123
  Margaret, 123
  Rebecca, 123
  Sarah, 123
  William, 123
TEMPLE
  James D., 177
TEMPLETON
  Abner W. M., 126
  Addy, 74
  Andrew J. C., 126
  Avus W., 127
  A. W., 126
  Clary J., 74
  Fany Bell, 74
  James P., 126, 127

TEMPLETON
J. H., 126, 127
John, 126
John D., 126
John H., 126, 127
John P., 74
John R., 126
Lucy, 73, 74
M. A. E., 74
Mary E., 126
Meedy Ann, 74
Nancy J., 126
Newton, 73, 74
Robert, 127
Robert H., 126
Sarah, 127
Sarah E., 126, 127
Telitha, 74
William E., 126
William P., 74

TERRY
E. Simpson, 180

THAXTON
Bessie M., 54

THOMAS
Betsy, 44
Bettie, 2
Daniel, 44
Margaret H., 63
Martha C., 69
Martin, 69
Mrs., 138
Mrs. James A., 136
Mrs. Reba, 48
Sarah C., 64
Warren, 1, 2
Y. W., 28

THOMPSON
Ada R., 49
Amey, 28, 32, 33
Ann, 102
Anna, 155
Bob Ford, 173
Calvin, 155
Chas. J., 120
Eliza, 155
Elizabeth, 155,
    157
Elizabeth G., 156,
    157
Elizabeth J., 32

THOMPSON
Eliza J., 33
Emma J., 156
Flonnie, 116
Frances J., 32
George W., 32
Harriet, 155, 156
Hattie F., 156
Isabella, 155
Jacob F., 32, 33
James, 155, 156
Jennie A. T., 32, 33
Jno. W., 119
Jo, 38
John, 32, 156
John A., 155, 156
John F., 28
John T., 156
John W., 32
John Wesley, 32
Joseph, 155, 156, 157
Joseph A. G., 32
Martha, 155, 157
Martha W., 32, 33
Mary, 104, 156
Mary A., 32, 33
Michel F., 32, 33
Minnie, 141
Mrs. Bessie, 182
Newcom, 32
Newcomb, 27, 33, 156
Newcom, Jr., 32
Newton C., 155, 156,
    157
N., Sr., 33
Patsey J., 155
Rev. Sam, 156
Richard, 156
Samuel, 156
Samuel A., 32
Sarah, 156
Theophilus, 156
Thomas, 143, 144
Thompson, 27
Tranquilla A., 144
W. C. B., 157
William, 32
William F., 155
William M., 32
Zilphia, 157

THORNEBERRY
Guy Elam, 47
Laura Lee, 47

THURMAN
Rev. E., 12

THWEATT
John Henry H., 6

TICKLE
Caleb, 77
Martha F., 77

TIGERT
John B., 19

TILFORD
David, 141
Elizabeth, 141
N. B., 141

TILGMAN
Silas, 27

TILLMAN
Barclay M., 61, 62
Charles C., 62
Elizabeth F., 61, 62
Henry A., 61, 62
Infant, 62
John, Sr., 61, 62
Lewis, 62
Lewis A., 61, 62
Louis, 162
Mary, 62
Mary E., 62
Rachel P., 62
Sally C., 25
Sally Clay, 62
Sophia A., 61, 62
William S., 61
W. S., 62

TILLY
Lacy, 1

TILMON
Cristena A., 28
George W., 28
Martha T., 28
Silas M., 28

TIMMONS
Ruby, 78

TITUS
Arthur, 19
Ebenizer, 18, 19
George, 19, 21
James, 19, 21
John, 19

213

TITUS
  Phebe, 19, 21
  Rachel, 18, 19,
    21
TOLLEY
  William P., 180
TOLMAN
  Dr. H. C., 153
TARWICK
  Rev. A. M., Jr., 119
TREADWELL
  Gustavus A. W., 114
TREESH
  Ira Joel, 139
TRIKLE
  Caleb, 45
  Martha F., 45
TROTT
  Abraham, 102
TROUPE
  Georgia E., 168,
    169
TROXLER
  Martha, 14, 15
TURNER
  Cora, 16
  Danl. B., 39
  Della, 116
  Hopkins L., 96
  Mrs. H. C., 112
  Roberta F., 105
TURRENTINE-TURRINTINE
  Absolom, 89
  Albert F., 87
  Alexander, 88
  Ann C., 86, 87
  Archelus, 87
  Belinda, 86
  Caroline L., 86,
    87
  Daniel, 87, 88, 89
  Daniel C., 86, 87
  D. C., 86
  Deborah, 88
  Eleanor, 87
  Elizabeth, 27, 86,
    88
  Fannie, 89
  Francis L., 86
  George, 86
  George E., 86, 87

TURRENTINE-TURRINTINE
  George R., 86
  George S., 87
  Harrison, 89
  James, 88, 89
  James F., 87
  James L., 86
  James, Sr., 86
  Jane F., 87
  Jean, 88
  John H., 87
  Josephine L., 86
  Joseph T., 86
  Joshua L., 86
  Katherine, 86
  Leila Irene, 87
  Liddia, 89
  Lillie A., 86, 87
  Louisa J., 86
  Lucy J., 86
  Lydia, 89
  Margaret, 87
  Martha, 88
  Mary, 88, 89
  Mary B., 89
  Mary E., 87
  Mary Elvira, 87
  Mary F., 87
  Mary J., 89
  Melinda C., 87
  Minnie E., 86
  Morgan C., 86
  Nancy, 86, 88, 89
  Nancy E., 87
  Phebe, 87
  Priscilla, 86
  Salena A., 89
  Sam'l, 88
  Samuel, 86, 87, 89
  Samuel A., 87
  Samuel W., 89
  Sarah, 88, 89
  Sarah C., 87
  Sarah J., 87
  Sarah Jane, 104
  Susanna, 89
  Thomas C., 86
  Virginia A., 86
  William, 86
  William A., 86
  William A. T., 87

TURRENTINE-TURRINTINE
  William J., 104
  William R., 88
  Wilson, 103
  Wilson E., 87
  Zerelda, 87

VANCE
  Col. David, 162
  David, 162, 164
  Dr., 84
  Elizabeth, 162, 166
  Jane, 164
  Jean, 162
VANNOY
  Anderson, 177, 178
  Andrew, 127, 128,
    177, 178
  Egbert, 128
  Eliza Ann, 128
  Elizabeth, 177, 178
  Isaac R., 128
  James H., 177, 178
  Jane, 178
  Jesse, 128
  Jesse F., 178
  Joel, 127, 128
  Joel, Jr., 129
  Joel, Sr., 129
  John, 128, 129
  Joseph H., 177, 178
  Margaret J., 178
  Martha S., 176, 178,
    179
  Mary, 128, 129
  Mary Ann, 178
  Mary Ann S., 128, 129
  Mary S., 128, 129
  Nathaniel, 127, 128,
    178
  Nealy P., 128, 129
  Sarah, 178
  Sarah J., 128
VAUGHAN
  America C., 174
  America C. S., 175
  Benjamin O., 175
  Charles A., 174, 175
  David A., 174, 175
  Elizabeth, 175

VAUGHAN
Elizabeth J., 175
Emmett O., 174,175
Ervin P., 174, 175
Florence V., 175
Harriet I., 174
Hattie, 175
James. 66
James D., 175
Kate A., 175
Martha J., 61
Mattie, 175, 176
Mattie D., 174, 175
Oscar, 175
Sarah, 66

WACASAR
Maggie E., 86
WADE
Edward, 27
WAITE
Robert, 126
WADLEY
John, 181
Mary, 181
M. P., 181
WALKER
A. T., 88
Christopher W., 47
James W., 88
Joseph H., 167
Orlin C., 47
Timothy G., 47
WALL
J. D., 181
WALLIS
Catharine B., 36, 103
WALTERS
Capt. Jacob, 23
James M., 66
Mary, 66
WARD
John H., 6
WARDLAW
E. J., 9
WARE
Mr., 41

WARREN
C. A., 155
E., 133
WATKINS
E., 178
William S., 178
W. S., 178
WATSON
Abigail, 69
Charles, 160
John, 69
Sallie, 1
Walter, 160
Wiley, 160
WATTERSON
William B., 165
WEATHERLY
Martha E., 25, 26
WEBB
Amrette, 6
Ann Eliza, 6
Bettie, 80
Charlotte, 6, 7
Effie B., 6
Floy F., 6, 7
Gordon W., 7
Isaac B., 6
James E., 7
James H., 6, 7
James H., 3rd, 7
Jean Marie, 7
John C., 7
Laura A., 7
Laura S., 7
Lillian A., 7
Lillian M., 7
Loraine, 6
Martha An, 7
Morgan C., 6, 7
Morgan C., Sr., 7
M. C., 120
Nell K., 6
Percy A., 7
Phyllis L., 7
Sarah L., 7
Shirley Ann, 7
Susan, 42
Tabitha W. M., 6
Tina S., 6
WEBSTER
Cleveland, 151

WEBSTER
Eliza D., 151
J. G., 151, 152
John G., 151
Robert P., 151
R. P., 150
WELCH
Amanda E., 113, 114
Buena V., 113, 114
Dorothy A., 113, 114
Helen M., 113, 114
Margaret J., 113, 114
Mary A., 113, 114
Mary A. V., 113, 114
Nancy M., 113, 114
Rebecca P., 113, 114
Robert W., 113, 114
Rosetta W., 113, 114
Sarah E., 113, 114
W. D., 135
WELDIN
Rachel, 89
WELLS
Agatha P., 83
Annie P., 83, 84
Edgar J., 84
Ethel, 83, 84
Henry C., 108
Hubert J., 83, 84
Jennie, 83, 84
John W., 83, 84
John Wesley, 83
Margaret C., 83
Mary P., 83, 84
Mary S., 83, 84
Othneil D., 83, 84
Sarah E., 83
Thomas E., 83, 84
Virginia, 84
Willie S., 83, 84
WEST
Anna J., 123
Tabby, 79
WHEELHOUSE
Alla, 105
Beta, 105, 112
Clemenza A., 104
Collumbus G., 104
Dennis, 105
Edna, 105, 112
Evie, 105, 112

WHEELHOUSE
  Isaac, 105, 112
  Joshua T., 104,105
  J. T., 105
  Laura, 105, 112
  Lila, 105
  Lilah, 105, 112
  Manda L., 104
  Mary Ann B., 105
  Mary E., 104
  Mattie, 105, 112
  Miles C., 104
  Mrs. R. F., 112
  Parthena, 104, 105
  Roberta F., 105
  Sarah Ann L., 104, 105
  Thomas, 104
WHITAKER
  _, 75
  Ambie L., 171, 172
  America F., 180
  Charles L., 179
  Coleman R., 171, 172
  Delia, 180
  Holland B., 171
  I. B., 171
  Isaac B., 171, 172, 180
  James C., 180
  James F., 171, 172
  John F., 180
  John M., 171, 172
  Laura F., 180
  Margaret L., 171
  Mark, 179
  Mark, 3rd, 180
  Mary, 171
  Mary J., 180
  Mary L., 171, 172
  McDaniel, 171, 172
  Rebecca M., 180
  Rosanna, 180
  Ruth Ann, 180
  T. L., 149
  Vic, 170
  Victoria J., 180
  Virginia K., 180
  William B., 180

WHITE
  Dr., 94
  Frank, 139
  I. H., 98
  Isaac, 94
  Mary, 139
  Virginia, 95
WHITESELL
  Kate, 76
WHITESIDE
  H. C., 119
WICH
  Miss, 93
WICHE
  Miss, 90
WICKSTROM
  Charles C., 21
  Harry, 21
  Helen C., 21
  Joanne H., 21
WIGGINS
  Nell, 68
WILHOIT
  _, 80
WILLIAMS
  _, 75
  Cassander, 51, 53
  Charles F., 113
  David, 103
  E. L., 16
  Emit M., 113
  Eva F., 103
  George P., 103
  H. Young, 112
  Isaac, 79
  James H., 113
  Jarmon W., 113
  John E., 113
  Lewis C., 113
  Marilda J., 113
  Mary, 106, 107
  Mary E., 113
  Mattie M., 113
  Michael F., 104
  M. M., 112
  Mrs. Willie L., 142
  Nora B., 112
  Rev. James, 75
  Robert, 106, 107
  Robert T., 113
  Samuel B., 113

WILLIAMS
  Sarah Ann, 113
  Sarah Annie, 113
  Terenia, 65
  Tom, 65
  William, 23
  William T., 113
WILLIAMSON
  Addie D., 166
  Allen D., 166
  George, 154
  Margaret E., 143
  Robert A., 142, 143
  William B., 166
WILLINGHAM
  Fannie, 91
  Matchie, 90, 91, 100
  Paul D., 151
  Thomas, 91
WILSON
  _, 75
  Anderson, 89
  Ann, 89
  Ann H., 38
  Caleb, 89
  Charles, 89
  Elizabeth, 89
  Elizabeth M., 38
  Faney, 89
  Foster, 97
  George, 97
  Harvey, 96, 97
  Hugh, 97
  James, 163
  Jane, 89
  J. C., 97
  Joe, 97
  John, 97
  John W., 89
  Josiah, 89
  Kate, 97
  Mamie, 97
  Margaret L., 25, 26
  Mary H., 29
  Miller, 97
  Robert, 89
  Robert L., 38
  Thomas, 89
  Violet, 167, 168
WINDROW
  Zilpha, 155, 157

WINFORD
  Rev. Jerome, 98
WITT
  Ben F., 3
WINSETT
  Mary Ann C., 106
WOMACK
  Catherine, 106
  Catherine A., 161
  Charles W., 136
  David D., 136
  Frances J., 136
  John W., 136
  Katie A., 136
  Mariah H., 136
  Michael, 136
  Mike, 160
  Nancy, 136
  Tacy, 136
  Wade H., 136
WOODARD
  Addie, 169, 170, 172
  Andrew B., 172
  Buena A., 172
  Galen D., 172
  James L., 172
  John R. 172
  Mary, 172
  Mary E., 172
  Milton W., 172
  Mrs. Mary, 169
  Mrs. Sallie, 99
  Robert S., 172
  Sallie, 172
  Willie K., 172
WOOD
  Lant, 109, 110, 111
  Minnie L., 122
WOODFIN
  Laura K., 108
  Lillian, 108
  Mary, 61
  Mary J., 59
  Mrs. Walton, 108
  Walton C., Jr., 108
WOODS
  James A., 155
  Jenie, 33
  T. H., 119

WOODWARD
  John H., 96
  Sallie, 96, 97
WOOSLEY
  Henry W., 119
  Mrs. Bryant, Sr., 30
WORD
  Gracie F., 46, 54
  Gracy F., 50, 51
  Henry, 50
  Mary E., 50
  Mary M. E., 50
  Thomas S., 169
WORTHAM
  Duke, 95
  Heath, 95
  Jane, 95
  Nancy, 94
  Nancy H., 95
  Robert, 95
  Tom, 95
  William, 95
  Zachariah, 95
WRIGHT
  Annie E., 151
  David K., 176
  Elizabeth, 93
  Miss, 90

YANCEY
  Lizzie, 30, 31
YATES
  Riley, 160
YEATMAN
  Thos., 40
YEISER
  Dr. Watt, 154
YELL
  Mary S., 121, 122
YINGER
  Dennis, 146
  Lizzie, 146
YORK
  Alvin C., 92
YOUNG
  A. M., 98
  Bernice, 56, 57
  Eddie C., 56
  Edward, 56
  Ella, 56

YOUNG
  Emily K., 56
  Ethel, 56
  Fannie, 56
  Gotha A., 56
  Gothie, 56
  James, 56
  James M., 55, 56
  Josie, 148
  Katherine W., 56
  Lizzie, 56
  Malinda E., 55, 56
  Margarett J., 55
  Mark M., 55, 148
  Martha E., 56
  Mary F., 55
  M. M., 56
  Nellie, 56
  Nettie, 56
  Rev., 84
  Sarah E., 55
  Virgie C., 56
  W. A., 56
  Will, 56
  Willie A., 56

www.ingramcontent.com/pod-product-compliance
Lightning Source LLC
Chambersburg PA
CBHW021902020426
42334CB00013B/447